AN ADAMS BUSINESS ADVISOR

Accounting
for the
New
Business

Other titles in
THE ADAMS BUSINESS ADVISORS

Bob Adams books are appropriate for professional development seminars, training programs, premiums, and specialized reprint activities. They can be ordered through retail outlets everywhere, or by calling the Special Sales Department at 800-872-5627 (in Massachusetts 617-767-8100).

AN ADAMS BUSINESS ADVISOR

Accounting for the New Business

HOW TO DO YOUR OWN
ACCOUNTING SIMPLY,
EASILY, AND ACCURATELY

CHRISTOPHER R. MALBURG, CPA, MBA

BOB ADAMS, INC.
Holbrook, Massachusetts

Acknowledgments

Every honest author has a small group of people who make a book like this more practical and down-to-earth. For me those people are John Watters, John Cameron, Alan Zusman, Kathy Tucker, Christine Wentz, Ann Ammerman, Lisa St. Germain, and Julie Roensch. Many thanks for giving freely of your time and professionalism.

Published by Bob Adams, Inc., 260 Center Street, Holbrook, MA 02343

ISBN: 1-55850-350-1 (hardcover)
ISBN: 1-55850-349-8 (paperback)

Printed in the United States of America.

J   I   H   G   F   E   D   C   B   A   (hardcover)
J   I   H   G   F   E   D   C   B   A   (paperback)

Library of Congress Cataloging-in-Publication Data
Malburg, Christopher R.
    Accounting for the new business : how to do your own accounting simply, easily, and accurately / Christopher R. Malburg..
        p.   cm. — (An Adams business advisor)
    Includes bibliographical references and index.
    ISBN 1-55850-350-1 : $29.95 — ISBN 1-55850-349-8 (pbk.) : $10.95
    1. Small business—Accounting. 2. New business enterprises—Accounting. I. Title. II. Series.
    HF5657.M2295   1994
    657—dc20   94-8710
                                                                                              CIP

This publication is designed to provide accurate and authoritative information with regard to the subject matter covered. It is sold with the understanding that the publisher is not engaged in rendering legal, accounting, or other professional advice. If legal advice or other expert assistance is required, the services of a competent professional person should be sought.
        — From a *Declaration of Principles* jointly adopted by a Committee of the American Bar Association and a Committee of Publishers and Associations

Cover design: Marshall Henrichs

This book is available at quantity discounts for bulk purchases.
For information, call 1-800-872-5627.

Other books by Christopher R. Malburg:

The All-In-One Business Planning Guide (Bob Adams, Inc.)
The Cash Management Handbook (Prentice-Hall)
The Professional Investor's Tax Guide (Prentice-Hall)
The Property Tax Consultant's Guide (Prentice-Hall)
Business Plans to Manage Day to Day Operations (John Wiley and Sons)
How to Fire Your Boss (G.P. Putnam's Sons)
The Controller's and Treasurer's Desk Reference (McGraw-Hill)
How to Write a Knock-em-Dead Book Proposal (Writer's Resource Group)

To Lynne Cohen

You're more than just a relative; you're a treasured friend.

Table of Contents

Introduction

Accounting for the New Business shows how to set up a workable and simple accounting system, one that provides the information owners and managers of small businesses need to make everyday decisions. You don't have to be a CPA to use the methods and techniques demonstrated here. In fact, I assume you aren't.

The book provides a comprehensive look into the accounting operations of small companies. It addresses the unique accounting information needs of small-business managers. *Accounting for the New Business* takes the mystery out of establishing a simple, useful accounting system.

We'll begin with the basic concepts needed to understand small-business accounting. Then we'll progress to creating a steady flow of information in the various *modules* of your new accounting system. Beginning in Chapter 5, we'll actually set up each component of your new accounting system. The later chapters demonstrate ways to use the accounting system to prevent fraud and theft and to report financial results to investors, partners, and lenders. Finally, you'll learn how to use the information produced by the accounting system as a profit management tool.

The book uses examples and illustrations to make concepts clear and workable. Very little of the material is of a technical nature. Where concepts may be foreign, the book identifies them, puts them into understandable terms, and walks you through easy-to-use applications that are likely to be relevant to your situation.

Regardless of your position or responsibilities, creating and understanding your company's accounting is a necessity. This book delivers the *what* and *how* essentials. We won't waste time on things that are of little or no direct use to managers of small companies establishing an accounting system. That's why, for example, eight chapters are devoted to showing, explaining, and helping you establish these components of a small-business accounting system:

- General ledger • Accounts receivable • Accounts payable
- Order entry • Inventory control • Cost accounting
- Payroll • Fixed assets

Purpose of the Book

Accounting for the New Business serves two functions:

- It shows you how to set up a simple, efficient accounting system that's usable right now in your business.

- It furnishes a handy reference guide that you can pick up, use to quickly answer a specific question (such as, how do you determine in thirty seconds flat whether your financial statements are right or wrong?), then put back on the shelf until the next question.

Everywhere practical, real-life examples are used to simplify and illustrate the presentation. The understandable style purposely separates accounting issues into their component parts. Once each has been explained, then its relation to other parts of the accounting system is added. Even people who already have some knowledge of accounting will benefit from the streamlined and simplified explanations, thus accelerating the task of busy decision makers as the accounting system takes shape and begins to provide useful information from day one.

Scope

The book explains the theories and concepts you need in order to understand, establish, and improve the accounting system in your company.

This isn't an accounting textbook. I don't intend to make an accountant out of you. However, I can promise that the subjects included here will show you how a small-business accounting operation *should* work. It won't waste time on subjects that probably aren't relevant right now to a company the size of yours. Instead, the book focuses on how to install an effective accounting information system that will help you to make more informed management decisions.

Who Can Benefit from the Book?

This book was written for a variety of individuals:

- People whose job it is to set up the accounting system at their company
- People newly promoted into the accounting department or who have been moved up within the department to a position of higher authority and need to understand how the system should work

Accounting for the New Business helps bridge the gap between the technical and the financial sides of the company. It explains in plain English how each area in the accounting department relates to the other departments. This is done purposefully to illustrate how the other departments affect the company's accounting system and vice versa.

How the Book Differs from Others

The style emphasizes a user-friendly approach. The objective is quick access to simplified techniques for installing and operating a modern small-business accounting system. You won't find long, irrelevant discussions on the theory behind each issue—that's for textbooks. Instead, we'll describe how each component works, the best ways to install it and operate it, and then move on.

Each chapter employs major and minor headlines for the topics to help you locate the exact discussion you want without wasting time thumbing through the parts you don't need right now. All examples and illustrations appear within the text where they'll be of most benefit, not elsewhere in the book where space permits.

Features of the Book

Along with the use of streamlined heads and concise discussions, often followed by examples that demonstrate the techniques, you'll see aides like these:
Charts and diagrams that demonstrate

- Month-end financial reporting
- Computation of useful financial ratios
- Checklists for installing a system of internal accounting controls

Worksheets that help you define the requirements of your company's accounting system. Copy these worksheets and use them for the design and implementation of your own accounting system.

Examples offering practical illustrations that quickly clarify a technique by showing how someone in a similar situation solved the problem. Some of the examples

- Demonstrate the best numbering scheme for your chart of accounts
- Identify the best size for batches of journal entries
- Determine whether it's cost effective for you to subscribe to a payroll processing service

How to Use the Book

There are three features of the book designed to help you locate the exact topic, problem, or issue in which you're interested. These are

- The master Table of Contents at the front of the book
- The Index at the back
- The head structure within each chapter

To locate a subject, look first in either the Master Table of Contents or the Index. Then locate the exact discussion using the head within the text.

Additionally, the book also was intended for reading from cover to cover. Each topic builds on what was discussed before. The chapters begin with the basics and progress to state-of-the-art practices in the field of small business accounting.

Chapter Summaries

Chapter 1: The Language of Accounting

This chapter covers basic terms and concepts used in small-business accounting. In it we clarify the difference between a debit and credit. We'll show how asset, liability, income, and expense accounts are increased and decreased. Chapter 1 includes examples of transactions that explain the terms and descriptions used later. It is the basic building block you'll need to understand how to set up and operate your accounting system.

Chapter 2: Components of the Accounting System

Chapter 2 identifies the elements of a modern small-business accounting system. It covers each of the disciplines: receivables, payables, order entry, cost accounting, payroll, inventory control, and internal control. These are the *modules* we'll be setting up in your company.

Chapter 3: Information Flow

Chapter 3 shows where in the company the necessary data comes from and how the accounting system processes it. From there, the chapter identifies the products of the accounting system used in managing a small business.

Chapter 4: Department Relationships with the Accounting System

Different areas of the company need information from the accounting department after the transactions are recorded. The granting of credit to customers is an example. Before allowing a higher line of credit, the decision makers must see the customer's payment history as processed and reported in the accounts receivable subledger.

Chapter 5: Setting Up the Chart of Accounts

Chapter 5 describes the chart of accounts, and discusses how to set one up and how to use it. Included are such tips as account numbering schemes that can be easily converted later to those used by automated accounting systems.

Chapter 6: The General Ledger

This chapter shows how to set up a general ledger. It details the uses of a general ledger, how to make journal entries, and the various types of accounts found in it. Emphasis here is on the G/L acting as the hub of the accounting system, with the other components trading information back and forth as if they were spokes of a wheel.

Chapter 7: Accounts Receivable

This chapter describes how to set up and then make entries into the A/R subledger. This subledger's purpose is to keep track of who owes what to the company. Specific instructions are given on how to record sales, credit memos, returned merchandise, payments, and to write-off of bad debts. Sample reports are provided that show how to track delinquencies for use in granting credit and accelerating collections.

Chapter 8: Accounts Payable

This chapter describes how to set up an A/P system and make the entries that keep track of which vendors are owed what. Specific instructions are given on how to record purchases, credit memos, returned merchandise, and payments to vendors. Sample reports are provided that show how to control disbursements from the A/P system to maintain compliance with purchase terms and to avoid missing trade discounts.

Chapter 9: Order Entry

The emphasis of Chapter 9 is on how to establish a link between the information needed by the people who take the orders and what sort of information that should flow from the point of order back into the accounting system. Included in this chapter are issues such as granting of trade credit, review of payment history, and recording the order in the income accounts as well as in A/R. It moves further along the accounting process by demonstrating how to remove the goods that were sold from the inventory system and place unavailable goods on back-order.

Chapter 10: Inventory Control

Most manufacturers have three kinds of inventory: raw material, work in process, and finished goods. This chapter sets up a simple inventory control mechanism. It identifies the special accounting treatments associated with inventory throughout the production and sale process. Additionally, the chapter demonstrates how to take a physical inventory and the role the physical inventory plays in computation of cost of goods sold and in internal control.

Chapter 11: Cost Accounting

Chapter 11 emphasizes the simplicity of accounting for the costs of production at a small business. This chapter describes how to establish a simple cost tracking mechanism designed to assist in production control for profit-making purposes.

Chapter 12: Payroll

Chapter 12 steps you through the decision-making process that determines the cost-effectiveness of using a payroll service. The chapter goes on to illustrate how to set up and run a simple payroll system. It describes the various types of payroll computations you are likely to encounter, such as salaries, bonuses, hourly wages, and piecework payments. Payroll tax liabilities are described, as are year-end tax reporting requirements.

Chapter 13: Fixed Asset Accounting

Even at small companies, fixed assets generally include cars, trucks, manufacturing machinery and equipment, and sometimes building improvements and real estate. Chapter 13 installs a foolproof system that categorizes fixed assets by type and economic life for easy computation of depreciation expense. The system also assists small businesses in assessing their property tax liability in tax districts where there is a personal property tax as well as a real property tax.

Chapter 14: Internal Accounting Controls

Small businesses are just as susceptible to fraud and embezzlement as their larger counterparts—more so, in fact because staff usually wear several different hats. This often gives individuals complete access to valuable assets with little or no oversight. Chapter 14 describes the control procedures for preventing such common embezzlement as check lapping, inventory shrinkage, and theft of assets. It describes common cash controls and management of petty cash funds. All are implemented through the accounting system.

Chapter 15: Monthly Financial Results

Chapter 15 shows how to extract financial performance information from the accounting system. Included in this chapter are the preparation of the balance sheet, income statement, statement of cash flows, and statement of changes in working capital. This is a lay person's approach to the production and use of the most common accounting reports. Chapter 15 emphasizes what these reports tell us about the company and their use in managing profitability.

Chapter 16: Accounting for Profitability

Added profitability is the most important byproduct of an efficient accounting system. Chapter 16 illustrates how to use key pieces of accounting information (such as cost of goods sold and production costs) to manage profitability.

Chapter 17: Selecting an Automated Accounting System

Chapter 17 walks you through the process of identifying your company's automated accounting needs, the availability of information, and the capability of staff. It then shows how to match those three attributes with the types of automated accounting systems designed for small businesses.

Read this book; use it as a reference source. If you're a senior manager, make sure your staff gets a copy. This work represents the current thinking, techniques, methods, and observations on small-business accounting systems. Rely on it for answers to the complex accounting questions you encounter every business day. Once you use this book, you'll seldom allow it beyond arm's reach. I hope this book is as enjoyable for you to use as it was for me to write.

— C. M.

The Language of Accounting

OVERVIEW

Chapter 1 introduces the basic terms and concepts used in small-business accounting. You don't have to be a CPA to understand this discussion. The book employs lots of examples to help solidify each new concept. Remember, the purpose of this book is to enable you to set up and use your accounting system for the decisions facing you each business day.

We'll set to rest any confusion over the differences between debits and credits and how they are used.

ACCOUNTING: A NECESSARY EVIL?

Many of the small-business managers I know view accounting this way. It's overhead and really doesn't contribute to the bottom line. Or does it? The people who run the accounting system speak in an unintelligible blur of debits and credits. They have little grasp of the operation that generates the money to pay their salaries.

Sound familiar? Maybe you're one of the entrepreneurs who share these thoughts. Welcome. I'm not out to convert you to the good of accounting. However, my guess is that once you see how to set up an efficient accounting system for your small business—one that really does contribute to overall profitability— you'll convert yourself.

Information Means Profits

The purpose of the accounting system is to *communicate*. It produces useful information (not raw data) that tells specific things about the company. To those who understand what this intricate system is saying (and you'll be one of them by the end of this book), it's like money in the bank.

Suddenly, information that you need to run the company is at your fingertips. Of course, this information is couched in financial terms. That's the language your accounting system uses. But it's not complicated and—with help from this book—it's not foreign.

Here are two examples that prove this.

Overdrawing TDO's bank account

TDO Enterprises fabricates the chassis boxes for computers. It always seemed that there wasn't enough money in the bank to pay the bills. A quick look at the aging of accounts receivable revealed that customers paid on average two weeks after the time stated in the terms of sale.

Rather than dip into its line of credit again, TDO's solution was to mount an aggressive collection campaign. The company used its accounts receivable system to monitor progress toward getting and keeping customers current.

Within the space of two months, TDO's bank account balance had risen to a point where it could pay its bills regularly without having to draw on its credit line.

MAG's eroding profit margins

MAG Partners, Ltd. sells grass seed on a wholesale basis. Profits recently turned down for no apparent reason. However, the partners were savvy enough to investigate the sales department's ability to pass on recent price increases to customers.

Comparison of the sales prices for MAG's grass seed with what MAG had to pay for it showed a 20 percent decline in gross profit margin (sales - cost of goods sold = gross margin). The solution was to dock sales commissions for the amount under the company's list price. Profits miraculously rebounded.

Knowing What to Look For

Was the language the accounting system used to describe these two problems foreign? No. Was the solution a great mystery? Again, no. For TDO, the answer was simply to collect receivables faster. The accounting system identified the delinquent customers. For MAG, the answer was to raise prices. Once again, the accounting system showed which products and salespeople weren't following company policy.

All management needed was an understanding of the *information* available in the accounting system to help run the company. That's how we'll use your accounting system.

WHAT YOU WANT FROM YOUR ACCOUNTING SYSTEM

The kind of information we found in the prior examples is what you want from your accounting system. This feedback must

- Be accurate
- Fulfill management's requirements
- Be easy to use

We can employ information like this in solving problems and running the business. As well as having the attributes of accuracy, relevancy, and simplicity, our accounting system ought to be set up in such a way that it does not require an inordinate amount of time to maintain. Remember, you aren't an accountant, and we don't want you to spend your time trying to do accounting.

Further, your accounting system should not require a CPA to operate it or to interpret the output. Some of the popular automated accounting systems require specific knowledge not only about computers but about the field of accounting as well. Make sure that those running the system have the background needed to install and operate it. If they don't, get a package that is more in tune with your firm's capabilities.

Further, if you are using an automated accounting package, it must run on the computer equipment that is either currently in place or to be acquired in the near future.

If you choose to use an automated accounting system, this book will be of immense help in teaching you the basics of how it works. Whether manual or automated, all accounting systems use debits, credits, a general ledger, and subledgers. All entries are posted the same way. The only difference is which buttons to push. The last chapter demonstrates methods of selecting the proper automated accounting system for your company.

ACCOUNTING FOR THE BUSINESS CYCLE

The business cycle is nothing more than the flow of transactions needed in your business to complete a sale and collect the proceeds. It's important to setting up your accounting system. We want to know what types of transactions are involved and the accounting entries to make along the way. Most companies business cycles progress something like this:

1. Purchase raw materials.
2. Enter goods into raw materials inventory.
3. Begin the manufacturing or assembly process.
4. Enter goods into work in process inventory.
5. Pay suppliers or pay employees (at service companies).
6. Complete the manufacturing or assembly process.
7. Enter goods into finished goods inventory.
8. Sell the inventory.
9. Collect payment for credit sales.

Briefly, here is the way your accounting system interacts at each stage of the business cycle.

Purchase Raw Materials

What happens when you buy the raw materials used to create your company's product? You receive the goods, and you either pay cash for the goods or obligate the company for future payment. Both transactions require these accounting entries:

- Increase raw materials inventory
- Decrease cash (if you paid on the spot)
- Increase accounts payable (if you didn't)

At this point, we've covered the first two steps of the business cycle listed above.

Begin the Manufacturing Process

When we use raw materials to make our product, the accounting system transfers the inventory from raw materials to an intermediate stage called work in process (WIP for short). This transaction explains the third and fourth steps of the business cycle.

Pay Suppliers

Sometime during the production process we must pay our suppliers if we bought the raw materials on credit. The accounting entry for this transaction does two things:

- Reduces accounts payable • Reduces cash

Complete the Manufacturing Process

At last, we have completed our manufacturing process. Now we can move the product from the work in process inventory to the finished goods inventory. This transaction particularly interests the sales staff, since it means that the product is now available for sale, and that's what generates their commissions. The entries into the accounting system that record this event go like this:

- Reduce work in process inventory
- Increase finished goods inventory

We've now completed the sixth and seventh steps of the business cycle.

Sell the Product

At last we're ready to make a sale. If it's a credit sale, our accounting system must record these transactions:

- Reduction in finished goods inventory
- Increase in accounts receivable
- Increase in sales revenue

If this was a cash sale, replace the increase in receivables with an increase in cash. We just finished the eighth step of the business cycle.

Collect the Receivable

The final stage of the business cycle is conversion of the receivable (which is an asset) into spendable cash. When the customer pays, the accounting system records a decrease in receivables and an increase in cash.

This ends the business cycle and the various accounting transactions involved. The accounting system we're setting up will cover every one of these transactions.

COMPONENTS OF THE ACCOUNTING SYSTEM

Think of the accounting system as a wheel whose hub is the general ledger (G/L). Feeding the hub information are the spokes of the wheel. These include

- Accounts receivable • Accounts payable • Order entry
- Inventory control • Cost accounting • Payroll
- Fixed assets accounting

These modules are ledgers themselves. We call them *subledgers*. Each contains the detailed entries of its specific field, such as accounts receivable. The subledgers summarize the entries, then send the summary up to the general ledger. For example, each day the receivables subledger records all credit sales and payments received. The transactions net together then go up to the G/L to increase or decrease A/R, increase cash and decrease inventory.

We'll always check to be sure that the balance of the subledger exactly equals the account balance for that subledger account in the G/L. If it doesn't, then there's a problem.

Differences between Manual and Automated Ledgers

Think of the G/L as a sheet of paper on which transactions from all four categories of accounts—assets, liabilities, income, and expenses—are recorded. Some of them flow up from various subledgers, and some are entered directly into the G/L through a general journal entry. An example of such a direct entry would be the payment on a loan.

The same concept of a sheet of paper holds for each subledger that feeds the general ledger. A computerized accounting system works the same way, except that the general ledger and subledgers are computer files instead of sheets of paper. Entries are posted to each and summarized, then the summary is sent up to the G/L for posting.

ORGANIZATION OF THE ACCOUNTING DEPARTMENT

Organize your small-business accounting system by function. Often there's just one person there to do all the transaction entries. From an internal control standpoint, this isn't desirable. Having too few people doing all the accounting opens the door for fraud and embezzlement. Companies with more people assign functions in such a way that those done by the same person don't pose a control threat.

Having the same person draft the checks *and* reconcile the checking account is a good example of how *not* to assign accounting duties. We'll talk extensively about internal control later. However, for now, small businesses often can't afford the number of people needed for an adequate separation of duties. The internal control structure that we'll install in your new accounting system helps mitigate that risk through *mechanics and procedures* rather than expensive people.

Assignment of Duties

Here's your first assignment: Figure out who is going to do what in your new accounting system. The duties and areas of responsibility we need to assign include

- Overall responsibility for the accounting system
- Management of the computer system (if you're using one)
- Accounts receivable
- Accounts payable
- Order entry
- Cost accounting

- Monthly reporting
- Inventory control
- Payroll (even if you use an outside payroll service, *someone* must be in control and responsible)
- Internal accounting control
- Fixed assets

Figure 1-1
Sample Accounting Questions

Question	Answer
Give me the accounting entry for a credit sale.	Debit accounts receivable; credit sales.
Give me the accounting entry to record depreciation expense.	Debit depreciation expense; credit accumulated depreciation.
What is the best size for a batch of invoices posted to the accounts payable system?	The smaller the batch, the better, because if it's out of balance, we don't want to have to wade through volumes of transactions to find the error. If you want numbers, try to keep the batch size down to twenty or so.
What reports do you want your receivables system to produce?	Aging, roll rates, ten highest-balance accounts, accounts over their credit limit.
What reports do you want your payables system to produce?	Aging, listing of past due vendors, cash requirements to stay current within the next week, month, etc.
Explain the *grandfather, father, son* method of backing up automated accounting data.	We have three back-ups on disks or tapes. The oldest is the grandfather and it is used to make the newest—the son—when the next back-up is done. In this way we can always recover either a day, week, or month back if something happens to our primary and one or more of our back-ups. To further safeguard the back-ups, store the father and grandfather off-site.
What is the entry to record a cash sale?	Debit cash; credit inventory.
What is the entry to record a credit memo?	If it's a return of merchandise, then debit inventory and credit cash for the amount given the customer. If it's a reduction of the receivables account, credit accounts receivables and debit the income account credited in the original transaction.
What's the difference between an accrual and a cash basis accounting system?	Accrual basis recognizes noncash transactions such as credit sales and purchases and depreciation; cash basis goes strictly on cash transactions.
What is a negative cost variance?	It means that your production costs exceeded the standard costs established by management.
What types of inventory methods are there?	LIFO, FIFO, and average cost.
What are the entries to record retained earnings in a partnership?	None. Partnerships have no retained earnings. Instead they have partners' capital accounts.
What are the entries to record a write-off of a bad debt?	Credit accounts receivable; debit bad debt expense.

In many cases the same person will do many of these things. However, these are the areas we'll be dealing with in setting up the accounting system. The person you assign to be in overall charge of the system should be the one who is most familiar with accounting. If you are just starting your company, you might want to think about the background of some of your new employees. At least one should have the capacity to run the accounting system.

If you find it difficult to determine someone's expertise in a field with which you are unfamiliar, here are some solutions:

1. Have them interviewed by an expert. Your own CPA will probably be glad to interview a few for you.
2. Carefully check references from past jobs. Ask detailed questions on exactly what they did in the accounting function. Compare the answers with what they *say* they did.
3. Ask them some accounting questions. It may sound odd that you (of all people) should be asking such questions. However, even if you can't judge the technical merit of the answers, you *can* get a feel for how comfortable they are with the subject and the authority with which they answer. Figure 1-1 provides some sample questions and answers to try out.

These are just a few of the questions you might ask. I'm sure you can come up with many more that are specifically relevant to your company.

Basic Terms and Concepts

There are a few (and only a few) things you need to understand in order to make setting up your accounting system easier. They're basic (trust me), and they will probably clear up any confusion you may have had in the past when talking with your CPA or other technical accounting types.

Debits and Credits

These are the backbone of any accounting system. Understand how debits and credits work and you'll understand the whole system. Every accounting entry in the general ledger contains both a debit and a credit. Further, all debits must equal all credits. If they don't, the entry is out of balance. That's not good. Out-of-balance entries throw your balance sheet out of balance.

Therefore, the accounting system must have a mechanism to ensure that all entries balance. Indeed, most automated accounting systems won't let you enter an out-of-balance entry—they'll just beep at you until you fix your error.

Depending on what type of account you are dealing with, a debit or credit will either increase or decrease the account balance. (Here comes the hardest part of accounting for most beginners, so pay attention.) Figure 1-2 illustrates the entries that increase or decrease each type of account.

Figure 1-2
Debits and Credits vs. Account Types

Account Type	Debit	Credit
Assets	Increases	Decreases
Liabilities	Decreases	Increases
Income	Decreases	Increases
Expenses	Increases	Decreases

Notice that for every increase in one account, there is an opposite (and equal) decrease in another. That's what keeps the entry in balance. Also notice that debits always go on the left and credits on the right.

Let's take a look at two sample entries and try out these debits and credits:

In the first stage of the example we'll record a credit sale:

Accounts Receivable	$1,000	
Sales Income		$1,000

If you looked at the general ledger right now, you would see that receivables had a balance of $1,000 and income also had a balance of $1,000.

Now we'll record the collection of the receivable:

Cash	$1,000	
Accounts Receivable		$1,000

Notice how both parts of each entry balance? See how in the end, the receivables balance is back to zero? That's as it should be once the balance is paid. The net result is the same as if we conducted the whole transaction in cash:

Cash	$1,000	
Sales Income		$1,000

Of course, there would probably be a period of time between the recording of the receivable and its collection.

That's it. Accounting doesn't really get much harder. Everything else is just a variation on the same theme. Make sure you understand debits and credits and how they increase and decrease each type of account.

Assets and Liabilities

Balance sheet accounts are the assets and liabilities. When we set up your chart of accounts in Chapter 5, there will be separate sections and numbering schemes for the assets and liabilities that make up the balance sheet.

A quick reminder: Increase assets with a debit and decrease them with a credit. Increase liabilities with a credit and decrease them with a debit.

Identifying assets

Simply stated, assets are those things of value that your company owns. The cash in your bank account is an asset. So is the company car you drive. Assets are the *objects, rights and claims owned by and having value for the firm.*

Since your company has a right to the future collection of money, accounts receivable are an asset—probably a major asset, at that. The machinery on your production floor is also an asset. If your firm owns real estate or other tangible property, those are considered assets as well. If you were a bank, the loans you make would be considered assets since they represent a right of future collection.

There may also be *intangible* assets owned by your company. Patents, the exclusive right to use a trademark, and goodwill from the acquisition of another company are such intangible assets. Their value can be somewhat hazy.

Generally, the value of intangible assets is whatever both parties agree to when the assets are created. In the case of a patent, the value is often linked to its development costs. Goodwill is often the difference between the purchase price of a company and the value of the assets acquired (net of accumulated depreciation).

Identifying liabilities

Think of liabilities as the opposite of assets. These are the obligations of one company to another. Accounts payable are liabilities, since they represent your company's future duty to pay a vendor. So is the loan you took from your bank. If you were a bank, your customer's deposits would be a liability, since they represent future claims against the bank.

We segregate liabilities into short-term and long-term categories on the balance sheet. This division is nothing more than separating those liabilities scheduled for payment within the next accounting period (usually the next twelve months) from those not to be paid until later. We often separate debt like this. It gives readers a clearer picture of how much the company owes and when.

Owners' equity

After the liability section in both the chart of accounts and the balance sheet comes owners' equity. This is the difference between assets and liabilities. Hopefully, it's positive—assets exceed liabilities and we have a positive owners' equity. In this section we'll put in things like

- Partners' capital accounts   • Stock   • Retained earnings

Another quick reminder: Owners' equity is increased and decreased just like a liability:

- Debits decrease   • Credits increase

Most automated accounting systems require identification of the retained earnings account. Many of them will beep at you if you don't do so.

By the way, retained earnings are the accumulated profits from prior years. At the end of one accounting year, all the income and expense accounts are netted against one another, and a single number (profit or loss for the year) is moved into the retained earnings account. This is what belongs to the company's owners—that's why it's in the owners' equity section. The income and expense accounts go to zero. That's how we're able to begin the new year with a clean slate against which to track income and expense.

The balance sheet, on the other hand, does not get zeroed out at year-end. The balance in each asset, liability, and owners' equity account rolls into the next year. So the ending balance of one year becomes the beginning balance of the next.

Think of the balance sheet as today's snapshot of the assets and liabilities the company has acquired since the first day of business. The income statement, in contrast, is a summation of the income and expenses *from the first day of this accounting period* (probably from the beginning of this fiscal year).

Income and Expenses

Further down in the chart of accounts (usually after the owners' equity section) come the income and expense accounts. Most companies want to keep track of just where they get income and where it goes, and these accounts tell you.

A final reminder: For income accounts, use credits to increase them and debits to decrease them. For expense accounts, use debits to increase them and credits to decrease them.

Income accounts

If you have several lines of business, you'll probably want to establish an income account for each. In that way, you can identify exactly where your income is coming from. Adding them together yields total revenue.

Typical income accounts would be

- Sales revenue from product A
- Sales revenue from product B (and so on for each product you want to track)
- Interest income
- Income from sale of assets
- Consulting income

Most companies have only a few income accounts. That's really the way you want it. Too many accounts are a burden for the accounting department and probably don't tell management what it wants to know. Nevertheless, if there's a source of income you want to track, create an account for it in the chart of accounts and use it.

Expense accounts

Most companies have a separate account for each type of expense they incur. Your company probably incurs pretty much the same expenses month after month, so once they are established, the expense accounts won't vary much from month to month. Typical expense accounts include

- Salaries and wages • Telephone • Electric utilities • Repairs
- Maintenance • Depreciation • Amortization • Interest
- Rent

MAKING JOURNAL ENTRIES

You'll be making lots of journal entries into your accounting system. That's how you record the transactions that occur. Regardless of whether you're using a manual or an automated accounting system, the same principle applies for journal entries.

All a journal entry (called a *J/E* for short) consists of is the debits and credits to the appropriate accounts. Usually there's a short explanation of the entry and some sort of reference indicator so that you can find the source documents that prompted the entry in the first place. Smart accountants try to group like-kind J/Es together into one as much as they can. This grouping saves time and keeps the number of J/Es flowing through the general ledger to a minimum.

However, there's no rule that says how many J/Es you can make. Make as many as you want. When major entries are complex and involved, many accountants make them stand-alone entries and don't include any others.

General Ledger Journal Entries

All J/Es are eventually posted to the G/L. Some go directly there; others begin in the receivables, payables, cash receipts, or disbursement subledger and are posted to the G/L as part of a *net* transaction. Automated systems do this posting for you automatically.

An example of a direct journal entry into the G/L might be recording depreciation expense for the month (recall that this was one of the questions asked earlier of a prospective accountant):

Depreciation Expense	$1,000	
Accumulated Depreciation		$1,000
Total:	$1,000	$1,000

Explanation: Records depreciation expense for the month of August 199X for these assets:

Leasehold improvements:	$250
Autos:	350
Machinery and equipment:	400
	$1,000

Entries to Subledgers

Did you notice how each entry to the G/L is double sided—for every debit there's an equal and offsetting credit? When we make entries into subledgers that's *not* the case. Think of the subledger as just an accumulation of detailed information that we want to keep straight and that eventually flows up to the G/L in the form of a double-sided journal entry.

Let's record a receivable into the accounts receivable subledger, then watch how it flows up to the G/L:

Accounts Receivable Subledger
Record credit sales to Tobby and Riley:

Accounts Receivable Subledger

Cust. Acct. #	Cust. Name	Date	Amt. of Sale	Description
1234	Tobby	5-24-9X	$524.34	Prefab alum. boxes
5678	Riley	5-24-9X	$756.92	#24 packed bearings
		Total	$1,281.26	

These two sales post to the A/R subledger to increase Tobby's and Riley's balances owed. Now watch how the A/R subledger flows up to the G/L:

General Ledger

G/L acct. #	Description	Date	Debit	Credit
250	Accounts Receivable	5-24-9X	$1,281.26	
475	Sales	5-24-9X		$1,281.26
		Total	$1,281.26	$1,281.26

See how both the asset account, accounts receivable, and the income account, sales, were increased using the double-entry accounting we spoke of earlier? That's all there is to it. All subledgers work this way. Their purpose again is simply to maintain the detailed information associated with their accounts, then pass summarized information up to the general ledger.

ACCRUAL AND CASH BASIS ACCOUNTING
You may have heard of these two types of accounting. All larger companies use the accrual basis—that's what we call *generally accepted accounting principles* for companies with annual revenues exceeding $5 million. Smaller companies have a choice. Here's the difference.

Accrual Basis of Accounting
Companies using the accrual basis of accounting simply record a transaction when it happens without regard to whether money actually changes hands. Credit sales are a case in point. When you sell your product to a customer who will pay

sometime in the future and you record the receivable, you are *accruing* the sales revenue. No cash changes hands, yet a real sale took place.

Accrual accounting presents a more accurate picture by matching income and expenses during the accounting period. The actual payment of money is incidental to the accounting for the transaction.

Cash Basis of Accounting

Very small companies often elect to recognize a transaction only when cash changes hands. For example, say you buy raw material from a vendor using trade credit. Under the cash basis of accounting, nothing has happened, since you haven't paid yet. You won't record a payable in the A/P subledger (chances are, you don't even *have* an A/P subledger). You don't record the purchase until you actually pay for the goods.

Deciding On the Basis of Accounting

In making this decision, you should consider the nature of your business. If you sell on trade credit to customers who pay in the future and if you buy your goods and incur expenses based on an agreement of future payment, then it makes sense to use the accrual method of accounting.

If, on the other hand, your business is of such a nature that most transactions are cash and your annual sales don't exceed $5 million, then you probably could use cash basis accounting. You needn't bother setting up receivables and payables subledgers, because you don't deal in them.

A final point here: Whichever method you chose, make sure you stick to it and don't change in the middle of the accounting cycle. Ever. If accounting is nothing else, it's consistent. You *must* consistently apply the basis of whichever accounting method you choose or you'll have a mess on your hands.

ACCOUNTING FOR DEPRECIATION AND AMORTIZATION

These occur only in accrual basis accounting systems since they involve *noncash* expenses. Depreciation and amortization represent the amount of an asset you've used up during that accounting period. Take the example of a delivery truck. The truck has a finite life—it won't last forever. Each month you move closer to the time when all the utility of the truck is used up.

Later on we'll go through the various ways of computing depreciation expense. For now, however, let's move on to the difference between depreciation and amortization.

Differences between Depreciation and Amortization

Both depreciation and amortization represent the using up of a portion of an asset's economic life. However, depreciation is generally associated with hard assets, such as vehicles, leasehold improvements, machinery, and equipment.

Amortization is associated with intangibles, such as patent rights, copyrights, loan origination fees, and goodwill. Theoretically both depreciation and amortization accomplish the same thing: recording noncash but no less real costs incurred during the accounting period.

INTERNAL ACCOUNTING CONTROL

Chapter 14 deals exclusively with internal accounting controls. These will keep you from having your lunch eaten by unscrupulous employees and outsiders.

By way of definition, in the language of accounting, the system of internal accounting controls is a structure of policies, procedures, checks, and balances that ensures transactions are executed, processed and recorded in accordance with management policies. Even when the system of internal control is working properly, it won't prevent fraud. It will, however, make fraud more difficult to execute and much more risky for the perpetrator. These two things help act as a deterrent. It also provides a mechanism by which management can verify that things are being done according to policy.

INVENTORY

For many small businesses, inventory is one of their major assets. As such we'll pay a lot of attention to establishing an effective inventory control mechanism in Chapter 10. For now, however, let's nail down the terminology used for inventory.

Raw Materials Inventory

These are the goods you buy to use in your manufacturing process. If liquid chlorine is used in the process of producing your salable goods, then it's considered raw materials inventory. If you make sheet metal cabinets for computers, then the unfinished sheet metal is raw material.

Work in Process Inventory (WIP)

WIP inventory is exactly what its name implies: somewhere between raw material and finished goods. Most companies have goods constantly in production. Usually not all the raw material purchased is converted to finished goods by the end of the accounting period. The balance sheet reports inventory still in production at month-end as work in process.

Finished Goods Inventory

Once the goods roll off your production line, they make the transition from WIP to finished goods. These represent the inventory you're ready to sell your customers.

Costing Inventory

You've probably heard of the various inventory costing methods:

- LIFO • FIFO • Average cost • Lower of cost or market

Briefly, here's what these mean.

LIFO

This is a commonly accepted inventory valuation method. It means *last-in, first-out*. It assumes that when you finish production of an inventory item and place it on the shelf with the rest of the finished goods inventory, you'll sell it before those produced earlier. Even though this may not always be your actual practice, for purposes of computing cost of goods sold, your accounting system may assume that this is true.

During periods of rising prices, a LIFO method of inventory valuation places higher costs in the cost of goods sold computation and therefore lowers net income. For tax purposes, this may be desirable.

FIFO

The *first-in, first-out* method is just the opposite of LIFO. It assumes that the inventory that's sold is the oldest inventory. A business that sells perishables would be a good example of a FIFO inventory user. During periods of rising prices, a FIFO method would produce a lower cost of goods sold, a higher net income, and a greater tax liability.

Average cost

Some types of businesses use an average cost for their inventory. Where prices are changing all the time, the most accurate measurement of cost of goods sold is an average cost. An example would be a company that sells *fungible* goods—those for which lots purchased can't be differentiated. A produce wholesaler would be a good example. You can't tell one lot of oranges from another. So if you're selling them, the average cost of all orange purchases is probably the most accurate.

Lower of cost or market (LCM)

Accountants use this method primarily for valuing inventory at the balance sheet cutoff date (probably year-end). We want a solid, conservative estimate of the inventory value. Using the LCM method gives us this realistic estimate. It guarantees that the inventory shown on the balance sheet, can be sold as of the balance sheet date for either it's reported value or its original purchase price, whichever is lower.

Chapter 2 identifies the various components of the accounting system.

Chapter 2

Components of the Accounting System

Overview

Chapter 2 identifies each component of your small-business accounting system. It provides an overview of how each works and shows the interrelationships between information generated by one component and that used by another. Of course, your company may not use each and every one of these components. For example, if all your sales are cash, without exception, you probably don't need to set up an accounts receivable module. If your taxes are sufficiently complicated that you employ an outside professional, you won't need to do much for tax accounting.

You will, however, need to maintain the records your outside professional needs to complete the company's tax return. These include not only the normal profit and loss figures associated with the company's operations, but also records concerning such things as asset purchases and fixed asset accounting.

It's important that you see the coordinated record-keeping effort we're establishing in your accounting system. By the end of this chapter you'll have an appreciation for the genius behind a modern double-entry accounting system.

There's nothing complex about the interrelationships among different components of the accounting system. Once established, they rarely change. Further, they are consistent. When you do something in one module, you can bet that what you expected to happen elsewhere did indeed occur, unless there was a mistake. Indeed, that's frequently how we check our work—look for the proper effect to make sure it's there.

Let's take a look at the various components of the accounting system and see how they work with one another.

Chart of Accounts

The chart of accounts is simply a list of all the accounts used by the accounting system. It usually contains

- Account numbers • Account descriptions • Opening balance
- Current balance

Think of the chart of accounts as simply a database of accounts to which transactions can be posted. Practically speaking, we don't routinely consult the chart of accounts once it is established. Instead, we look at the general ledger for a list of accounts to post.

General Ledger

Every account appearing on your chart of accounts is in the general ledger. This is your accounting system's clearinghouse for all transactions. It won't include all the *individual* transactions from subledgers. However, they'll be in the G/L at least in summary form.

The general ledger is the component of the accounting system from which we take all financial statements. At month-end, when we produce financial statements, we transfer the account balances from the G/L to the reports.

Here's where attention to the order in which the accounts are reported is important in creating the chart of accounts. Since the chart of accounts, general ledger, and financial statements are so closely related, it makes sense to use the same order for each. The reporting order for presentation of your monthly financial statements probably goes something like this:

- Assets • Liabilities • Owners' equity • Income
- Expenses

Doesn't it make sense to use this same order in setting up the chart of accounts and general ledger? Sure. Because then, you just lift off the section of accounts you want to report on, summarize any lead accounts, and produce the report.

Source Documents

The general ledger employs source documents to provide a basis for each entry made. The rule is simple and one that you should follow: No source document, no entry. That's because we may need to refer back to the reasons for many of these entries long after we've forgotten them. Further, people other than those who actually made the entries might be looking through your accounting system for an explanation. Without a source document, it would be impossible for them to tell what happened.

A source document may be nothing more than a journal entry form explaining why a particular entry was made, when, and who did it. That's fine. Just so it provides a sufficient *audit trail* for use later to support the entry. We can trace most journal entries to an actual document that came from outside the firm. An invoice from a vendor is a good example. A batch of checks received from customers along with a confirmed deposit slip from the bank is another.

Keep in mind that preparing monthly financial statements is only half the utility you'll get from your accounting system. The other half comes from its ability to record and keep straight every financial transaction that goes on inside your company. It can tell you—long after everyone else has forgotten—just why each transaction occurred. We also use it to recreate entries made in error and then correct them. That's why we'll pay a lot of attention in Chapter 6, "The General

Ledger," to the mechanism we set up to trace and locate original source documents used in making G/L entries.

Journals

Many companies with large volumes of similar entries that require more detail than the general ledger provides use journals. These are really just subfiles of the general ledger. We design them to keep the details of each small transaction straight, then post the information to the general ledger, where it's recorded in summary fashion.

Some of the more common journals used to support the general ledger are the

- Payroll journal • Cash receipts journal
- Cash disbursements journal

Transitions in these are recorded (*posted* is the term accountants use) in detail in the individual journal. Then the transactions for the day are summed up and posted to the general ledger as a summary entry. The G/L contains a reference to that specific batch of entries in the journal.

For an example of how this works in the cash disbursement journal, let's say that today we're going to pay twenty of our vendors a total amount of $1,000. The cash disbursement journal is really the accounts payable subledger. From this we know to whom we owe what. We also have a record of each invoice.

So we select those vendors that we're going to pay. In the A/P subledger we record the payments and reduce the balance owed to each of those lucky vendors. The total reduction in A/P is $1,000. We also record the check numbers we used for payment and the date. This becomes a component of our check register—the outgoing side. We'll use it later to help reconcile the bank account. The incoming side for use in bank account reconciliation is usually the cash receipts journal.

At this point we have a complete list of our payments and the checks we have written. We keep the list with the A/P subledger. These transactions reduce the account balance for each vendor we owe by the amount paid. The next step is to post this information to the G/L. This is a simple entry; there are only two accounts involved: A/P and cash. Here it is:

Accounts Payable	$1,000	
Cash		$1,000
Records A/P batch #15 on 6-12-9X.		

With help from the reference below the entry in the G/L, we can go back to the A/P subledger and identify each vendor paid in this batch. Further, there's no extraneous information (such as the name of each vendor, its account number, and invoice numbers) to clutter the G/L—it's all contained in the A/P subledger.

That's how the G/L interrelates with the other modules of the accounting system. One clean entry is made for their summarized transactions. Of course, there are times when we bypass the subledgers and make an entry directly to the G/L. These are usually for less frequent transactions than cash receipts, disbursements, and payroll. A more likely direct entry into the G/L might be recording the purchase of a new and expensive piece of production machinery.

ACCOUNTS RECEIVABLE

We want a solid mechanism to keep straight who owes us what. That's the A/R subledger. It feeds summary information on transactions affecting it to the general ledger. Most of the detailed activity associated with individual credit customers is recorded only in the receivables subledger.

Sources of Information

The A/R subledger receives three types of source documents that account for the bulk of transactions affecting its accounts:

- Sales slips and invoices
- Payment received chits
- Credit memos

Process each type of document in a separate batch to keep straight the type of transaction that's being recorded. This makes it easier to refer to later. We can just look up the appropriate sales, payment, or credit batch and go right to the transaction in question.

Since the receivables system is usually the end point for these source documents, store them in the receivables department. Ready access also makes it easier to retrieve the necessary information about customers who dispute the balance they owe. We want to be able to find the sales slip or invoice proving the purchase for which we're requesting/demanding payment.

Information in the A/R Subledger

The receivables subledger contains a variety of information about each customer. Some of the automated systems on the market contain a complete sales history. However, all that's really required are the following:

- A/R account number
- Customer name, address, and phone number
- Balance owed

For collection purposes and to feed into the order entry system, it's often nice to have a history of the customer's credit transactions, a record of the highest credit balance, the credit limit, and any incident of nonpayment or dispute. The sales staff could also use a complete history of what each customer has purchased and when. However, these things aren't necessary to do the *accounting* for receivables.

For tax purposes, we want to keep track of where we've earned our income. If your company is a partnership or sole proprietorship, you'll need to know who owes you a Form 1099 at year-end to prove that the income you've recorded is correct. (By the way, corporations don't receive 1099s.)

Are you getting a sense of the kinds of information the accounting system captures that the rest of the company can use? This isn't surprising, since the function of the accounting system is to maintain specific records in an orderly fashion for future reference. The best accounting systems are those that allow for flexibility in reporting—not just in the financial statements, but in the ability to access some of the history available within the system. Accounts receivable is a good example.

Many automated accounting systems provide for user designed reports that access the system's history files. Some of the more sophisticated systems provide for the conversion of accounting records into spreadsheet files. Using these, a knowledgeable person can create virtually any analysis required.

As you continue through the components of the accounting system, please think about the various *nonaccounting* uses for some of the information we're generating. Even if you choose to use a manual accounting system, there are some things you can do in designing it that will make future access to this information easier. If you employ an automated system, consider some of the other uses of all this information and make sure the system you choose has the ability to provide it to you.

Accounts Payable

This is the flip side of the receivables subledger. Mechanically it works much the same way. We record all the invoices received by the company. The A/P mechanism tracks them according to due date or date of payment needed to take advantage of a trade discount. The A/P subledger pays each payable when due. The ledger summarizes these transactions then posts them to the general ledger.

Sources of Information

The best source document for entry into the A/P system is the vendor's invoice. This usually includes most of the information needed to feed the A/P system. Many firms require that each invoice be either approved by the person who ordered the item or matched with a company purchase order.

Another document often used to validate a vendor invoice is a company receiving slip (sometimes called a *receiver*). Someone on the receiving dock signs the receiver to confirm receipt of the item and its entry into inventory or wherever else the firm uses it.

The point is that before we blindly enter a payment request into the A/P system we want to be sure that

- We ordered the item.
- The item was received in good condition.
- Someone in the company is knowledgeable about the purchase.

Information in the A/P Subledger

For most small businesses, the information needed in the A/P system is less extensive than that in accounts receivable. That's probably because this is a liability rather than a valuable asset. Nevertheless, a well-run disbursement mechanism gives your company credibility with its vendors and helps you manage your cash flow.

Here are the basic pieces of information we want to record into accounts payable from each vendor's invoice:

- Vendor account number (in our A/P system)
- Vendor name, address, and phone number
- Amount owed
- Regular due date, trade discount percent, and trade discount due date
- Vendor's invoice number
- Description of the item
- Expense or asset general ledger account number to hit

With this information, our payables system can track the invoice and make sure it's paid according to our purchase terms. We can identify the specific invoice later by its number and retrieve it from our files. We know the item and which account number in our accounting system to use when we post the A/P batch to the general ledger.

Nonaccounting Needs

The person in your company who keeps track of the cash balance uses the payables system too. A valid question often asked is, How much in the A/P system right now needs to be paid in the next _____ days to stay current with our vendors? Some of the better automated A/P modules produce a specific report that addresses such cash management questions. If cash is tight for your company, whether you use a manual or automated system, this is a question you'll probably want to answer with a minimum of effort.

Vendor history

We'll want the A/P system to provide some sort of vendor history for us at least through the current year. This is most important for tax purposes. At year-end, we need to send a Form 1099 to noncorporate vendors from whom we've purchased more than $600 in goods or services.

To generate this information, we need the ability to tally total expenditures for each vendor, then determine if that vendor qualifies to receive a 1099. Some of the more sophisticated computerized A/P modules ask if a new vendor you're setting up should receive a 1099. If so, the module will also request the vendor's social security number or tax payer ID number (for printing on the 1099 form). The A/P system then proceeds to keep track of year-to-date purchases from each vendor that is to receive a 1099. At year-end the system actually prints the 1099 forms for you.

Purchase history

Sometimes it's nice to know which vendors you're giving your business to. Buyers use this information to negotiate more favorable purchase terms by citing a profitable past relationship. It also identifies those vendors who give purchase discounts and those who don't.

ORDER ENTRY (O/E)

Here's where the rubber meets the road. All your company's sales efforts and advertising come down to that person on the telephone taking customer orders. Alternatively, your sales staff may also act as order takers. They may draft sales agreements on the spot and submit them to an order processing desk.

Regardless of who actually does it, O/E is responsible for converting often complex sales arrangements into

- Warehouse pull requests for inventory
- Back-order requests for inventory sold but unavailable
- A sales invoice
- The information needed to enter the transaction for entry into the accounts receivable system

There are also some decisions your O/E staff needs to make. They cannot do their job without specific knowledge of the customer and its financial stability. They need access to the customer's receivables file.

Accounts Receivable Interface

Some of the more sophisticated computerized accounting systems have an *interface* between order entry and accounts receivable. The O/E staff has *read only* access to each customer's accounts receivable history. If the current balance plus the intended purchase exceeds the customer's established credit limit, the O/E person can decline an order. This can save a great deal in collection and bad debt expense.

Inventory Control interface

The O/E mechanism should ideally provide an updated listing of the availability status for each inventory item. It's much better to tell a customer about possible delays in delivery or projected shipping dates when the order is placed. This takes some of the guesswork out of buying from you. Further, the O/E person is often the first to know about back-ordered items. There's no one better to flag the item to the company's purchaser.

Substituting goods

Another benefit of linking order entry with the inventory system is the ability to automatically see which goods can be substituted for others that may be currently unavailable. Something to consider when designing your O/E and inventory mechanisms is how much (if any) benefit having this information at someone's fingertips would be.

For companies that can use it, when goods are unavailable, the automated O/E system interface with inventory control provides a list of substitutes that might work. This prevents losing a sale because the product isn't available. The substitute satisfies the customer's needs, and the company makes a sale.

Of course, the more sophisticated these automated accounting modules are, the more information they require in their setup. Substitutions are a case in point. Part of the new item entry menu for each inventory commodity is a list of possible substitutes. Of course, this prolongs the setup of the inventory control system. It also opens the door for error if someone isn't familiar with the company's inventory. However, when used properly, this can be a powerful tool.

INVENTORY CONTROL

Since inventory is often one of a small business's largest assets, control of inventory is near the top of everyone's priority list. Buying too much of the wrong item or not having enough of a product that's currently hot whittles away your profits.

Likewise, your inventory control (I/C) mechanism helps in figuring out how much of each item to order. For example, many managers try to strike a balance between bulk discounts from larger than normal orders and working capital tied up in excess inventory. If the deal is good enough, it often makes sense to buy more than you need right now.

Safety stock is another concern of inventory control. We want enough extra inventory on hand to meet *reasonably foreseen* excess demand. Holding stock beyond that point fails to balance the risk of missing out on a sale with the cost of carry for the safety stock. Chapter 10, "Inventory Control," addresses each of these points and shows how to compute the optimum levels of stock to order and hold.

Controlling Inventory

The inventory control system works in much the same way as the receivables and payables subledgers. Its purpose is to keep straight a lengthy and complicated set of items having numerous transactions every day. The net of all inventory transactions each day (or whenever you choose to do it) is posted to the general ledger as a simple double-sided entry.

The basic activities accounted for in the inventory control system include

- Entry of inventory stock receipts
- Tracking of inventory items as they progress through the production process from raw materials to work in process and finally to finished goods
- Exit from available inventory when a sale occurs

Providing Management Information

The activities listed above are only the basic duties of a good inventory control system. If the information is available and if you know how to use it, your inventory subledger system can provide a new dimension to managing one of the largest assets your company has.

Computing cost of goods sold

The basic cost of goods sold equation goes like this:

Beginning inventory *plus* purchases *less* ending inventory *equals* cost of goods sold

The balance sheet should be able to tell you the beginning inventory number. However, the inventory control mechanism should provide the purchases made during the accounting period. If you are using a manual ledger, perhaps all that's needed is an additional column beside the inventory items. Sum the column at the end of each month and you have all the purchases.

Automated I/C systems work the same way. They provide reports on purchases at the touch of a button. Further, the computer tracks the cost of each inventory item and the value added by any manufacturing activity.

Determine ending inventory from the records in the I/C system. Alternatively, take a physical count of the ending inventory. Usually some sort of reconciliation process takes place between the inventory records and a physical count. In any case, your I/C system should provide ending stock numbers along with the total value of the ending inventory.

Most systems do this for each inventory transaction. We call the process a *perpetual* inventory system. The system updates the number of goods available after every change. Certainly for companies with an active inventory turnover, it is beneficial to know

- Stock on hand
- Inventory just received
- Requirements to fill an order

History and status

From a management standpoint, we often want to know which inventory items are moving and which are simply gathering dust while gobbling up our working capital. Modern I/C systems provide information on the movement of each item. The factors that influence the amount of inventory most small businesses carry include

- Demand for the item
- Duration of the production process
- Raw material or critical component availability
- Durability of the finished good
- Method of distribution

Further, in a single place there's a good chance we'll find the following for each inventory item:

- Number of items on hand • Date the items were received
- Price at which each was purchased • Vendor's reorder number
- Back order status • Warehouse location
- Minimum safety stock recommended • Suggested quantity order

Obsolete and slow-moving inventory

Some sophisticated computerized inventory control systems have the ability to conduct ad hoc inquiries of the entire warehouse stock or any particular item. Frequently asked questions concern obsolete and slow-moving items. These are too expensive for small businesses to keep on hand without selling. Remember, the objective of inventory control is to keep this costly asset turning. We want to have our inventory on hand for as little time as possible.

Cost Accounting

This segment of the accounting system has a reputation for being difficult to master. I suspect the reason is that managers often think they were unfairly allocated a cost that doesn't belong to them. The intent of the cost accounting component of the accounting system is to track what it costs the company not only to make a product but to

- Stock it • Sell it • Ship it
- Collect the receivable • Absorb bad debts
- Pay for indirect management and other overhead items

We'll use the cost accounting system partly as a benchmark to keep production costs in line. To that end, we'll generate a simplified version of standard costs. These are compared against actual costs, and the variances are investigated. Small businesses can't afford to let their production costs spin out of control for even a short time. The cost accounting system spots deviations and draws management's attention to them.

Allocating Indirect Costs

We cannot attribute indirect costs to any one production item. The salary of the shop foreman is an example. The foreman spends time on all the items produced. To say that more or less of that person's salary should go to a particular product is difficult.

That's why the cost system *allocates* a share of each indirect cost to each salable item. It's this process of allocation that helps us arrive at a minimum sales price for our products. Sales below that price would cause us to lose money.

Payroll

People often view payroll as excessively complicated because of tax reporting and the various forms filed with the federal and state governments. That's why commercial payroll processing companies have enjoyed so much success. The fact is, however, that payroll isn't that complicated, especially for a small business with only a few employees.

The first decision that Chapter 12, "Payroll," walks you through is the determination of *who* should do your payroll. For many small companies the added effort doesn't justify what little cost a professional payroll processing service charges. Indeed, many banks offer this service to their customers.

The decision boils down mostly to the cost of a service versus the time and capability of your staff. Additionally, you need a backup in case the primary person leaves or is ill on a critical day. I've known public accounting firms that hired an outside service despite (or maybe because of) the fact that they had many qualified professionals who could have done the job.

Another consideration—and one of the reasons professional payroll processing systems are so inexpensive—is that these services use your money. Not only must you fund the entire payroll well in advance of the release date, you must also fund all your federal and state contributions. In some cases this amounts to a significant increase in working capital requirements as much as two months ahead of the required payment date.

Manual vs. Automated Payroll

If you choose to do your own payroll, you still have another decision: manual or automated. The answer usually depends on the background and familiarity of the persons doing the job. Usually these people gravitate to whatever method they used last time.

However, if the decision is to use a manual payroll processing system, remember that all the payroll and tax entries and employee payment records are also manually kept. Automated systems, on the other hand, automatically update your general ledger, keep track of W-2 information for each employee, and record everyone's complete salary history. Further, they'll prepare most of your government reporting requirements for you. And most of them are relatively inexpensive.

FIXED ASSET ACCOUNTING

Here's another possible use of a subledger. Most companies have fixed assets—those assets that are durable and will last for many years. Leasehold improvements and motor vehicles are good examples. Just like the other subledgers we'll be setting up in your accounting system, this one takes a lot of detailed transactions and summarizes them for entry into the general ledger.

Fixed assets, however, have some special requirements. First, every month they have depreciation or amortization charged against them. The computation varies depending on the type of asset, its tax classification, and its economic life. The charges hit each fixed asset in the subledger. Then they're summarized, and the following entry flows up to the general ledger:

> Depreciation Expense $1,000
>   Accumulated Depreciation $1,000
> Records fixed asset depreciation expense for July 199X.

Another use of the fixed asset accounting system involves property taxes. Many states assess property tax on personal as well as real property. The fixed asset accounting system provides a mechanism that can easily report all the information necessary for the tax authorities when it comes time to prepare the return.

INTERNAL ACCOUNTING CONTROL

The system of internal accounting control is probably one of the most valuable mechanisms in your accounting system. However, it's also the most complicated, and its subject to error because it involves people. If small-business owners and managers did everything themselves, there would be little need for internal control. However, by its nature, a company depends on a number of people to perform their jobs in accordance with management's prescribed policies and procedures. That being the case, your firm risks

- Disregard for management policies and procedures
- Entry of bogus documents into the accounting system
- Loss or theft of vital documents
- Inaccurate or fraudulent reporting of financial transactions
- Theft or conversion of assets

Purpose of Internal Controls

Many people mistakenly take internal controls to mean *detection* of theft or fraud. That's only partly the purpose—and not really the primary function at that. Detection contributes to the real purpose of the control mechanism: *prevention* of unauthorized actions. The system we establish in Chapter 14, "Internal Accounting Controls," utilizes the *deterrent* effect that increased likelihood of detection provides.

The most any control system can hope to do is provide a deterrent. It's really there only to keep honest people honest. It won't do much good against a savvy and determined perpetrator. Nevertheless, we design our control system to make each act *harder* to commit and to limit the potential damage from each event. Further, the increased risk of detection that adherence to strict control procedures provides increases the likelihood that smarter operators will try someplace that's easier.

Interface with Other Departments

The system of internal accounting controls encompasses each department in the accounting system—and throughout the entire company, for that matter. Your control system affects procedures and individual responsibilities in every accounting discipline. Most controls are common sense. Almost all are easy and purposely inexpensive to maintain.

An example is cash disbursements through the payables system. Only a novice would allow the same person to enter invoices into the A/P system, draft the checks, *and then reconcile the checking account.* Even the most dim-witted thief doesn't need check signing authority to steal your money. Yet this necessary separation of duties gets ignored constantly in small businesses.

FINANCIAL REPORTING

The most visible effect of any accounting system is the monthly reports it turns out. Small businesses usually need the basic financial statements:

- Balance sheet • Income statement • Statement of cash flows

Additionally, for partnerships, we'll add the changes to partners' capital accounts. From an internal management perspective, the monthly reporting routine should produce reports addressing specific concerns. For many small businesses, these focus around accounts receivable, projected cash flows, and analysis of gross margin by product.

One of the increasingly important features of many automated accounting packages is the inclusion of comparative reports showing actual versus planned results. Another of the books in the Adams Business Advisor series, *The All-In-One Business Planning Guide,* focuses exclusively on preparation of a working business plan for small businesses.

USING OUTSIDE PROFESSIONALS

Outside financial professionals seem to paper the small-business landscape. Running the company occupies owners and managers of small businesses. Most are experts in their particular field. Few have the time or energy to stay current on the latest accounting, financial, and tax methods that could help them.

That's where the use of outside professionals—CPAs and tax planners—comes in. Some of the engagements for which small-business owners and managers use financial experts include

- Tax preparation
- Tax planning
- Audit, review, or compilation of financial statements
- Special projects

Tax Preparation

Federal and state tax laws are moving targets. Financial professionals have the time, background, and resources to keep up with the latest changes in the tax law. A good CPA looks at changes in the law and determines how they affect the company and can be used to its advantage.

Audit, Review, and Compilation

Most companies that have several partners or outside investors and lenders need some sort of independent accounting of the books and records. Independent CPA organizations perform these professional services. The key is their *independence.* People who rely on the company's financial statements don't want the CPA beholden to any of the company principals or the firm itself.

Briefly, the three levels of service provided are audit, review and compilation. An audit is the highest level of service a CPA organization provides. The objective is to render an opinion on the fairness of presentation of the financial statements. CPAs conduct extensive procedures to satisfy themselves that the statements are fairly presented. Audits are expensive and are not usually required by small businesses unless partners, investors, or lenders demand them.

A review, on the other hand, does not provide an opinion on the financial statements' fairness. Instead, the CPA conducts less extensive procedures. The purpose is to *review* the financial statements to see if anything comes to the CPA's their attention that leads him or her to believe there's a problem.

Compilations are the lowest level of service. Very small companies may lack any sort of financial staff. In this case, they may hire a bookkeeping service to *compile* their financial statements. A compilation provides no assurance that the statements are correct. The professional simply takes the information provided by the client and puts it into financial statement format. CPAs do not conduct procedures to verify the source information. Generally, compiled financial statements are not adequate for third-party use. However, they can be well used by internal management to run the company.

Special Projects

CPAs have the kind of technical financial background that's often useful to small businesses. For example, a review of a firm's system of internal accounting controls and recommendations for improvement can often give peace of mind to partners and investors. Alternatively, evaluation of the processing mechanism for receipt and collection of accounts receivable can sometimes accelerate cash inflow.

Chapter 3 defines the flow of information throughout the accounting system.

Chapter 3

Information Flow

OVERVIEW

The flow of information through the company to the accounting system can sometimes follow a convoluted path, especially in small businesses. Often we find that procedures for conveying information and the accounting treatment vary depending on who is in control of the transaction. Further, many small businesses have little if anything written down regarding what to do and when. That's what makes things complicated.

Chapter 3 demonstrates the flow of information throughout the company. We'll take a transaction-by-transaction approach. The first thing we'll determine is what kind of accounting entry each type of transaction should generate. Once we know that, it becomes a simple matter to identify the type of information the accounting system needs and who would normally provide it.

The flow of accounting information isn't very complicated unless people try to interject their *personal value* to the company or their *vast* knowledge of special situations. There are only a handful of transaction categories that most companies process every month. Further, only a few places in the company generate information about these transactions. So let's get started.

PURCHASE OF MATERIALS

The first thing most companies do in the business cycle is buy the materials they'll convert into salable goods. If yours is a service company, you'll bypass this step, probably replacing it with the salaries of those who do the work your company provides.

So, how do you purchase the raw materials or subassemblies that go to your inventory for later use on the production line? More formalized companies often issue a purchase order. Some have a separate purchasing department. Very small companies just pick up the phone and place an order. Any of these is fine at this stage of the business cycle.

Purchase Order Information

If your firm does use a purchase order (P.O.), the accounting and finance department can probably use some of the information on it. First, the person who manages the firm's cash might like to know the amount of money committed and its payment date. This is entered into the cash forecast.

Second, you might want to keep a copy of the P.O. and match it against the vendor's invoice before that invoice is entered into the accounts payable system. This provides assurance that

- Vendors aren't arbitrarily sending in invoices for items you never ordered.
- The invoice correctly adheres to the purchase terms.

Additionally, those in your company who placed the order might like to keep track of it. This helps in tracing delays in shipment and quickly identifying critical items for which there's an availability problem. However, an actual entry into the accounting system isn't yet required.

RECEIPT OF GOODS

When the firm actually receives goods from vendors at the receiving dock, two things need to happen:

- The inventory account needs to be increased by the amount of materials received.
- An offsetting entry to a liability account—usually accounts payable—needs to be made.

Most companies use a *receiver* or receiving slip. This paper verifies receipt of the material in acceptable condition by the receiving dock. Often the vendor includes the invoice with the shipment. This is routed to the accounting department as well.

Accounting Entries

The entry we're going to make using the receiver and invoice goes like this:

Inventory	$1,000	
Accounts Payable		$1,000
Records receipt of raw material inventory from receiver #123.		

See how both inventory and A/P were increased by the amount of the inventory received. The information flow begins at the receiving dock with the receiver and invoice.

Lacking an Invoice?

What happens if there's no invoice included with the shipment? How do you know for sure how much to pay? Some companies try using the packing list, which gives the extended cost of the materials received. However, these are sometimes wrong, and they almost always lack the pertinent information your A/P people need to enter the purchase into the A/P subledger. Further, there's the danger of double-counting the payable by also entering the invoice when it finally arrives. You'd run the risk of paying twice for the same items.

You might consider putting the offsetting inventory entry into a holding liability account. You could call it something like *holding account for items re-*

ceived with no invoice. This account, however, must be reconciled each month. We don't want liabilities hanging around the balance sheet that no one has any knowledge of. If you do use this kind of account, make sure that you can identify each receiver and packing slip that are included in its balance. Then, after receipt of the real invoice, the entry to A/P goes like this:

Holding Account for Items		
Received with No Invoice	$1,000	
Accounts Payable		$1,000

Records entry of invoice for items previously received on receiver #123.

This entry transfers the balance from the holding account to accounts payable—both are liability accounts.

RECEIPT OF PURCHASES INVOICE

Small businesses are fortunate in that the people doing the accounting are also familiar with the company's purchases. When an invoice comes in, they either know it's valid immediately or can quickly ask someone to make sure. However, your company may be large enough that there's a question about invoices when they arrive. The solution is to match invoices over a certain dollar limit with a copy of the purchase order sent from the purchasing department to the accounting department.

Of course, for this system to work, company policy must ensure that nothing over a certain dollar amount gets purchased without a purchase order. This makes for a more complicated purchasing procedure. However, it *is* one of the solutions used by slightly larger companies.

Recording the Invoice

Accounts payable now records the invoice into its subledger. Let's say you just received the telephone bill:

Telephone Expense	$1,000	
Accounts Payable		$1,000

Record telephone expense for May 199X.

From the telephone invoice received in the mail and forwarded to the accounting department, the entry increases the telephone expense and also increases accounts payable.

MANUFACTURING COST FLOWS

For some firms this is the most complicated information flow. That's because there's a lot happening on the production line. It's not always easy to assess the costs associated with production of finished goods inventory. These must come from the shop floor. Your accountants may not always understand the production process and therefore can't figure out how you came up with these costs.

Nevertheless, the information leaves a paper trail from the production line to the accounting department and documents the flow of manufacturing from raw materials to work in process and finally to finished goods.

Companies with strict control of the cost accounting system require a piece of paper when anything on the production line moves from one phase to the next. A copy of the transaction document goes to the accounting department.

Following the Manufacturing Flow

Let's watch the accounting treatment of a well-documented manufacturing operation:

1. Take the basic goods out of raw materials and put them into work in process. The accounting entry goes like this:

Work in Process Inventory	$1,000	
Raw Materials Inventory		$1,000

Record movement of raw material into WIP inventory on July 6, 199X.

2. Account for the direct labor and overhead expenses used in the production process. This information usually comes from the payroll department. Each unit of labor expense is allocated either to direct production costs or to indirect expense (overhead). Overhead gets allocated among the products produced. Here's the first part of the two-part entry:

Direct Labor Expense	$500	
Indirect Labor Expense	500	
Wages Payable		$1,000

Recognize shop labor expense.

This first part of the entry sets up the normal expenses for payment to the employees.

Work in Process Inventory	$1,000	
Direct Labor Expense		$500
Indirect Labor Expense		500

Move production wages into WIP.

This second part of the entry takes the expenses out of their normal expense categories and puts them into WIP inventory. We want to do this to include the labor as part of cost of goods sold.

See how records of activity on the shop floor *must* flow to the accounting department in a timely and accurate fashion?

3. The production process is completed. Now the product moves from WIP inventory to the finished goods inventory. Here's the entry:

Finished Goods Inventory	$2,000	
Work in Process Inventory		$2,000

Production work completed and moved to finished goods inventory on July 31, 199X.

You may ask, Where did the extra $1,000 come from? Finished goods inventory comes from the combination of raw materials and labor:

Raw Materials	$1,000
Direct Labor	500
Indirect Labor	500
Total cost of goods	$2,000

PAYMENT OF INVOICES

Few companies pay their invoices the day they receive them. Instead (in an accrual accounting system), they are recorded in accounts payable. The A/P system recognizes the liability and flows that and the expense item up to the general ledger for presentation on our financial statements. However, the company still owes the money to the vendor.

The A/P system also does something else. It tracks the due dates of our payables. We don't want to pay our vendors either before payment is due or after. Instead, we want to pay in accordance with the purchase terms. If the invoice has a trade discount for early payment and we elect to take it (as we almost always do), the A/P system flags that date for us too.

So, the information that tells us to pay an invoice usually comes from within the accounting system. If you're using a manual A/P system, chances are that a tickler file mechanism provides the information. Automated systems produce daily reports of what's due and when. Some automatically prepare a list of suggested invoice payment dates that will keep the company current.

Additionally, your purchasing manager may provide input regarding payment to specific vendors. Advice is often related to deals he or she is currently working on and provides a trade-off between your company and the vendor.

Regardless of where the order to pay a particular invoice comes from, when it's paid, here's the entry in the A/P subledger that is summarized for posting to the general ledger:

Expense Account	$1,000	
Cash		$1,000

Records A/P payment for batch #123 made on July 6, 199X.

Information in the A/P Subledger

The payables subledger provides a wealth of information about your vendors and the accounting for each payment. Here is some of the information that flows from it

- Vital statistics about each vendor
- Check number used to pay the vendor • Invoice number paid

- Date paid • Trade discount taken • Expense account debited
- Invoice retrieval reference number

Additionally, somewhere in the A/P department you should be able to retrieve the actual invoice, stamped "PAID" on its face so that there's no danger of paying it again. Along with the invoice, many firms include a payment approval form signed by an authorized signatory. Alternatively, the check signer is presented with not only the check ready for signature but all the backup documentation that supports it. This usually includes at least the invoice and sometimes the purchase order. Signing the check means approval of all the documentation supporting the payment. This method provides a good control and is relatively streamlined.

RECORDING SALES

Sales is an important part of the accounting system information flow. In Chapter 14, "Internal Accounting Controls," we'll get more heavily involved in the system of checks and balances to be sure all sales go for the benefit of the company and not into someone's pocket. However, for now we'll concentrate on the information generated, where it goes, and what it's used for.

Cash Sales

Most companies that sell retail or do a substantial amount of sales in cash use a cash register. This produces an external tape for each sale that goes to the customer as a receipt.

Modern cash registers also have an internal tape that tallies the amount rung up and (hopefully) gets put in the cash drawer. Access to the internal tape often requires a separate key held by an independent supervisor.

Here's the information flow in recording cash receipts from sales:

1. The supervisor counts the cash drawer, then verifies that amount against the amount rung up and reported on the internal tape. The two should match.

2. A bank deposit ticket is prepared, and the money is deposited in the bank.

3. A copy of the bank deposit ticket and the cash register tape are sent to the accounting department.

4. The entry is recorded in the accounting system:

Cash	$1,000	
Sales Income		$1,000
Sales for July 6, 199X.		

5. The bank sends the accounting department a deposit confirmation or the regular monthly bank statement. Either can be used to verify that correct deposit reached the bank.

Recording Credit Sales

This is usually the most common form of sale for companies that don't sell retail. The information flow must be timely and must accurately establish that the company has a new asset on its balance sheet—the customer's promise to pay some time in the future.

The best source document for recording a credit sale is almost always the invoice sent to the customer. By the way, make sure your company renders its invoices *immediately* after the sale. Many companies include the invoice with the shipment. Alternatively, they mail them out separately on the day of shipment. Waiting to render an invoice just unnecessarily prolongs the collection cycle. It drives up the receivables balance and eats up valuable working capital needed elsewhere in the company.

The invoice copy goes from the sales department to the accounting department. Sometimes a company uses a document that confirms the shipment to the customer. These are appropriately called *shippers*. They are often attached to the invoice that goes to Accounting. This way everything associated with each sale stays in one place, either in Sales or in Accounting. Often both departments keep their own copies, but that is a duplication of effort unless there's some overriding reason for keeping the same documents in two different places.

Entry into the receivables system

Using the sales invoice, the accounting staff is ready to record the credit sale. It goes first into the A/R subledger, which contains all vital information about the sale. If this is a new customer, here's the information provided by the invoice:

- All customer vital statistics
- Amount purchased
- Terms of sale—payment date and/or trade discount provided for early payment and the date
- Credit limit—nice to have, and helpful if you use an automated system that interfaces with order entry

Once posted to the A/R subledger, all this vital information is summarized, and the summary flows up to the general ledger.

Here's the entry made into the G/L to record the credit sale:

```
Accounts Receivable              $1,000
     Sales Income                          $1,000
     Records credit sales for July 6, 199X, A/R batch #123.
```

The accountants file batches of entries in the A/R archives for future reference. Perhaps they file the sales invoices and shippers along with them as well. That way they can trace the entire transaction if they ever have to.

Billing for a Service Company

Instead of selling a hard product that's kept in inventory and shipped out to customers, service companies sell their time. They may charge a fixed fee for the job or service, or they may charge standard hourly rates for employees extended by the time the job takes. Whether you are a doctor, lawyer, consultant, plumber, or electrician, that's the way it's done.

The flow of information that records your sales is only slightly different from that for companies that sell products. Here's how it works.

Time sheets or job orders

We need some way of accurately capturing the services rendered or the time spent on the job by our employees. Many firms use time sheets filled out by each employee that give the client number and the time expended on that client's job. These flow to a billing department that accumulates all the time spent by everyone in the firm. The time is extended by each employee's standard hourly rate. Senior people charge more for their time than those who are more junior. Additionally, any out of pocket expenses incurred by the firm on behalf of the client accumulate in the billing department and get added to the bill.

It works much the same way for companies that charge by the job. Charges for all the work done by the company for each client accumulate in the billing department. The company renders one consolidated bill to each client.

By the Way

Setting up a new billing system? You should provide for the ability to itemize the time and what each person did on each project your firm is billing the customer. More often than not, customers demand that information before paying.

The billing department sends out bills to the firm's clients with copies to accounts receivable.

Recording the receivable

From this point, recording the receivable for a service company is exactly the same as for any other type of firm. The invoices are posted to the A/R subledger. New clients receive a new A/R account. The receivable subledger is posted and the summarized entry flows to the general ledger:

Accounts Receivable	$1,000	
Sales Income		$1,000
Records credit sales for July 6, 199X, A/R batch #123.		

RECEIPT OF PAYMENT

From an accounting standpoint, payment received for an outstanding invoice requires just two actions:

- Subtract the part of the customer's receivable that's being paid.
- Record the receipt of cash.

To do this, we primarily use information sent in by our customers. Invoice copies are a good source of information regarding who has paid what and on which specific invoice. If you can get your customers to include either a copy of the invoice they are paying or a tear-off part that includes all the vital information for entry to your receivables system, you'll be ahead of the game.

Here's the information your A/R people look for:

- Customer name • Customer account number
- Invoice number for which payment is being made • Amount sent in

Recording Checks Received

Your mail room (or whoever opens the mail), should record all the checks received. Often, the person who does this is the same person who prepares the bank deposit. For control purposes, it is *not* the person who records the payment in the accounts receivable subledger.

Some companies copy the checks and attach them to the invoice copies or stubs customers include with their payments. Then they deposit the checks in the bank.

Entry in the A/R Subledger

The batch of checks received comes into the accounting department. The person responsible for maintenance of the A/R subledger records all the payments of the paying customers. These entries reduce the balances they owe the company.

Posting to the General Ledger

After posting cash receipts to the A/R subledger, summarize them and post the summary to the general ledger. Here's the entry that's made to the G/L:

Cash	$1,000	
Accounts Receivable		$1,000
Records cash receipts batch #123 on July 6, 199X.		

Bundle the list of payments entered into the A/R subledger with the invoice copies and check copies (if made) into a single cash receipts batch and store them by batch number for future reference. By using the batch number appearing on the G/L entry, finding it in the future should be no problem.

CREDIT MEMOS

It always seems that someone wants his or her money back. From a control standpoint, when we make the decision to comply, we don't want people just reaching into the cash drawer and handing over the money. Instead, it's better to have an orderly flow of procedures that separates the decision making authority from the cash (or check) disbursement.

Further, we want to communicate to the accounting system exactly what took place and why. Then there's the matter of properly crediting the customer's account. If we're handing the customer money to cancel a transaction, there already was one problem. We don't want to compound the issue by screwing up the credit entry too.

The best way to ensure an orderly flow of information into the accounting system is to use a *credit memo*. This is simply a piece of paper (usually a pre-printed form, often on colored paper to distinguish it from a debit transaction) used by whoever deals with the customers. Credit memos contain the following information:

- Customer name and address
- Customer account number in the A/R system
- Amount being credited
- Reason
- Signature of the person authorized to approve customer credits
- Invoice number that's being canceled

Additionally, many companies require that the original invoice accompany the credit memo. They do this so that they don't end up paying back the full retail price for goods bought on sale, with the customer making what amounts to an arbitrage profit.

Flow of Credit Memo Information

Many retail firms have a policy regarding payment of cash for returned merchandise. Small amounts we don't worry about. However, there's often a dollar amount cutoff beyond which the firm's accounting office must issue a check to the customer. This makes sense because of the possible risk of abuse by employees authorized to reach into the till and disburse cash to customers.

Once it has been completed and approved, attach the credit memo form to the original invoice and forward it to the accounting department. The accounts receivable clerk credits the customer's A/R subledger account for the amount of the credit memo. Some companies require a supervisor's approval for a credit entry into the A/R system. Some automated systems require a specific password from someone authorized to make credit entries into the system.

The A/R subledger receives a credit for the amount given back. If there are several credit memos, batch them together and run them through at the same time. The A/R system removes the amount from each customer's account and summarizes the entries for posting to the general ledger.

The general ledger entry goes like this:

Sales	$1,000	
Accounts Receivable		$1,000
Records credit memo #123 on July 6, 199X.		

But wait. The customer still hasn't been paid. We still must generate a check. The A/R people don't write checks, so the clerk issues a check request with the credit memo as back-up. Some companies set this up as a regular entry (like an invoice) into the accounts payable system. If this is the case, the entry to A/P would be

Customer Returns	$1,000	
Accounts Payable		$1,000

Records payment request for credit memo #123 issued on July 6, 199X.

Then, after issuing the check, we record it in the A/P system just like a normal payment:

Accounts Payable	$1,000	
Cash		$1,000

Records payment of A/P batch #123 on July 6, 199X.

Do you see how the system maintains a complete audit trail of the transaction? That's at least part of the purpose of your accounting system. Additionally, do you see how we keep control of cash payouts and how (whenever possible) the accounting system employs functions (like A/P) that have already been set up and are specifically designed to do what is needed? We've succeeded in converting a somewhat nonroutine transaction into one that flows through the accounting system just like any *routine* transaction. In this case we used the A/R system to record a credit memo as if it were a normal cash receipt. Then we used the A/P function to record the disbursement refund to the customer as if it were a regular A/P invoice.

TRANSACTIONS IN THE GENERAL LEDGER

We've already seen how many of the bulk transactions are summarized in the subledgers and then posted to the G/L as a single entry. This preserves the flow of information from the transaction source into the subledger, where it belongs. Within the subledger we can look up and reproduce any detailed transaction. However, the detail stays in the subledger and flows to the general ledger only in summary form.

General Ledger Entries

There will be occasions when you'll make entries directly into the general ledger. If you use subledgers for your receivables and payables, most of these will be nonroutine transactions. Let's say that you buy an expensive piece of equipment and want to enter it directly into the G/L. Of course, you could run it through the accounts payable system, since you're going to have to pay the invoice anyway. However, if you wrote the check and made the entry directly to the G/L, here's how you would do it:

Machinery and Equipment	$1,000	
Cash		$1,000

Records purchase of machine and payment via check #123 payable to XYZ vendor.

Bypassing the A/P system circumvents some of the normal flow of information. For example, how will the check number, amount, date, and payee get into the check register using this method? How do we set up this vendor in the A/P vendor history file so that it gets a Form 1099 at year-end if necessary? The answer is that you will have to remember to enter all this additional information in these records when you bypass the normal flow of information.

Normal general ledger entries

Here are some of the entries normally made directly into the G/L:

- Adjustments after bank accounts are reconciled.
- Issuance of capital stock.
- Recording of additional paid-in capital by partners and investors.
- Interest income from investments.
- Inventory adjustment after physical inventory.
- Depreciation expense each month—however, this might also come from the fixed asset subledger if you use one.
- Recording of gain or loss on foreign exchange conversion.
- Sale of assets—but again, if you use a fixed asset subledger, make sure the accounting gets done at that level too.

PAYROLL

Payroll takes some of its information from the production cost side of the business. At manufacturing companies, records containing the time each person worked and on what project usually come from the timekeeper and flow up to the payroll department. Sometimes companies insert an intermediate step and stop the records at the cost accounting department. There they are allocated to the appropriate work-in-process inventory. However, smaller companies often don't have a cost accounting department. Instead, they combine the labor cost allocation function with payroll.

At service companies, more people are on salary. That usually precludes allocating individual time to specific services sold. Professional firms such as law offices and accounting firms allocate the cost of their services to customers in the billing department rather than through the payroll system.

Setting Up New Employees

Generally the information needed to set up a new employee comes from the personnel department. If you don't have a personnel department, the person designated to keep employee records needs to fill out the proper paperwork. Employment applications usually have places for all the vital information so that you won't forget any of it. Among the needed information that goes to the payroll department is:

- Employee vital statistics
- Date of hire

- Completed and signed form W-4 including social security number
- Beginning salary
- Number of times paid per month
- Any information needed for direct deposit services

Though this is not part of the payroll process, you should also be aware that under federal law all new employees now must be able to prove they are who they say they are. To do this, the employee supplies a Form I-9. This tells the employer that a person has a legal right to work in the United States. Accompanying it is identification containing the employee's signature and photo. A U.S. birth certificate and driver's license will work. A valid passport that contains a signature and photo also works.

The payroll department is responsible for maintaining permanent payroll records for each employee for a period of between three and seven years after termination. Personnel—or whoever performs this function if you don't have a dedicated personnel department—is responsible for maintaining individual personnel records, such as performance reviews.

Salaried Employees

For salaried employees, the payroll process seldom changes unless they get a pay raise or a bonus. The payroll department sets up salary, and it doesn't change until it's time for a raise. What *does* change, however, is the amount of those taxes that reach a maximum limit sometime within the payroll year. The payroll person must be aware of these and execute the proper cutoff when the time comes.

Salaried employees are exempt from overtime compensation. They don't get paid extra for more than a standard forty-hour work week. However, some companies like to track—at least informally—the amounts of overtime their exempt employees accumulate. The company later repays them in the form of *comp* time. That is time off work with pay in exchange for working longer hours during crunch periods.

If your firm tracks overtime for exempt employees, it's sometimes better to do this outside of the payroll department. Don't forget, this is an informal program, one that's not sanctioned in the form of a dollars and cents payout.

Vacation and sick time

Custom entitles most employees to vacation and sick time. However, there's no law that says you *must* provide this benefit. If your company does, the payroll department usually tracks the accumulated vacation and sick time each employee is entitled to by company policy. When an employee is on vacation or takes sick time off, the payroll department is notified by the person's supervisor. The payroll department then docks the accumulated time for the category taken.

Hourly Employees

Many companies use time cards that are reviewed and approved by an employee's supervisors, then forwarded to Payroll. These may assist in the cost accounting effort as well, since some methods of timekeeping actually keep track of the amount of each employee's time spent on each project or work in process inventory item.

Beyond allocation for cost accounting purposes, the payroll of hourly employees is similar to that of their salaried counterparts. The real difference is that payment fluctuates with the number of hours worked extended by each employee's hourly rate.

Provision for vacation, sick time and overtime is made when necessary. The company docks each person's vacation and sick time accumulations as used.

Piecework Records

Some companies pay employees on the production line in the form of *piecework*. That's a certain amount paid for each piece of work completed. Garment manufacturers are famous (some say notorious) for this policy.

Payment for piecework operates in much the same way as payment for an hourly employee. Each employee completes a card containing a record of all finished items. Then it's reviewed by the supervisor and forwarded to Payroll. The person's wages are based on the number of items completed extended by the standard rate per item. As always, the payroll department deducts taxes and withholding.

Piecework employees are subject to the same labor laws as any other employee. The law entitles employees to protection against wages falling below statutory minimums.

Minimum wage

All employees, no matter how they are paid, must receive at least the minimum wage. This means that a piecework employee paid on the basis of the number of items completed must also make at least the minimum wage. At the time of this writing the federal minimum wage was $4.25 per hour. If the person's wage doesn't come up to that level, the employer must make up the difference.

Garnishing Wages

Orders for garnishment of employees' wages go directly to the payroll person or department. The clerk makes the deduction in accordance with the court-ordered garnishment. Payroll notifies the employee at the time of receipt that an order for garnishment of wages has been levied against his or her income. The check to the garniture is sent out with each payroll.

Garnishment is a very personal subject. Instruct your payroll staff that it is nobody's business but the garnishee's. They are not to discuss employees' garnishments with anyone. Just as with all payroll information, employees found releasing unauthorized information from the payroll department are subject to termination.

PAYMENT TO OWNERS, PARTNERS, OR INVESTORS

This is the purpose of running a business. We want to generate sufficient income to provide owners, partners, and investors with a competitive return on their invested capital. Accounting-wise, here's how this works.

Resolving to Make a Distribution

The board of directors or whichever body within the company makes these decisions resolves to distribute funds to owners, partners, and/or investors. The decision-making body executes a resolution at a regularly scheduled meeting. The amount and date of the distribution are entered in the meeting's minutes. The body instructs the company's CFO to execute the orders regarding the distribution.

The company's treasurer or whoever manages the cash is notified of the distribution, its amount, and its timing. That person makes sure that there is sufficient cash on hand on payment day to make the distribution. In practice, however, the treasurer or cash manager was probably consulted *before* the resolution was passed. After all, he or she is the one who knows the firm's capacity to pay out a dividend or other distribution.

Recording the Resolution to Distribute

The CFO also notifies the controller that the company has incurred a liability. The controller enters that liability into the general ledger. The source document authorizing this journal entry is usually a copy of the board minutes authorizing the distribution. The accounting entry in the G/L is

Dividend Declared	$1,000	
Dividends Payable		$1,000

Records dividend resolution by BOD on July 6, 199X.

Note that the dividends declared account appears under owners' equity. That's logical, since payout of funds to owners *reduces* owners' equity.

Recording Payment

On the payment date, the controller makes another journal entry. The accounting department cuts the checks. You could run this through the regular accounts payable subledger, too. If you do, make sure that the account debited is dividends payable and *not* the more normal trade accounts payable. Here's the entry:

Dividends Payable	$1,000	
Cash		$1,000

Records payment of dividends on August 8, 199X.

That's all there is to it. We've run through every common entry you are likely to encounter during a normal accounting cycle. Of course, there will be entries we haven't covered. However, most of them are likely to be variations of those discussed here. The information that causes every one of these entries flows in an orderly manner to the accounting department. Most such causal factors appear in writing. When they don't, the accounting department reduces them to writing and prepares a journal entry form that documents the reason for each entry.

Chapter 4 defines the relationship of the various departments in the company with the accounting department.

Chapter 4

Department Relationships with the Accounting System

OVERVIEW

Each department in the company has an information relationship with the accounting department. Usually it's a two-way path of communication. Not only do most departments feed the accounting department facts and figures about what they're doing, but they also need feedback—and not just feedback of their own information after the accounting department has processed it into a report format. Most departments need at least some sort of data from other departments after processing by the accounting department as well.

Chapter 4 identifies the relationships each department has with the accounting department. It also focuses on the informational relationships each department has with the others. The accounting department provides the common denominator.

As you set up your accounting system, it's these relationships between each department and Accounting and between departments using accounting information that you need to be aware of. If you can anticipate who uses certain pieces of data and how they use them, there may be some things you can do in the design stage to make the information more accessible and useful.

SALES

This is the top of the information pyramid. From an accounting standpoint, the sales department originates the flow of information once a sales transaction has occurred. Never mind the production people reminding us that Sales wouldn't have anything to sell if it weren't for them. Production would not need to make anything if Sales didn't sell it.

Like most departments, Sales has a two-way information relationship with Accounting and several other departments. Not only does it feed Accounting the sales information, but it needs certain data back as well.

Sales Information

Order entry is usually under the control of Sales. O/E funnels the sales orders to Accounting for posting to the accounts receivable subledger. The invoice contains the necessary information. This part of Sales's relationship with Accounting provides all the information needed to set up a new customer on the receivables system.

Credit Relationship

At the point of order, Sales needs to use its relationship with the person or department that does credit authorization. Here the relationship can sometimes become adversarial. The sales department wants (naturally) to make a sale. However, the credit person wants to avoid bringing on board a customer whose risk of delinquency or, worse, write-off is unacceptable. Sales and Credit must find a balance so that the company's policies regarding credit risk don't unduly hinder its ability to sell its products.

The relationship with Accounts Receivable also enters into decisions regarding credit policy. Credit criteria are adjusted depending on current collections and the firm's experience concerning the delinquency of customers similar to those that Sales now wants to bring on board.

Along with the current collections, credit policy depends on such things as

- Aging of accounts receivable
- Rates at which receivable accounts roll from one aging bucket to the next
- The amount of working capital tied up in receivables compared with what the company can afford

It's often up to the sales department to obtain for Credit Authorization the information necessary to make a credit decision on new customers. This includes such things as

- Financial statements
- Banking relationships and authorization to contact bankers
- References from other creditors

Small businesses are recognizing that sales that are made too easily are often the ones that prove impossible to collect. It's the credit department's job to determine the risk of selling to each customer and how big a credit line it is willing to extend.

Inventory Control

While we're still on Order Entry, let's touch on its relationship with Inventory Control. As the order desk books sales, the information flows from I/C. After all, before something is sold, the sales staff needs to make sure it's available from the warehouse.

If the stock is not on hand, O/E must know both the back-order status and the *projected* availability. For the O/E staff, this relationship with Inventory Control is vital. I/C should be able to provide Sales with information concerning

- When items were back-ordered
- From whom

- What alternative suppliers they used
- Price from alternative suppliers and the price to your customers
- Projected availability date

Certainly this isn't accounting information. However, it needs to come from two systems, O/E and I/C, both of which have a lot to do with the accounting system. Further, the changes made as a result of the relationship between these two departments *do* create accounting entries.

Sales Relationship with Accounts Receivable

The sales department targets its efforts. It doesn't want to waste time on prospects that are in trouble with the company. That's what makes a connection with Accounts Receivable useful. A/R tells which customers have not yet reached their credit limit. Further, if you use an automated system, chances are that the computer can sort this information geographically. Some companies can do it by zip codes, telephone area codes, cities, or states.

Additionally, the receivables system can provide Sales with information regarding customer purchase histories. The order entry mechanism does this automatically. Again, automated systems can provide a complete purchase history for each customer. Manual systems can accomplish the same thing by using a ledger card for each customer that has a handwritten record of all that customer's purchases. This information can be valuable if the accounting department has the ability to sort through its files and come up with all the customers who purchased a particular item.

It may be that the company has a new product that replaces an old one. Alternatively, there may be some enhancement that the firm sells as an add-on to that particular product. Regardless, the better the relationship between Accounting and Sales, the more each department will understand the needs of the other and be able to respond.

Sales Commission

Before we leave the receivables side, let's talk about sales commissions. Many sales departments don't trust their information relationship with Accounting. Consequently, they keep their own sales statistics and reconcile the accounting reports to them. Small businesses don't usually have the time or resources to keep two separate records of the same information.

This is where an understanding of the relationship between different departments like Sales and Accounting comes in handy. To the accountants, absolute precision in recording the right amount of sales for each salesperson may not be important. Recording the sale to the right income account and setting up the receivable for the right customer interests them more.

However, the sales staff earn their living from sales commissions. They view accounting errors that don't give them credit for a sale as someone stealing from them. That's why they tend to maintain their own sales records. The logic isn't hard to understand.

Nevertheless, if you can establish the kind of information relationship between Sales and Accounting that eliminates the necessity for maintaining two separate sales commission systems, you'll be that much further ahead.

Payment on net collected balances

There's another aspect of the special relationship between the sales department and Accounts Receivable. This one has to do with collection efficiency. This interests the sales department only if the company computes commissions on *net collected balances* rather than simply gross sales. It's true that sales may drive the company, but collection of receivables is what provides the cash to pay the salaries.

Reconciliation of sales data

Sales must trust Accounting to properly record all sales information and give credit to the appropriate salesperson. One way to accomplish this is to have competent people in the accounting department. If they don't understand something about a sales transaction, they'll stop and ask. They take pride in accurately recording *all* the information, not just the information that is important to their accounting task.

Another way is to produce the sales reports and have someone in the sales department review them, maybe even reconciling them to the invoices that went out that month. The more time that goes by with no mistakes, the more a trusting relationship is likely to develop and the less reliance there will be on keeping a separate commission calculation system.

Sales's Relationship with Cost Accounting

Production costs have a lot to do with how much a company needs to charge to maintain acceptable profit margins. The sales price of a product is something near and dear to the heart of every salesperson. To the extent that sales prices respond to the market, the firm may find itself in a more competitive position.

Further, who knows better what customers want than the salesperson whose proposal was turned down because the product didn't have a particular feature? The sales staff often works with the engineering and cost accounting staffs to help design products manufactured at a competitive cost and priced to sell.

Material variances provide some of the most profitable opportunities for change. Often the cost accountants discover unavoidable material variances. Sometimes it happens that a product needs too much of an item. The alternative is to go to a different material. The sales staff can quickly predict the customers' response to such a change. That combined with input from Engineering can help hold production costs down and boost sales.

Sales by Product

One of the best bits of information coming out of the Sales-Accounting relationship is the analysis of sales and profit by product. The marketing and sales staff want to emphasize those products that generate the most commission and the highest number of sales. The company wants to sell products with the highest profit margin. Often these are not the same items.

The accounting system can easily produce sales reports by product. It generates the profit margin for each product using information from Cost Accounting. With this information, it's easier to create an incentive that rewards the sales staff for selling the high-margin products.

A similar use of the Sales–Inventory Control relationship provides information about obsolete or slow-moving merchandise that is just sitting on the warehouse floor gathering dust. A quick look at the inventory reports shows how much of each product is on hand. The sales department knows about how long it should take to move these goods. From there, overstocked items become obvious. Discount programs, more lenient sales terms, and other sales incentives to buyers can be focused on these specific goods.

The sales staff also knows what items are in danger of falling out of favor with customers for reasons ranging from technological obsolescence to a new product introduced by a competitor. Again, properly designed incentive programs can move these goods out of the warehouse while there's still some demand.

CREDIT AUTHORIZATION

Credit Authorization has an accounting information relationship with three areas of the company:

- Finance and accounting • Sales • Inventory

Most companies designate a specific individual as responsible for granting credit to the company's customers. The purpose is to consolidate the flow of information needed and the application of company credit policy at one point. Here is how Credit's relationship with each of these three areas works:

Finance and Accounting

The credit department receives its policy directives from the finance department, usually from someone in the controller's or treasurer's office. That person seeks to formulate a credit policy that will keep accounts receivable and the risk of loss within acceptable bounds.

To that end, management establishes procedures for evaluating credit customer and authorization levels outside of the credit department. All the credit people do is execute those procedures in accordance with policy. They base their determination on a set of decision rules. For example, customers with a net worth below a specified amount can have a specified maximum credit limit. There's little room for negotiation. In special circumstances , if the customer demands a higher credit limit, the request can always go up the chain of command.

Sales

The sales and marketing department often has some input into the shaping of credit policy. It provides information regarding the credit practices of the firm's competition. We don't want to make credit decisions in a vacuum. Excessively (and perhaps unnecessarily) restrictive credit criteria may put the company in the position of not being competitive.

Additionally, there are often circumstances associated with specific customers that Sales is aware of that may not be readily apparent to someone in Credit reading an application. The sales department can go to bat for a customer. Perhaps the cosignature of the customer's parent company allows the needed credit limit to be granted. Alternatively, the sale could go directly to the parent, but the delivery of product could be delivered to the subsidiary that needs it.

The point is that by bringing in the information relationship between the sales and credit departments, we can make better credit decisions.

Inventory

Though knowledge of the inventory balance may not always be relevant to all credit decisions, it can be of some help on occasion. Here's how: Let's say that we have a customer who wants to buy part of our inventory of a certain product. We would not normally grant this particular customer a credit line as large as it is asking for. However, this item is overstocked. Further, the sales staff says that our competition is introducing a new product that will make ours more difficult to sell.

These are factors that shift our risk. On the one hand, the customer may not pay as fast as usual. That reduces our profit margin by kicking up our receivables balance and the amount we need to borrow on our working capital line. Additionally, our risk of incurring a bad debt may rise. However, mitigating that risk is the possibility of having to discount this particular inventory item. The result of including these informational relationships in this credit decision may result in a better determination of how much to give and still maintain the required profit margin.

GENERAL LEDGER

Recall our analogy of the general ledger being the hub in a large wheel that is the accounting system. As the hub, the G/L has a relationship with every department in the company. There isn't a transaction that occurs in the firm that does not get reduced to dollars and cents at some point. Regardless of which subledger it hits (if any), everything flows up to the G/L.

The general ledger channels information from inside the company and reports it to the outside in the form of financial statements. In this regard, the G/L is the best *top-level* form of information for senior executives, investors, limited partners, and lenders. Additionally, if your company is in a regulated industry that requires periodic financial reporting, the G/L is the source for most of that information as well. For example, the securities brokerage industry's NASD requires something called a FOCUS report. The banking industry requires a CALL report. Both use information directly from the general ledger, formatted in the manner prescribed by the regulators.

Internally, the general ledger provides the detail for certain transactions that are not run through any of the subledgers. An example would be the purchase of an expensive piece of production equipment by a company that doesn't use a fixed asset subledger. The journal entry to the G/L would set up the asset on the books as well as recording the payment. The journal entry form that documents this transaction would most likely contain all the information necessary to begin recording depreciation expense as well.

Cost of Goods Sold

We established earlier that computation of the cost of goods sold was

Beginning inventory *plus* inventory purchases *less* ending inventory *equals* cost of goods sold

This number is hugely important to the company and to each individual associated with the production and marketing of its products. The information relationship established between the G/L and inventory control ensures accurate reporting of cost of goods sold.

Relationship with the Subledgers

By definition, most subledgers contain the record of the transactions done in a specific department of the company. Inventory, fixed assets, accounts receivable, and accounts payable are all examples. These subledgers must balance exactly to what's in the G/L for the accounts they control.

Their purpose is to provide the details of each transaction affecting the subledger and to make sure the information flows up to the general ledger. The G/L reports these transactions on the firm's financial statements.

For purposes of retrieving the transaction detail that's not shown on the general ledger (but may nevertheless be of interest), there's a special *reference* type of relationship. Here's how it works.

The general ledger contains a record of the posting of each transaction batch that comes from each of the subledgers feeding it information. Remember, the G/L is the hub of the wheel and the subledgers are the spokes. Let's say you want to see if this month's accounts receivable balance in the G/L contains a very large payment from one of your customers.

The first step is to look in the A/R subledger to verify receipt and posting of the customer's payment. Once the payment has been processed, the customer's account history should indicate the cash receipts batch in which it was posted. These batches are usually numbered sequentially throughout the month. We'll probably want to look up the hard copy detail of this batch to check two things:

- That the payment from the customer in question was in fact included in the cash receipts batch
- The amount of the batch

Next, we look at the accounts receivable batches posted to the general ledger. We search through all the transactions made during the month until we find the batch of cash receipts that we've already determined that our customer's payment was in. If the amount of the cash receipts batch we got from the A/R subledger agrees with the amount the G/L shows as having been posted from that batch (and there's no reason they should ever be different), then we've proved that the customer's payment is indeed reflected in our balance sheet.

Why would an entry made in a subledger *not* get recorded in the general ledger? There's no good reason. The problem can arise with cutoff dates. Let's say that the payment we just looked up came in on the last day of the month. Depending on how strictly the accounting department adheres to month-end cutoffs, it may have been pushed forward into the next month.

Accounts payable and sales are good examples of accounts with potential cutoff problems. Companies that use an accrual basis of accounting try to match the income and expenses *associated with a particular month*. For example, assume that a company makes sales on the last day of the month, but doesn't mail out invoices until the first or second day of the new month. There's a potential cutoff problem. The same holds true for payables. You may actually buy something or incur expense in a given month but not receive the invoice until the next month.

In both cases, the accounting system should *accrue* for the income and expense transactions incurred in that month. For the sales not yet invoiced, here's how we do it: Accumulate all sales made before the cutoff in the G/L using the following entry:

Unbilled Accounts Receivable	$1,000	
Sales		$1,000

Records sales made prior to July 31, 199X cutoff but not invoiced until August.

Then in August, when the invoices actually hit the accounts receivables subledger, the entry in the general ledger *for these sales only* is

Accounts Receivable	$1,000	
Unbilled Accounts Receivable		$1,000

Records invoicing through A/R subledger of sales made prior to July 31, 199X cutoff but not invoiced until August.

Notice that the account *unbilled accounts receivable* has a zero balance after these sales are invoiced and recorded in the A/R subledger. Knowing exactly what's in these accrual accounts is important. We don't want to double-count a sale or expense by first accruing it and then later recording again when the invoice is processed. In other words, what goes into these accounts must eventually come out.

The technique identified above works for accounts payable as well. For expenses that we know were incurred prior to the month-end or year-end cutoff but for which the invoice has yet to be received, just accrue the expense in a G/L account called *uninvoiced accounts payable.*

This method of accrual establishes a relationship between the general ledger and transactions that definitely occurred during the operating period being reported but for which no documentation was received by the appropriate subledger. We really should report these transactions, since they occurred in the period. Lack of paperwork rarely excuses the existence of things like unrecorded liabilities.

However, in small businesses that are not required to having a certified audit, such transactions usually aren't material. Month-to-month cutoff problems are rarely an issue. However, they can become a problem at year-end. Especially if the IRS finds that sales were unrecorded for the purpose of reducing net income and, therefore, evading tax liability.

Accounts Receivable

Your company's cash manager is one of the biggest users of the information the receivables system generates. The receivables system communicates the probable cash inflow from collections. Whoever is responsible for maintaining sufficient balances in the checking account closely monitors the collection information.

Further, if the receivables department is on its toes, it can provide a continuous projection of what should be collected each week from each aging bucket. That kind of information may enable a cash manager to forgo drawing down funds from the line of credit. Perhaps it can peg the commitment for the line of credit lower than it would have otherwise and save in the cost of commitment fees.

Order Entry

Receivables has a mutual relationship with the order entry department. First, O/E often is responsible for generating the invoices that A/R needs for posting to its subledger. The lag between the sales date and the time invoices actually go out to customers concerns the accounts receivable manager. Any lag makes the collection effort appear sloppy. If the invoice date is the date of sale and there's a time lapse between this date and the date the invoice is sent out, the firm has automatically built that time into its collection cycle.

This relationship goes the other way too: from A/R into order entry. It makes sense to provide customer balance information to the Order Entry person. That way he or she can tell immediately if a customer who wants to place an order is current or delinquent with the account.

Accessing a manual system

In a manual system, access to customer receivables balances by Order Entry works something like this: The O/E person receives a listing of each customer, the current balance, maybe the credit limit, and delinquency aging, if any. For quick reference, the listing should be alphabetical. Update the list as often as practical. Naturally, the more frequent the update, the more accurate the information.

Accessing an automated system

We mentioned earlier that any automated relationship between O/E and the receivables system should use a *read only* format. If we give someone other than the person specifically responsible for maintaining data integrity the ability to make changes, we've lost control.

What some of the automated receivables and order entry systems do is pull selected pieces of receivable data each day. That way there's a file separate from accounts receivable in the order entry system after each day's work. Alternatively, the more sophisticated systems access receivables balances on a *real-time* basis. This provides up-to-the-minute information from Accounts Receivable.

A point to note here is that regardless of how frequently the order entry system gets its delinquency, credit limit, and customer balance information from Accounts Receivable, it won't be often enough. Customers wishing to place an order who are told that their accounts are delinquent or that they are over their credit limit invariably have an excuse. Why is it that their checks always seem to be in the mail or already at the company but just haven't been processed?

The O/E person is at a disadvantage even with an up-to-the-minute informational relationship with Accounts Receivable. The company faces possibly losing a sale for no reason other than the firm's own internal processing inefficiency. Here's where another dimension of the A/R relationship with Order Entry comes in.

First of all, it should be common knowledge around the company just how long it takes to process a customer's payment from the time it arrives in the mail to the time it gets posted to the customer's accounts receivable balance. This shouldn't be more than a day or so. This knowledge helps forestall customer complaints of internal inefficiency. If an order taker knows that there's no more than a two-day processing lag for recording customer payments and the customer claims it mailed a payment two weeks ago, it's probably not the company's fault.

For situations where the O/E person wants to save a sale, there should be a line of direct communication to the A/R person. It would be nice to be able to determine on the spot if a customer's payment was received and is currently in the queue for entry into the accounting system. This question shouldn't be a regular event because the A/R person has other work to do. However, if needed, that relationship should exist.

ACCOUNTS PAYABLE

Like Accounts Receivable, Accounts Payable has a relationship with the person who manages the company's cash. To maintain an efficient use of cash, it's not a good idea to keep more money in the bank than you need to clear the checks expected for presentation *each day*. We can't predict this without accurate information from accounts payable as to what was sent out, when, and to whom.

Maintenance of an Accounts Payable–Cash Management relationship requires information beyond the balance in the accounts payable portfolio. We want more detail. For instance, some of the modern automated A/P systems provide reports showing the cash disbursements required to keep all vendors current. The accounting system produces these reports for almost any period of time. We base the account selection criteria the computer uses on the payment due date entered by the A/P staff.

Using this information, the cash manager can match the cash outflow requirements against what the accounts receivable system says should be flowing in over the same time frame. That's how we project the cash we're likely to need in the form of borrowing or the size and term of our investment of excess cash.

Determining Float

Another factor in the relationship between Accounts Payable and the cash manager is *who* was paid and how long it usually takes that customer to receive our check, deposit it, and get it presented to our own bank for clearing through our checking account. This time lag is called *float*. With enough of the right kind of information from the A/P system, we can use float without risk of overdrawing the checking account.

We'll get more heavily involved in the computation and use of float in Chapter 8, "Accounts Payable". However, for now be aware of this important factor in the relationship between A/P and the treasurer's department.

Maintaining Purchasing Records

There are two record-keeping relationships between the accounts payable department and Purchasing. The first has to do with keeping track of purchase orders and being able to match them in the payables department against vendor invoices that come in. The system does this before an invoice is posted to the A/P subledger. Once it is there, the system treats it as a valid invoice. The only way to discover a problem is if the check signatory notices it before signing the check and mailing it out.

The second part of this relationship relates to compliance with the purchase terms established by whoever bought the goods. Some purchases are on the installment method. Some are based on progress made toward completion of the item purchased. Regardless of how each invoice should be paid, the payables person must be aware of it. Further, if special long term payment commitments have been made, the cash manager must be told so that they can be included in the cash forecast.

Aging Policy

Accounts Payable does not determine the company's policy toward automatic aging of its invoices prior to payment. That's usually done at the more senior levels of the finance department. However, A/P does execute this policy. It must have a relationship with those who decide how long to age each invoice prior to payment. Further, they must have feedback from A/P that the policy is being complied with.

If there are complaints from specific vendors or if the company's reputation for creditworthiness is in danger, the system communicates that as well. Usually this goes to the person who does the company's buying. Perhaps the company needs to change its purchase terms, especially if they don't match company policy on the aging of payables.

ORDER ENTRY

We've already covered the informational relationship that Order Entry has with Accounts Receivable. Included in this, however, should be the conduit to the credit department. It's even better if the O/E person can pull up a customer's credit limit at the same time the receivables balance comes up. Using these two pieces of information (taken from different departments within the firm), the order person can determine whether the proposed order puts the customer over the credit limit. There at the point of sale, the order taker has a clear set of policy guidelines to follow regarding procedures for granting credit that exceeds a customer's limit.

That's how small businesses need to control their receivables—using departmental relationships between order entry and the credit department. If you employ a computer system, this relationship is usually automated and becomes an automatic part of every order review.

Relating O/E and Inventory Balances

Once the order person determines that a customer has the *capacity* to purchase the goods, there's a second step. Does the company have the goods to sell? Many small businesses maintain the absolute minimum levels of inventory possible. This is particularly true in the off seasons for cyclical companies.

There are going to be stockouts. Often the warehouse cannot fill an entire order from a customer. In the earlier discussion of the relationship between Sales, Order Entry, and Inventory Control, we established the linkage that tells an order taker just what's available *at the point of sale*. That's when this informational conduit can be useful.

Many customers allow a partial shipment. In this case, the O/E person can sell what's available in the warehouse; the system automatically back-orders the remainder of the order. Some of the more sophisticated back-order systems have the ability to reserve back-ordered items when they come in. The system automatically prepares a pull sheet instructing the warehouse staff to pull the recently arrived items. The system then prepares a shipper and an invoice to the customer for whom the back-order was placed. The items are shipped, and the sale is recorded in the accounting system.

Automatic Substituting

An extremely useful relationship between Order Entry and Inventory Control is the automatic suggesting of possible substitutes for items that are presently out of stock. Employees who are familiar with the company's products and what's on hand in the warehouse can often do this in their heads. However, because of employee turnover or the technical sophistication of the company's products, such knowledge isn't always possible. If the inventory system has a list of substitute items—almost like a parts interchange list—there's a chance of losing fewer sales as a result of stockouts of the primary item.

For the practice of substitutions to work, there must be a direct relationship between Order Entry and Inventory Control. When a product isn't available, the system should offer the order taker a list of possible substitutes that *are* available.

Reducing Inventory

O/E doesn't reduce any inventory balances until an item is shipped. After all, the goods are still on the warehouse floor. Indeed, the inventory control department should be the only group with the ability to make entries to inventory.

However, once O/E takes an order for an item, there needs to be some mechanism to tell other order takers (or to remind your one and only) that a certain number of items have already been spoken for and that shipment is imminent. Using this dotted-line relationship, O/E has the ability to reserve certain inventory items when it sells them. It does not have the ability to make any sort of accounting entry to an asset it doesn't control.

INVENTORY CONTROL

We've already discussed most of the relationships Inventory Control has with other departments within the firm. To summarize them, I/C sends information to

- *Sales* regarding product movement and availability and obsolete and slow-moving items
- *Order Entry* regarding stock on hand, stock already reserved for shipment, substitute items in stock, backorder status
- *Cost Accounting,* which monitors the cost of each phase of inventory, transfers inventory from raw materials to WIP to finished goods, and tracks the carrying cost of inventory during each phase of production
- *Credit* to identify inventory overstock to assist in judging potential risk of loss

Inventory Purchases

A relationship we haven't talked about yet is that between Inventory Control and the purchasing department (or person). There's no real transaction required when an inventory item is purchased but not yet received. Sometimes the system gives the inventory department or the production line a back-order status update so that they can plan for the item's arrival or make other arrangements if projected delivery is too far in the future.

Receipt of an inventory item triggers the normal procedures within the accounting department:

1. The goods are checked in with a *receiver.*
2. The paperwork goes to Accounts Payable, where it's matched against a valid purchase order.
3. The items are entered as an increase to payables and as an increase to inventory.

COST ACCOUNTING

Cost Accounting tracks the manufacturing costs of the company's products as they proceed through the production cycle. To this end, Cost must have a solid relationship with the production and manufacturing departments as well as with Inventory Control. Cost must know not only all the materials going into the products, but the labor associated with the manufacturing operation as well.

The cost accounting department must also have a relationship with the accounting department. The inventory control subledger records inventory transfers, additions, and value added from labor during the production process.

In addition, the cost accounting department controls the cost of production. It monitors these costs against preset standards. When the costs begin to vary (as they often will), the cost accounting department steps in and helps Production bring them back into line.

If Production is unable to bring costs back into line, the sales department is consulted regarding possible price increases. The cost accounting department is an important member of the team whose job it is to maintain profit margins.

PAYROLL

The payroll department has a relationship with every single department in the company that has employees. Their time cards, piecework chits and salary sheets all come to Payroll.

This department communicates to the cash manager the amount needed to fund the payroll account each payday. Additionally, it causes checks to be cut for withholding tax payments and to pay tax expenses.

FIXED ASSET ACCOUNTING

A company's fixed assets are generally its most valuable assets as well. Fixed asset accounting at small businesses, however, is usually not very complicated. We'll talk about it as if it were a department (in fact it is a department within the accounting system). However, accounting for fixed assets usually doesn't take more than a small part of one person's time each month.

The relationships between fixed asset (F/A) accounting and the rest of the company stay close to the purchasing department. When fixed assets are acquired, Purchasing provides the details of what is purchased to F/A accounting. The system records the purchase on the fixed asset subledger (if one is used) and then posts it to the general ledger.

As fixed assets are sold, the opposite entry is made to remove them from the books. This information, however, usually comes from the department that cut the deal to sell the asset. A gain or loss on the sale is recorded from the fixed asset subledger into the general ledger.

Every month, when depreciation is recorded, the entries are made in the fixed asset subledger to reduce each asset and increase its accumulated depreciation account. The entry flows up to the G/L, where depreciation expense and accumulated depreciation are both increased.

INTERNAL ACCOUNTING CONTROL

Internal Control has relationships with almost every department in the company. Though no accounting entries come out of Internal Control, its presence is felt in management's policies and procedures.

Internal Control sometimes adjusts the tasks of certain people who do the accounting entries to fit better with commonly practiced control procedures. For example, the back door of the warehouse may be locked as a result of internal control procedures.

Chapter 14, "Internal Accounting Controls," provides an extensive guide to ways to reduce the risk of transactions not being executed in accordance with management wishes or policies.

RECORDS RETENTION

Most accounting departments maintain their records for a period of at least seven years. Beyond that, unless the company is involved in fraud, which has no statute of limitations, it's not likely that these records will be needed.

There are usually two levels of storage used when we talk about retaining records, ready access and off-site storage. Records from last year and perhaps the year before are usually maintained on-site and readily available. After two years, many companies box up the records and store them off-site in a professional archive facility. They are available if required, but it may take a day or so to get them.

Here is a short list of the accounting records usually saved:

- Complete general ledger and all detailed subledgers
- Financial statements
- Tax returns: income, property, payroll, and any others
- Canceled checks and bank statements
- Journal entry backup documentation, including J/E forms
- Computer media to reconstruct the entire books and records if necessary

COMPUTER SYSTEM

The accounting department is often the major user of small-business computer systems. If that's the case at your company, chances are that the accounting department will also be in charge of running the computer.

The relationship of the computer system with other parts of the company may be one of convenience. For example, many small businesses with multiple computer users in different departments employ a local area network. This is simply a group of microcomputers linked together by networking software and a large mass storage device called a file server.

With this configuration, the accounting department has its work on the computer, but so do the other departments. More often than not, along with accounting, the computer applications at small businesses include engineering, word processing, and spreadsheet applications.

Most users want their files protected from unauthorized entry and update. This is particularly important for the accounting and proprietary engineering files.

Let's begin the first step in actually setting up your company's accounting system. Chapter 5 shows how to create a working chart of accounts.

Chapter 5

Setting Up the Chart of Accounts

OVERVIEW

Chapter 5 describes the chart of accounts. We'll identify the reasons for setting one up in the first place. There are particular numbering schemes that different companies use for their charts of accounts. Additionally, if your firm has more than one division or if you want to keep track of a specific group of costs within a single category of accounts, a properly numbered chart of accounts can be a great help.

Finally, many small businesses begin with a manual accounting system but plan to convert to a computer one day. There are things you can do when setting up your chart of accounts that will make that process easier.

Why Set Up a Chart of Accounts

The single overriding reason to establish a formal chart of accounts is to maintain consistency of accounting entries. Chances are that more than one person in your company will make accounting entries. Even if this isn't the case, most likely other people will look at the financial statements.

This being the case, those working with the accounting system have to know the different categories of accounts they may choose from when making entries. The more knowledge your accounting people have about the system via its chart of accounts, the less likely they are to misapply entries to the wrong accounts.

Would such misunderstandings make the financial statements wrong? Probably not, unless the firm's accounting principles are so haphazardly applied for such a long period of time that we couldn't really tell what is going on. However, for most small businesses that's not the major issue.

We want to know and control the various accounts contained in the chart of accounts. For example, suppose there is no formalized chart of accounts. Instead, the accounting staff just makes entries into the accounts in the G/L that they are familiar with. Now suppose that two of the expense categories are *utility expense* and *office expense*. Now the telephone bill arrives. One month the first A/P clerk enters it into the utility expense account. The next month a different A/P clerk enters it into office expense. Is the income statement wrong? No. It still tells us the company's expenses.

However, we really have no idea what our telephone expenses are. For some companies that's not a problem. For others, such as securities broker/dealers, telephone is one of their largest expense categories. That's how they make their living—on the phone. Since there is no chart of accounts directing the accounting staff to *consistently* use the same accounts every single month for the same type of entries, it's difficult to know how much the firm spends on telephone service.

Use the chart of accounts as a map to determine the type of accounting entries that go in each account category. If there's a doubt, all the accountant needs to do is go to the chart of accounts and look up those accounts that are most likely to be applicable. Then look at the G/L detail for those accounts and see which ones were used in the past for the entry in question.

This maintains the consistency of application for the accounting system. There are very few mistakes the accounting system cannot correct *as long as they were made consistently.* The problems come when people don't make errors the same way twice. Correction requires analysis of every entry in every account. Errors made consistently, on the other hand, usually just require a few journal entries to correct.

Defining the Chart of Accounts

Think of the chart of accounts as a master list of all those accounts within the accounting system that you can make entries to. Usually there are four parts to the chart of accounts:

- Account number • Account description • Opening balance
- Current balance

Account Numbering

The biggest thing to consider about your chart of accounts is its numbering system. We don't want to box ourselves into a corner by numbering accounts consecutively. That makes it difficult to add new accounts in the same section of the chart of accounts. We'll leave plenty of room in various categories of accounts for the new ones you'll add over the course of time.

Account Descriptions

The descriptions of the accounts are important, since you'll probably use them more often than the number designators when talking about a particular account balance. We want precise and brief account descriptions. Don't forget, you'll probably be writing these out on each journal entry form. We don't want you to get writer's cramp.

Account Balances

Often when we're bringing on a new accounting section or setting up an accounting system for an ongoing company, each account already has a balance. The system must recognize this somewhere. The chart of accounts is as good a place as any. The accounting system then takes these opening balances and produces an opening balance sheet. This ensures that everything gets into the new accounting system correctly.

If you are converting from a manual accounting system to a computer or from one automated system to another, it's essential that your new chart of accounts begins as a mirror image of what your old one ended with. Comparing the opening balance sheet of the new system with the closing balance sheet of the old one accomplishes that goal.

Further, if you are doing the conversion in the middle of an accounting period—something that's *not* advised—the comparison of opening balances needs to go beyond the balance sheet accounts. In this case your new system needs to mimic the complete trial balance of the old system. The trial balance is a report that lists the balance of every single account in the chart of accounts—assets, liabilities, owners' equity, income, and expenses. Compare the old and new trial balances to make sure *all* account balances made it into the new system.

Setting Up the Chart of Accounts

The general rule when entering accounts in the chart of accounts is to include each account you *think* you need to track. If you miss one, you can always add it later. Having said that, we should also note that compactness can be a virtue when reading financial statements.

Don't forget that your accounting system will include each of the accounts in your chart of accounts on the financial statements. Therefore, we want to choose our accounts carefully so that we don't end up making similar entries several different accounts just because we couldn't remember which one we used the last time.

Choosing Accounts

So, which accounts do we put in the chart of accounts? Start by picking those that you want to see on your balance sheet and income statement. For example, say you have several pieces of machinery on your shop floor that you want to show as separate assets on your balance sheet. Include a separate account for each in the fixed asset section of the chart of accounts. Don't forget, however, the depreciation for this equipment. For each asset account, you also need to establish an accumulated depreciation account for *that* piece of equipment. Each month that account receives a credit and the depreciation *expense* account receives a debit to record depreciation of that asset. The same holds true for intangible assets amortized each month. An example of such an intangible asset would be the free rent some real estate companies offer to new tenants as an enticement to locate their business in that building. Accountingwise, the company does indeed incur a lease expense for office space each month, even though it doesn't pay it. We take the free rent as a reduction in the present value of the committed lease payments over the life of the lease. This amount is amortized each month. We place its value in the chart of accounts as an asset.

Expense Accounts

Expense categories are often the most extensive part of any chart of accounts. Beginning accountants often want to track every single expense. It's almost as if each vendor has its own particular type of expense that's different from every other expense, so they set up a separate account for it.

When you need an expense account, of course set it up in the chart of accounts. However, keep in mind that the purpose of your accounting system is to communicate the firm's financial results. For most companies it makes little difference if the CEO can tell the cost for letterhead stationery *and* the cost for envelopes. All he or she usually cares about is the total stationery costs. And sometimes even that's too detailed—maybe office supplies expense is sufficient.

The point is to include those accounts that effectively communicate the costs paid by the company that have a material effect on the firm's net income. If a particular cost—like paper clips—is so small that it's immaterial, put its cost into a larger expense account like office supplies.

On the other hand, we want to strike a balance between providing the detail needed to run the company and bombarding those who read the financial statements with useless (and confusing) data. It doesn't make sense to put in one expense called utilities, expecting to include telephone, electrical, gas, and refuse, then do through every entry each month trying to segregate the telephone expense. A better way to make your accounting system work for you would have been to just put in a telephone expense account in the first place and use it to enter all telephone-related expenses each month.

Roll-up of Subaccounts

You can have the best of both worlds with a little thought in setting up the chart of accounts. Say that you want to track each individual utility expense but don't really want to show them all on the income statement. Smart managers put in a lead account called utilities. All the individual expense accounts (telephone, electricity, etc.) are put under it in separate *subaccounts*. On the income statement, the accounting system reports only the lead utility expense account, which has accumulated (rolled up) all the individual expenses contained in the subaccounts beneath it. However, you can track each component expense separately just by looking at the subaccount transaction activity.

Alternatively, if you don't want to set up a separate subaccount but *do* want to track an expense, here's another idea. Many automated payables systems keep an excellent record of all purchases made by the firm from each vendor. That's how the system accumulates annual expenses for the 1099 form. Since many vendors sell your company just one thing (or items in just one expense category), let the A/P system track the detail of this expense. Just look in the vendor activity file to find out how much you paid for this expense and when.

Deleting Accounts

Many automated accounting systems won't let you delete accounts once they have received entries. Even if an account has no balance, it has a transaction history that the system wants to preserve. If you deleted an account, you would lose its history. So once you begin using an account, plan on not deleting it from the chart of accounts.

Of course, you can always make a journal entry to transfer the balance in an unwanted account to a different account. Then you can change the account description to something like "DO NOT USE." For many of the automated systems, accounts with a zero year-to-date balance are not printed on the financial statements.

NUMBERING SCHEMES

Regardless of whether you're using a manual or an automated accounting system, the numbering scheme is important. Let's take a few minutes to consider the impacts of specific decisions you're about to make in setting up your chart of accounts. They will have an impact on the level of detail your accounting system is able to provide.

How Many Accounts?

The first, most basic question you need to answer is, how many accounts are you going to want in your chart of accounts? If you're using an automated system, find out the maximum number of accounts it allows. That gives you an indication of any limitations you might have. Remember, the more accounts you have, the more work it is to produce financial statements and reconcile the accounts.

Most people begin by listing the separate accounts they want to track. We'll go about it in a slightly more systematic manner. First, break the accounts down into their categories; then list them. Here are the categories:

    Assets:
        Current assets
        Fixed assets
    Liabilities:
        Current liabilities
        Long-term liabilities
    Owners' equity
        Retained earnings
    Income
    Expense

Determine which accounts you want in each category. After you have done this, you will have a good indication of how many accounts you're going to need in your chart of accounts. Additionally, you've taken a giant step toward completing your chart of accounts. A point to remember is that you need include only those accounts that have a material impact on the company. You can easily lump others that are immaterial into another larger account.

Numbering Options

Most accounting systems use at least a three-digit numbering scheme. Some use four. Others use a prefix of two or three digits followed by a dash or space, then another three or four digits. Some even allow for the use of a suffix. However, that's getting more sophisticated than most small businesses require.

Three-digit systems

If you use a three-digit account numbering scheme, establish a consistent number range for each category of account. Figure 5-1 shows one such scheme.

Of course, a three-digit scheme allows only a finite number of accounts within each category. If you need more (and if your accounting system allows more), you can always assign a longer range of numbers to a single account category. For example, assets can run from account 100 to account 299.

Figure 5-1
Three-Digit Chart of Accounts

Account Description	Account Number
Assets	100
Current assets	110-159
Fixed assets	160-199
Liabilities	200
Current liabilities	210-259
Long-term liabilities	260-299
Owners' equity	300
Retained earnings	400
Income	500
Expense	600

Four-digit systems

Numbering systems using four digits allow more flexibility. Now you have plenty of room to keep everything separate in 1,000-number categories. Figure 5-2 shows an example.

Figure 5-2
Four-Digit Chart of Accounts

Account Description	Account Number
Assets	1000
Current assets	1100-1499
Fixed assets	1500-1999
Liabilities	2000
Current liabilities	2100-2499
Long term liabilities	2500-2999
Owners' equity	3000
Retained earnings	4000
Income	5000
Expense	6000

There's another advantage to using a four-digit system. It allows plenty of space between individual accounts. When you need to insert a new account between two already existing ones, it's easy to do so. For example, say our company rarely extends loans or notes to anyone. That's not our business. However, somehow we find ourselves with three notes receivable from the sale of production line equipment. Now we have to put these notes on our balance sheet. Normally they would just go into a single account called *notes receivable*. However, these are so unusual for us that we want to separate them so that no one forgets to collect them. Here's how the current asset part of our chart of accounts looks:

1100	Cash
1200	Accounts receivable
1300	Allowance for uncollectibles
1400	Inventory

Notes receivable should go between allowance for uncollectibles and inventory. So, let's number our three new accounts like this:

1300	Allowance for uncollectibles
1310	Notes receivable: Maggie
1320	Notes receivable: Autumn
1330	Notes receivable: Tobby

That's the advantage of using a four-digit system. There's enough room between accounts that we don't have to number consecutively. We can leave space between accounts to allow for possible inserts later.

Prefix systems

We use prefixes to distinguish between subsidiary accounts or departments that roll up into a lead account. For example, let's say that we want to keep all labor expenses for the sales and production departments separate. Figure 5.3 shows how the prefix system works for salary expense.

Figure 5-3
Prefix System for Labor Expense

100-6100	Labor expenses (lead account)
100-6120	Hourly wages (lead account)
100-6130	Exempt salary (lead account)
100-6140	Temporary help (lead account)
200-6100	Labor expenses (sales dept.)
200-6120	Hourly wages (sales dept.)
200-6130	Exempt salary (sales dept.)
200-6140	Temporary help (sales dept.)
300-6100	Labor expenses (production dept.)
300-6120	Hourly wages (production dept.)
300-6130	Exempt salary (production dept.)
300-6140	Temporary help (production dept.)

Notice that the prefix 100 is used for the accounts in which all the various categories of labor expenses from both departments are rolled up. This includes the four types of labor expenses for the sales and production departments.. We can use them to track the various components of labor expense for both departments. We can also roll them up to the lead account individually for each type of labor expense. For financial statement presentation, we'll probably want to roll all labor expenses up to the single account 100-6100, labor expenses, and present them as just one number.

By including departments in the chart of accounts, we allow ourselves the option of preparing complete financial statements for each department if we want. That's helpful to companies with multiple locations run as autonomous profit centers. Income and expense items are posted to the general ledger just once using that particular profit center's prefix.

If you are using an automated accounting system that allows for prefixes, it probably also has the ability to prepare departmental financial statements; you simply specify the account prefix. Then when you want to see how the company as a whole did, you can produce consolidated financials that roll each department prefix up to the parent company level.

Alternatively, if your system doesn't have the ability to print complete financials from the accounting system, you can probably still download the account activity to a spreadsheet program. From there it's an easy matter to select just those accounts whose prefixes you wish to report.

Suffix systems

Some of the more sophisticated automated accounting systems employ suffixes after the primary account number. They use these to designate *subaccounts* of a major account category.

For example, let's say your primary account for cash in bank is account 1010. However, you have accounts at three banks and a repurchase agreement investment account at one of those three banks. Here's how to use suffixes to separate the transaction activities in those accounts:

1010-00	Cash in bank
1010-01	Cash in bank—B of A
1010-02	Cash in bank—Chase Manhattan
1010-03	Cash in bank—Mechanics National
1010-04	Cash in bank—Mechanic's repo account

Using the suffixes to designate subaccounts of the primary account, your accounting system tracks all the specific entries to each of these accounts. The financials can report each subaccount balance or simply roll them up to the lead account—in this case, account 1010-00, cash in bank.

Combinations of numbering systems

Probably the most complicated chart of accounts numbering system is one that employs three different categories in the same account number and separates them with dashes or spaces. The purpose is usually to allow for entry of different divisions, locations, or profit centers. The automated systems that allow for this often give you the option of entering alpha-numeric characters as well.

Let's say our combination numbering system goes like this: XXX-AAA-XXX. The first series of X's is used for the general account category, say office supplies expense. The series of A's designates the profit center. The final series of X's designates the department within the profit center.

Here's an example showing the use of a combination numbering system:

3520-EST-250	Office supplies—Eastern region—Accounting
3520-EST-350	Office supplies—Eastern region—Sales
3520-WST-250	Office supplies—Western region—Accounting
3520-WST-350	Office supplies—Western region—Sales

Using this numbering scheme, we can pretty much get whatever combination of account activity reporting we want. In this case, our reporting options would include

- Consolidated account activity for the entire company
- Account activity just for one region
- Consolidated account activity for the entire company just for one department category such as sales
- Detailed reporting for just one account of one department category

LINKING THE CHART OF ACCOUNTS TO FINANCIAL REPORTS

When you prepare your financial statements, somehow a linkage must exist between every account number in the chart of accounts and some line on the financial statements. Many of the automated accounting systems provide for this linkage at the point where you enter your chart of account information. This tells the computer which of the various accounts in the chart of accounts to add to produce each line in the financial statements.

Even if you use a manual system, the concept of *linkage* isn't a bad idea. It makes creating the financial statements that much easier. What you're telling the report writer is, simply, take these account balances, add them up, and place them on this line of the financial statement.

If more than one account goes on a single line of the financial statement—like the four cash in bank accounts described earlier—all the statement preparer has to do is add them together. Automated accounting systems work in much the same way.

CONVERTING FROM A MANUAL TO AN AUTOMATED SYSTEM

Most small businesses either employ some sort of computer system from the day they open their doors or convert to a computer within the first few years. Usually some of the first applications for a new computer involve automating the accounting system. That being the case, even if you intend to begin using a manual system, chances are you'll want to switch at some point in the future.

Paying attention to the way you set up your manual chart of accounts can really pay off in the future if you decide to switch to a computer. The key is to establish a numbering system from the beginning that is compatible with that used by the type of automated system you are most likely to use if you decide to switch.

Deciding on the Numbering Scheme

The most forward-looking small-business owners take a quick look at the various automated accounting systems on the market even if they fully intend to begin with a manual system. Choose several that at least appear to do what your company needs its accounting system to do. Here are the operations most often selected by small businesses using a beginning accounting package:

- General ledger • Accounts receivable • Accounts payable
- Order entry • Inventory control • Cost accounting
- Fixed asset accounting • Payroll

Take a look at the numbering requirements for the two or three systems that you think might work for your company. Find out if they are three-digit or four-digit. Do they provide for department prefixes or suffixes? That's about all you need to find out. Now, model your manual numbering scheme after the one those automated systems use.

Setting Up a Manual Chart of Accounts

Many companies enter their chart of accounts on a multicolumn sheet of accounting paper. Here are the column headings:

- Account number • Account description • Opening balance
- Ending balance for each month

Be sure to leave plenty of room between accounts. This is true not only of the account numbers, but also of their physical location on the paper. You don't want to have to erase or to cram new accounts between those that already exist.

When it comes time to convert your manual chart of accounts to an automated system, chances are that your existing numbering system either provides an exact match or is easily converted. Indeed, if you did enough research on the front end, your existing chart of accounts can probably be used as the source document for input into your automated chart of accounts.

SAMPLE CHART OF ACCOUNTS

Every company uses a different chart of accounts. There's no single format that's better than another. Indeed, even companies in the same industry often have very different charts of account. It all depends on what level of detail you need to run the company and the type of financial reporting you want. Some of the new automated accounting systems on the market will even prepare a chart of accounts for you automatically from a preprogrammed selection list that asks you for the type of business you're in.

Figure 5-4 provides a sample chart of accounts so that you can see what one looks like. Don't use this to set up your own chart of accounts. The accounts listed are probably not what your firm needs—they're too general. However, the broad categories might provide a good framework for you as you begin.

Figure 5-4
Sample Chart of Accounts

TDO Enterprises, Inc.
Chart of Accounts
As of July 6, 199X

Account Number	Account Description
1000-1299	Current assets
1000	Cash—roll-up account
1050	Petty cash
1060	Cash in B of A acct #32456
1070	Cash in World Bank acct #4568
1080	Repo investments—Kidder #6789
1090	Marketable securities
1100	Accounts receivable—trade
1110	Allowance for uncollectibles
1150	Notes receivable—Maggie
1160	Funds on deposit—Valley Escrow
1165	Funds on deposit—Robinson Helicopter
1200	Inventory—roll-up account
1210	Raw materials inventory
1220	Work in process inventory
1230	Finished goods inventory
1300-1349	Tax refunds receivable
1310	Federal tax refunds receivable
1320	State tax refunds receivable
1350-1399	Prepaid expenses
1360	Prepaid insurance
1370	Prepaid federal taxes
1380	Prepaid state taxes
1400-1499	Other current assets
1410	Tenant deposits receivable
1500-1699	Property, plant and equipment
1510	Land—1200 Via Anacapa
1520	Building—1200 Via Anacapa
1530	Accumulated depreciation—1200 Via Anacapa
1540	Leasehold improvements—1547 Magnolia
1560	Production line equipment—line #1
1570	Production line equipment—line #2
1580	Motor vehicles
1590	Accumulated depreciation—motor vehicles

Account Number	Account Description
1600	Other fixed assets
1700-1999	Other assets
1710	Loan origination fees
1720	Accumulated amortization of loan origination fees
1730	Fire sprinkler system
1740	Accumulated depreciation—fire sprinkler system
1750	Computer equipment
1760	Accumulated depreciation—computer equipment
1800	Landscaping on office building
2000-2199	Current liabilities
2010	Accounts payable—trade
2020	Accounts payable—raw materials
2030	Salaries and wages payable
2040	Accrued property taxes payable
2050	B of A line of credit
2200-2299	Payroll taxes payable
2210	SDI payable
2220	FICA payable
2230	State withholding payable
2240	Federal withholding payable
2300-2399	Current portion of long-term debt
2310	Chase Manhattan loan
2400-2499	Note payable
2410	Note payable to J. Watters—production equipment
2420	Note payable to B. Cohen
2430	Notes payable to officers
2500-2599	Accrued income taxes payable
2510	Accrued federal income taxes payable
2520	Accrued state income taxes payable
2600-2699	Other accrued expenses
2610	Accrued interest expense
2620	Accrued bonuses
2700-2799	Noncurrent portion of long-term debt
2710	Chase Manhattan loan
3000-3999	Equity
3100	Common stock issued and outstanding
3110	Common stock dividends declared
3200	Preferred stock issued and outstanding
3210	Preferred dividends accrued
3250	Additional paid-in capital
3300	Retained earnings
4000-4999	Income
4010	Income from product #1
4020	Income from product #2
4030	Income from product #3
4100	Interest income

Account Number	Account Description
4200	Gain on sale of assets
4300	Miscellaneous income
5000-5999	Selling expenses
5100	Advertising
5200	Promotion
5300	Sales travel and entertainment
5400	Sales discounts and allowances
5500	Sales commissions
6000-6999	General and administrative expenses
6050	Office salaries
6075	Executive salaries
6080	Bonuses
6100	Depreciation
6110	Amortization
6120	Electricity
6130	Telephone
6140	Gas
6150	Auto expenses
6160	Dues and subscriptions
6170	Temporary help
6180	Water and refuse
6190	Janitorial
6200	Insurance—worker's comp
6210	Insurance—general liability
6220	Insurance—product liability
6230	Insurance—director's and officer's
6240	Interest expense
6250	Legal
6260	Accounting
6270	Postage and messenger service
6280	Repairs and maintenance
6300	Property taxes
6310	Federal income taxes
6320	State income taxes
6330	Federal payroll taxes
6340	State payroll taxes
6400	Licenses and filing fees
6410	Rent—office
6420	Equipment rental
6430	Gardener
6440	Pest control
6500	Other expenses

Chapter 6

The General Ledger

OVERVIEW

The general ledger acts as the hub of the company's financial wheel. Information flows from the other parts of the accounting system as well as from the entire company. Everything is funneled into the G/L. Chapter 6 describes the general ledger. We'll take you through the techniques used to set up your own G/L and show you how to make the accounting entries needed to track your company's performance.

Since accounting isn't a precise science, we'll also show you how to reason your way out of confusion with complex journal entries. Most important, you'll see how to draw from the general ledger the kind of accounting reports and financial statements you, your investors, and lenders need to monitor the company.

USES OF THE GENERAL LEDGER

The general ledger is the most important part of the accounting system. The G/L records all transactions that occur anywhere within the company. Lose the general ledger and you've lost the firm's ability to recreate its financial history.

Most small businesses use the general ledger not only to record individual transactions that happen infrequently but also to track bulk transactions. The subledgers process and summarize these everyday entries—like cash receipts and payments—before sending them to the general ledger.

The general ledger has four main uses:

- It records each transaction.
- It acts as the book of original entry for all accounting transactions.
- It provides an audit trail so that individual transactions can be traced.
- It is the source of all financial reports.

Books of Original Entry

The G/L is the heart of the company's books of original entry. The subledgers record detailed transactions and then feed them upward to the general ledger. We add to these books the supporting documentation, such as journal entry forms and invoices; all these components along with the company's system of internal accounting control make up what's known as the *accounting system*. The general ledger remains at its center, though. The accounting system does most of its work for the purpose of recording entries to the G/L.

Recording Transactions

The general ledger acts as the master file for all accounting transactions. Many are simply entered directly into the G/L. Others are detailed elsewhere and then summarized in the G/L. Regardless of where entries come from, the general ledger records everything financial that happens in your company. If it's *not* there, then the firm (at least financially) didn't recognize the event.

Providing an Audit Trail

Chances are that you've heard of the importance of an audit trail. Few nonaccountants know what one is. Fewer still have ever used one. Your general ledger needs to have a mechanism for tracking down the actual source of every recorded entry. Later in this chapter you'll see how to set up the audit trail mechanism.

Source for Financial Statements

We draft the company's financial statements directly from the general ledger. Every account that's needed on the balance sheet, income statement and statement of cash flows comes directly from the trial balance of the general ledger.

If you created the chart of accounts to mimic the order of the financials (balance sheet accounts first, then income statement accounts), creating the financial statements is easy. Regardless of the G/L account order, however, transactions that aren't entered in the general ledger won't be seen on the financials.

What about the footnotes we so often see after the financial statements? These do not reflect accounting entries of the firm whose reports they accompany. Instead, they clarify items on the statements that require further explanation. Often footnotes include points of particular interest, such as accounting policies. Notice that these aren't accounting entries that should have gone into the G/L. If they were, they'd be in the G/L and on the financials.

Contingent liabilities are an often-cited footnote. These reflect *potential* liabilities that *may* have an impact on the company's balance sheet, like a pending lawsuit against the firm. However, the company hasn't incurred the liability yet. Therefore, the G/L didn't need an accounting entry.

Since we're on contingent liabilities, you should know that auditors usually look closely at the *probability* of incurring a liability. If an event is highly probable, we may need to establish a reserve against the loss on the firm's balance sheet. We do this in the interests of presenting the financial statements of the company fairly. Otherwise, disclosure of the liability's existence in a footnote is sufficient.

INTERACTION WITH OTHER PARTS OF THE ACCOUNTING SYSTEM

Accounting transactions flow into the G/L through a process called *posting*. This is nothing more than transferring the summarized transaction previously recorded in the subledgers. However, a summarized transaction comes into the G/L as only half an entry—the part associated with the subledger used to record the detail.

The other half of the entry comes from the general ledger itself. The person doing the posting must know where the other half goes. This isn't difficult. Most small-business accounting systems have just one *offsetting* account used for any given subledger posting, and they rarely have more than a handful. Later in this chapter we'll walk through an entire G/L posting.

Transactions Not Using a Subledger

The G/L also records those accounting entries that aren't run through a subledger. These are usually not bulk entries, such as those associated with accounts receivable or payable. Instead, they involve just a few accounts and don't happen all that frequently.

An example of a transaction that's posted directly to the G/L might be notification of a dishonored customer payment check. If your accounts receivable subledger doesn't provide for such events (or if you don't use an A/R subledger), make the entry directly to the G/L. Here's the entry:

Accounts Receivable	$1,000	
Cash		$1,000
Records NSF check on A/R account #1234.		

Notice that an increase in the receivables account reinstated the asset. Further, cash decreases, since we didn't really get the money after all. To maintain the audit trail, attach a copy of the dishonored check to the journal entry form and file it for future reference. The firm sends the original rubber check back to the deadbeat customer with a note requesting payment in another form, such as a cashier's check.

Many other transactions go directly into the G/L. These include such things as

- Acquisition of assets • Sale of assets • Drawdown of loans
- Repayment of loans • Investor capital contributions
- Customer payments that bypass the A/R system
- Vendor payments that bypass the A/P system

Of these, be especially careful of the last two. Many accounting systems, if they employ any subledgers, use either A/R, A/P, or both. Bypassing the subledger and making an entry directly to the G/L opens the door for throwing these accounts out of balance. We'll talk later about this balancing act. However, be sure to get in the habit, when making entries directly into a G/L account that uses a subledger, of also recording the entry in the subledger.

Better yet, it's usually easier just to make the entry in the subledger in the first place and post it to the G/L. That way you know everything stays in balance.

Posting to the G/L

Posting to the general ledger means nothing more than making a *permanent* entry. The entry may come from a journal entry form that is posted directly to the G/L. It may come as a summary of many transactions already detailed in a subledger. The point is that any entry posted to the G/L is (or should be) permanent.

Once posted, an entry cannot be deleted. So how do you fix an error in a posted entry? By making another entry—a reversing entry. This happens frequently in accounting systems. However, to preserve the audit trail we don't erase wrong journal entries. It's easier just to fix an error by making a correcting entry. This preserves proof that the correction was accurate.

SETTING UP THE GENERAL LEDGER

Let's set up a general ledger. It isn't hard, especially if you followed the order suggested in Chapter 5 for your chart of accounts. The customary order of financial statement presentation goes

- Balance sheet • Income statement • Statement of cash flows
- Statement of changes in financial position

The order in which these accounts appear in the financial statements is the order recommended for your chart of accounts. The G/L follows this order. Remember that accountants are *consistent*. That consistency begins with the chart of accounts and flows to the general ledger and on to the financial statements.

Businesses that are very small tend to orient their general ledger around their checking account. They reason that right there in the check register is a place for the information needed to run the company:

- Cash balance • Income • Disbursement

However, the check register doesn't provide any place to record sales made on account (and, therefore, identify who owes you money). Further, it doesn't provide for any transactions that are not cash-related, such as depreciation. Finally, a check register cannot be used to create a balance sheet.

We won't orient your G/L to the check register. Instead, we'll use the reverse order:

- Cash coming in is recorded as a sale or a payment on accounts receivable that is *also* recorded to the cash account in the G/L.
- Payments going out either buy an asset or reduce an account payable and are *also* recorded to the cash account.

You can be sure that the G/L records everything that happens in the check register. Using this method, the transaction history of your cash account becomes your check register. Either accounts payable or the cash disbursements subledger contains the preprinted numbers of disbursed checks. We'll record deposits in either accounts receivable or the cash receipts subledger. Using these pieces of information, it's still easy to reconcile your checking account. Further, record the transaction causing an entry into the check register in

- The appropriate G/L account
- The customer account (if it belonged to A/R)
- The vendor account (if it belonged to A/P)

Using a Manual System

If you're just starting a small business and you don't want to install an automated accounting system, you'll need a manual G/L. Complete kits for manual G/Ls are available from most business supply stores or well-stocked stationery stores. These mostly consist of a book with some sort of removable mechanism so that you can take out and insert columnar paper.

The heart of the manual G/L system is a long columnar piece of paper. Down the left edge are the days of the month. Across the top are the G/L accounts. Balance debits and credits against one another to ensure that they're equal either for each day or for each entry. Some accountants balance both to be sure.

With the manual G/L, you can also maintain subledgers if your company has large volumes of similar transactions. The most common subledgers for a manual system are receivables, payables, and sales. There's a general ledger account for each subledger. The subledger summarizes daily transactions. Then they're posted (transferred) to the G/L account.

Avoid unnecessarily bulky books. Most small businesses have a separate book for the G/L and one for each of the subledgers they use. This prevents having one monumental book for everything. Besides that, they're easier to work with.

Pegboard Systems

Small businesses that are on the cash basis of accounting, as many physicians' offices once were, use a system commonly called a pegboard. This system assumes that every transaction flowing through the G/L has something to do with cash.

The convenience of the pegboard is in the little carbon strip on the back of both checks and bank deposit tickets. Completing the check or deposit ticket automatically enters the description, check or deposit ticket number, amount, date and G/L account.

Here are the main points to remember in a manual G/L:

1. You must be able to make debit and credit entries to all accounts conveniently.
2. The system must make balancing all entries easy.
3. For all subledgers, you must be able to summarize the detail and post it to the G/L easily.
4. The current balance of each account must be easily seen.

The specific items of information associated with each entry include

- Date
- Source document retrieval number
- Accounts debited and credited
- Amounts
- Identification of accountant who made the entry
- Brief reason for entry

Using an Automated System

Most automated accounting systems automatically transfer the chart of accounts information into the general ledger module. This makes setting up an automated G/L a simple matter. However, any errors made on the chart of accounts are transferred to the G/L as well.

Establishing a New G/L

If your company is brand new (i.e., has no balance sheet), then the automated chart of accounts has no balances in any of the accounts. It's up to you to make the initial entries. Generally these record owners', partners' and investors' initial cash contributions. The entry credits the equity side of the balance sheet and debits cash.

From that point, the general ledger records all the transactions of the company as it gets itself up and running. The asset accounts of the balance sheet record acquired assets. Each purchase decreases cash. As the firm makes commitments for leased equipment and office space, the G/L records the liabilities.

Establishing an Existing G/L

If your company already has an operating history, it also has current general ledger account balances. Automated systems usually ask for the existing account balance when you set up the chart of accounts. These balances automatically are transferred to the G/L when that module is brought on-line. Therefore, when you first turn on your general ledger, you should get a full set of financial statements.

Indeed, that's how we make sure that no errors occurred when we entered the current account balances. Print a complete trial balance and a full set of financial statements. Compare them with the last ones produced by the old accounting system. They should be identical. If they are not, then there is a mistake.

> *Before doing anything else in the new automated G/L, find and fix that mistake. The new trial balance must exactly equal the old trial balance.*

An important point to note before leaving the G/L setup is how it treats subledger balances. Some systems allow the balance of a subledger to be entered as an opening balance of the G/L. These systems provide a step in subledger setup that keeps opening balances there from being transferred up to the G/L again, thus double counting.

Other systems ask that G/L accounts with subledgers not have an opening balance entered. When the subledger is created, the G/L automatically posts the opening balance.

Whichever method your automated system uses, be sure to take note so that you don't double-count the opening balance of your subledger accounts in the general ledger.

Setting up Subledgers

Most of the better automated G/L systems have a setup menu that walks users through the procedures necessary to get started. Two first steps are establishing the chart of accounts and making sure that all existing account balances exactly mirror the ending balances from the old system. Next, the menu asks which subledgers to establish.

Subledgers or journals are just additional computer files containing the detailed transactions that make up the general ledger balance. The computer automatically creates a command path between the subledger files and the G/L file. Automated systems posting transaction subledgers to the G/L use these common journals:

- Accounts receivable • Accounts payable • Cash disbursement
- Cash receipts • Payroll • Sales • Nonfinancial data

Accounts receivable subledger

If your company is ongoing, the receivables subledger needs to have the customer list and current balances recorded. That's how the A/R subledger is tied to the G/L. Once again, take special care that after all customer account balances are entered, the whole A/R subledger isn't posted to the G/L.

Sometimes the data entry instructions aren't clear on how to enter the balances for the first time without having them posted to the G/L. If you have any questions, consult the technical support staff of your accounting software system.

Along with the subledger, many automated systems use a standard *control account* and a *contra* account. These are simply the G/L accounts that the subledger uses. The control account is the G/L account that usually corresponds to the subledger. The contra account is its offsetting account. The debits and credits are automatically entered when the source journal is established. One of your menu selection items for, say, the A/R subledger will be the G/L account numbers to which these transactions are posted.

For example, when recording credit sales, all the entries for each customer go into the A/R subledger. The subledger summarizes the transactions, then sends them up to the G/L as a debit to accounts receivable (that's the control account). However, there must be an equal and offsetting credit. The contra account receives the entry. In this case it's the sales account. Likewise, in a cash receipts batch to record customer payments on accounts receivable, the entry looks like this when posted to the G/L:

Cash (contra account) $1,000
    Accounts receivable (control account) $1,000
Records cash receipts batch #1234.

Accounts payable

We set up the A/P subledger the same way as the receivables subledger. However, instead of customers, A/P uses vendors. The company still has current balances owed each vendor. Most accounting systems ask for:

- Vendor list
- Current balance owed
- Due date

Be sure to enter the firm's year-to-date purchase volume for vendors receiving a Form 1099.

> *Vendors get a Form 1099 if the vendor firm is a partnership, a sole proprietorship, or any other entity that is not a C corporation and your purchase volume is $600 or more for the year. When in doubt, send a 1099.*

For those vendors who receive a 1099, you'll also have to enter the taxpayer identification number or social security number into the A/P system.

Purchase history is usually optional. Once again, make sure the A/P balance isn't posted to the G/L account and thus double counted if it was already entered during the chart of accounts setup.

For accounts payable, the *control account* is the accounts payable account in the general ledger. The *contra* (offsetting) *account* depends on the transaction. If you are entering invoices, the contra account is whatever expense account the invoice belongs to. If you are paying off the firm's payables, the contra account is cash in the bank account.

Inventory

The last of the modules we'll deal with in setting up the G/L is inventory. Like the other two, the inventory module usually goes through an input menu for each item in inventory. Again, there may be a danger of double-posting the new inventory balance to the general ledger if you're not careful.

Entering the information required for the inventory module can be extensive, depending on the capabilities of the computer system. Chapter 10 describes the requirements of the inventory control system.

MAKING JOURNAL ENTRIES

The general ledger system and the subledgers that feed it detailed information are now ready to record transactions. Every entry into the G/L begins with a source document. The rule is: no source document, no entry. Even if the source document is just a journal entry form that documents the *reason* for the entry, it's still necessary. Avoid (at all cost) entries going into your accounting system for no apparent reason.

The flow of information described in this section includes both subledger transactions that flow up to the G/L for posting and single entries that are posted directly to the G/L. The information flow looks like this:

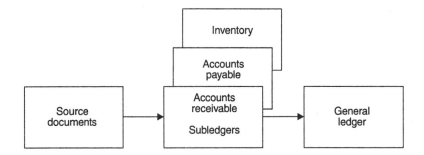

Source Documents

Source documents used for making journal entries provide the reasoning behind each transaction being recorded. It's usually straightforward. Recording an addition (debit) to accounts receivable that resulted from a sale is a simple transaction. However, recording the mathematical computations required to accrue a reserve against bad debts is not so straightforward. For these reasons, we want a *retrievable* document that describes the transaction.

There's also another reason. Many accounting transactions are repetitive. Rather than reinvent the wheel when recording complicated transactions, it's better to duplicate the prior period entries. All that's required is a quick look at the G/L and the transaction's underlying paperwork.

Journal entry forms

Whether you set up an automated or a manual accounting system, you should use standard journal entry forms. Once you get used to them, you'll be able to find the information you need quickly. Further, forms prompt you for all the information that should be included, and so you won't run the risk of forgetting something that could later prove important. Figure 6-1 (page 98) shows a sample J/E form (they're really simple).

Notice that the bottom of the form shows where to locate the backup documentation. The best place is attached to the J/E form itself. File the forms according to journal entry form number. For entries made directly into the G/L, enter the J/E form number as the primary source of information regarding the transaction. Indicate where to find additional information in the reference at the bottom.

Also notice that there's a place to total all debit and credit entries. *These must be equal.* Most automated G/L systems won't let you enter an unbalanced journal entry. The balance sheet won't balance if an unbalanced entry gets into the G/L. This reduces the financial statements' credibility to zero. *Make sure your journal entries balance.*

Batching Entries from Subledgers

Subledgers batch their entries for a single posting to the general ledger. That's the purpose of using a subledger in the first place—to summarize similar transactions. Try keeping your batches small—say twenty or so entries to a batch. If a

Figure 6.1
Journal Entry Form

J/E form #: _____

Company Name: _____   Date:_____

Preparer: _____

Journal Entry Form

Account #	Account Description	Debit	Credit
	Total		

Explanation:

Reference document located at:

---

batch is unbalanced (and some will be), it's much easier to find the problem in a small batch than in a large one. Also, for future research, it's faster to read through a small batch than a large one.

Automated systems usually give you a chance to review the entire batch before you transfer it to the G/L for posting. Unless you're positive that the batch is exactly as you want it, review the batch before posting.

If you print the batch out, that document becomes the hard copy record of the transaction. The G/L reference is to that batch. You'll need it in the future when you are searching for details of the transaction. Be sure to file it.

The batch goes to the G/L. The net result is posted to all the accounts affected.

Single Entries into the G/L

Journal entry forms support entries made directly into the G/L. You can make direct journal entries to any G/L account. Once again, if you make them to an account with a subledger, be sure to update the subledger. Do not allow the system to automatically transfer the update to the G/L, causing a double posting.

Note that accountants often use more than just two accounts in a journal entry. Often several accounts complete an entry. Particularly complex entries may use many accounts. Here's an example using just three.

Say a new partner has entered the company. The capital contribution consists of cash, common stock of a publicly traded company, and some production line equipment. The journal entry would be

Cash	$100,000	
Common stock	250,000	
Equipment	175,000	
Partner's capital		$525,000
Records capital contribution from TDO Enterprises.		

Balancing the G/L with Its Subledgers

The most important thing to remember when working with a G/L that's supported by subledgers is that *they must balance.* If they don't, then a transaction was posted to one account and not the other.

G/L Account Balance Exceeds Subledger Balance

No matter how careful people may be, it's likely that sometimes a G/L account won't match its subledger. Of these instances, accounts receivable is the most serious. You can't tell who owes that money if the G/L receivables account exceeds the A/R subledger. Finding the phantom customers can prove difficult, since only the subledger contains their names and account numbers.

If this does happen, try these steps:

1. Identify the amount by which the two accounts are out of balance.

2. Review the G/L transaction detail and see if a single entry or a group of entries adds up to the amount out of balance.

3. Review the transaction detail for these suspected entries and identify the customers.

4. Update the A/R subledger with the missing customer transactions.

5. *Do not* post these transactions to the G/L. Doing so will double-count them and perpetuate the problem. Instead, post the correcting batch to the subledger, then delete it before posting to the G/L.

This technique works regardless of which subledger disagrees with the G/L.

Subledger Balance Exceeds General Ledger

This situation is more irritating than anything else. As long as you can prove the balance in the subledger with actual customers (receivables), vendors (payables), goods (inventory), or fixed assets (fixed asset subledger), a correcting journal entry can be made to the G/L.

The trick, however, is to correctly identify the contra account in the general ledger when you make the adjusting entry. If this type of error happens in your accounting system, try these steps:

1. Determine the amount by which the subledger balance exceeds the general ledger account.

2. Check the last few batches to see if an entire batch failed to get posted to the general ledger. This situation sometimes happens in systems that don't automatically post subledgers to their general ledger control accounts. Alternatively, but less likely, a portion of a batch may have failed to post properly. A power interruption in the middle of a posting run could cause that.

3. Most systems allow queries for unposted batches. If a batch just hasn't been posted yet, it's a simple matter to post it to the G/L.

4. If no batches are still open, then somehow the batch was deleted before it could be posted to the G/L. Such an error can happen if there's a computer glitch in the middle of posting. Make sure the correcting entry to the general ledger includes the entries to both the control account and the contra accounts. Be sure to clearly document it on the journal entry form for future reference.

Closing Entries

Think of the balance sheet and all its accounts as a snapshot of the company at a particular point in time. Think of the income and expense accounts as an *accumulation of activity* during a particular period of time. The difference is important. Balance sheet accounts never get zeroed out at year-end. You out income and expense accounts in order to begin tracking the accumulation of activity for the next accounting period.

Year-end closing entries accomplish this zeroing out process. Whether you run a manual or an automated system, the process is the same. Here's what actually happens:

1. Make entries to all income and expense accounts. The entries are equal and opposite to the balance in the accounts at year-end.

2. Add all debits and credits together. If the net result is a credit, the company made a profit; a debit means a loss.

3. Enter the net debit or credit in the retained earnings account in the owners' equity section on the liability side of the balance sheet.

Automated systems usually have a special menu item that does the year-end closing entries for you. It also sets up the next year's general ledger. It does this by transferring the year-end balance sheet numbers to the new year's G/L as its opening balances.

Figure 6-2 shows an example of a simple closing entry.

Notice how the closing entry reverses the accumulated balances in the income and expense accounts and puts the difference—a $1,500 profit in this case—into retained earnings.

CREATING THE AUDIT TRAIL

Historians say that their mission consists of proving past occurrences. They sift through evidence that substantiates the record. A good audit trail does the same

Figure 6-2
Closing Entry

Assume the following period-ending balances in these accounts:

Revenue product A		$1,000
Revenue product B		3,000
Cost of goods sold	$1,000	
General & administrative expenses	1,500	

Closing entry made:

Revenue product A	$1,000	
Revenue product B	3,000	
Cost of goods sold		$1,000
General & administrative expenses		1,500
Retained earnings		1,500
Total entry	$4,000	$4,000

thing. It provides documentary support for the entries made to the general ledger and all subsidiary ledgers.

The audit trail is just as significant a part of an accounting system as the books of original entry and the procedures that provide internal control. Without an adequate audit trail, people must take the accountant's word for the accuracy of the company's financial statements.

Lack of an audit trail makes duplicating the logic behind journal entries impossible. People have a habit of forgetting over time why they made a particular accounting entry. The audit trail is designed to guide you straight to the original if need be to figure out why something was done.

Auditors seek to verify past financial events. Without adequate audit trails, they'll find it difficult (that's CPA jargon for *expensive*) if not impossible to audit your company. Imagine the impression a company makes on investors and lenders when it must disclose that its accounting records are in such a mess that its CPA firm can't audit it.

The general ledger provides the first step in working through the audit trail to find specific transactions. Often the search ends at the G/L. The transactions in small businesses are often of such a nature that all someone needs is a reminder.

For entries made directly to the G/L, the reasons that caused the entry are readily available. All one needs is the journal entry number and a quick search through the files.

Other transactions, however, must be traced to the subledger where they originated. From there, the search progresses to the particular batch in which the entry was transferred to the G/L. The search ends at the specific document that caused the entry in the subledger in the first place. The question may have to do with a payroll adjustment. Perhaps we need to know if last month's expense accrual included property taxes. Maybe we want to be sure that an especially large customer payment made it into the receivable account this month and wasn't pushed into the next month. An audit trail makes this type of research fast and accurate.

Components of the Audit Trail

Audit trails have four components:

- General ledger reference • Journal entry • Subledger batch
- Actual supporting documentation

Depending on the nature of the question, the audit trail can start from any of these points. The sign of a good audit trail is that each component has references to both the step that came before and the step that was taken after.

For example, let's say a vendor gives us a duplicate invoice and claims that we failed to pay it. It looks familiar, and something tells us we already paid it. But how to prove it quickly?

Step one: general ledger search

Identify the most likely expense account for the invoice to have hit had it been paid. In the general ledger, look up the transaction detail for that account. We find that indeed there was a payment batch from the A/P subledger that debited (increased) that expense account during the period in question.

Step two: subledger search

Since the G/L account has references to the batch numbers of all subledger entries, we now have a specific batch to search for. We can go to the A/P subledger and look up that batch. List the batch by vendor name (and sometimes vendor number). If we used an automated system, the list probably shows several more pieces of information, including

- Date paid • Amount • Invoice number paid
- Check number that paid the invoice

Step three: search of documentation supporting the batch

Now it looks as if we did indeed pay the invoice. However, so far all we have are our own internally generated records. That's not sufficient proof to an outsider. We must provide both the paid invoice and the cancelled check. A good audit trail retains the original for all entries. So we'll look up the for this particular A/P batch and pull out the *cancelled* invoice. Note that our A/P people cancelled it so that there would be no chance of its being repaid again in error.

The last piece of supporting evidence is the cancelled check. We know the number of the check that paid the invoice from our search of the subledger batch. Now we'll look through the bank statement for the month in which the check probably cleared. If the check cleared, then either we'll have the cancelled check or we can get it from the bank.

Our search has ended, and it produced persuasive evidence proving the payment. The evidence is persuasive because we built it on two external documents: the invoice and the cancelled check. Further, our accounting system processed these documents consistently and provided references each step along the way to prove it.

If this sounds like a lot of work just to prove one payment, you're right. Audit trails and their maintenance require some effort. Nevertheless, if this was a huge invoice, no amount of work would have been too much to prove we paid it. Besides, in actual practice, this whole process would probably have taken just a few minutes.

Shortcuts

Like so many other things in accounting, there are some shortcuts to this process. Continuing with the invoice example, here's an alternative. Say this particular vendor is one we've been doing business with for some time. All we have to do is go directly to the A/P vendor file. If you're using an automated system, it's probably called the vendor history file. It contains records of each vendor transaction. Chances are it will tell you when the invoice in question entered the A/P system and when it was paid. From there you can go directly to the bank statement to retrieve the canceled check.

USING T-ACCOUNT ANALYSIS

There's an age-old method of analyzing accounting transactions. It's called *T-account analysis*. Using this technique, it's easy to see all the accounts affecting a transaction and the various debit and credit entries to them. T-account analysis is especially useful when there are many different accounts affecting a transaction and you know what the ending balance *should* be in at least one of the accounts.

Here's how the procedure works. Say we have to make property tax payments for three properties. The payments are to come out of one checking account. However, we must transfer the funds from another account to fund the payment. T-account analysis would look something like this:

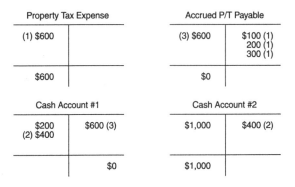

Analyzing the Transaction

Beginning balances: Notice that both cash accounts have a beginning balance. Cash account #1 has $200, and cash account #2 has $1,000. Since #1 is the account that pays the bills, we'll eventually have to transfer sufficient funds to cover the property tax payment.

Transaction #1: This begins the process. Accrue the three property tax expenses in the accrued property tax payable account. This sets up a future payable and recognizes the property tax expense for the current period.

Transaction #2: The funds necessary to cover the $600 expenditure are transferred into cash account #1. Notice that we transferred only the amount needed to cover the payment, $400.

Transaction #3: Make the property tax payment for all three properties using one check. The entry removes the payable, leaving a zero balance, and also takes the money out of Cash account #1. We didn't touch the expense account. We recorded property tax expense when making the accrual.

If you're unsure of which accounts to debit or credit for a particular transaction, try using the T-account method. It's elementary, but it might save you some time in reasoning out a problem.

Chapter 7 moves into the first subledger that feeds information into the general ledger, Accounts Receivable.

Chapter 7

Accounts Receivable

OVERVIEW

The receivables system we'll establish in Chapter 7 records credit sales. However, it's also designed to perform for several other functions:

- Accelerate cash inflow
- Project future cash flows
- Improve collections
- Identify problem accounts
- Provide a source of collateral for financing

The system is easy to operate and places a premium on account organization. These two attributes maximize the information gained from successfully managing accounts receivable.

SETTING UP ACCOUNTS RECEIVABLE

Throughout the book we've described several subledgers. Accounts receivable is one of them. Information flows into the A/R system from sources throughout the company. Receivables processes it, summarizes it, then sends it up to the general ledger for posting. The G/L lacks the capacity to detail the account balance for each customer. That's the job of the A/R subledger.

Manual Receivables Systems

Manual systems come in a variety of types depending on the company. However, they all must have the ability to record every transaction for every customer. When the firm sells a product to a customer that doesn't pay at the point of sale, the system records a receivable. Conversely, when a customer pays for a previous purchase, the system removes the receivable.

Customer cards

Some manual systems use a card file—one card for each customer. This method records each sale and payment along with all other transactions. Alphabetize the cards for easy reference. The drawback comes when reproducing the cards. For companies with hundreds of customers it's a big job to make a duplicate set of customer ledger cards. Especially when you realize that the stack you copied yesterday is out of date today. Further, only one person can work on the customer cards at a time.

A/R subledger summary

Along with the customer cards, there must be a way to summarize all the transactions processed on through the individual customer cards. The manual method works best for companies without many customers. The receivables transactions are posted to a columnar page that has these column headings:

- Customer • Purchase description • Date • Amount
- Sale accounts—these are the G/L sales accounts to which the sales are posted
- Cash • Accounts receivable

The page serves as a summary of all customer receivable transactions. Additionally, it acts as a source document for posting to the general ledger. The accountant summarizes all transactions daily. Some companies post the summary transactions to the G/L daily; others wait until month-end.

Recording Transactions

A manual system for recording accounts receivable requires several checks and balances to be sure that no transaction gets lost. Unfortunately, some of these require duplicating entries in different places. Let's assume that you've set up the customer card system described above. For any receivable-related transaction, use these steps:

1. Record the transaction on the customer card.
2. Foot the customer card to show a new balance after each day's entries.
3. Record the transactions for each card on the A/R subledger summary sheet. This shows entries to the cash account, accounts receivable and various sales accounts. Make sure that all debits equal all credits.
4. Balance the cash account entries against the daily bank deposit ticket. If they don't balance, there's a mistake someplace.
5. Post the A/R subledger summary sheet to the general ledger.

Automated Receivables Systems

Automated receivables systems use these same steps. Instead of customer cards and columnar sheets of paper for the subledger, however, they use electronic computer files. The advantages of using an automated receivables system include the following

- Identical information isn't entered twice since computer files share data.
- Manual customer balance computations are unnecessary since the computer does them.
- Receivables tracking reports are done automatically.
- Posting from individual customer files to A/R subledger files and to the general ledger is automatic.

If you use an automated system, chances are that its menu walks you through the procedures for recording receivables transactions. During setup of the system, you established these items:

- Customer files
- A/R subledger files
- Default G/L files to which the receivables system posts specific types of transactions, such as sales, customer payments, and credits

Transaction recording for an automated system begins at the customer level. The customer history file retains the details of the transaction. If it's a sale, record the invoice number, date, items bought, and amounts. The A/R subledger summarizes all the transactions into the customer files. It creates a batch detailing all receivables transactions by customer. It also balances the batch according to the G/L accounts the subledger intends to post. The system flags wrong entries or out-of-balance batches for correction.

Most automated systems make transaction recording routine and almost foolproof. All transactions go to pre-established G/L accounts. The system offers the default account originally set up for posting. It usually asks if this is the account you want the transaction to use. The answer is usually yes, but there are occasions when you'll want to change a transaction account to something else.

Linkage with other systems

Many of the sophisticated A/R systems are linked with the order entry and invoicing systems. This linkage eliminates the need for someone in Accounts Receivable to enter sales orders in the A/R system. Instead, the order entry system automatically accesses customer files in the A/R system and records the sale. The receivables staff reviews the transactions, making sure that invoices were mailed out and that the proper accounts were posted. From there the batch goes directly to the G/L for posting to sales and accounts receivable.

Additionally, many A/R systems provide a link with the cash receipts system. Indeed, some A/R systems have cash receipts as a subsystem. Accounts Receivable processes customer payments when they arrive. It posts the individual customer accounts. Then it summarizes the cash receipts and posts a credit to accounts receivable and a debit to cash.

CONTROL POINTS

Regardless of whether you use a manual or an automated receivables system, there are six control points the system must address. Keep these in mind as you continue setting up the receivables system.

Control Point 1: Verifying A/R Balances

The ledger cards or computer files should contain sufficient information to reproduce each transaction. Different types of transactions require different supporting documentation. Here is the required documentation:

- Sales require access to the invoice.

- Payments need the cash receipts batch, deposit ticket, or bank statement.
- Credits usually require the credit memo.

Somehow the customer detail file (or card) needs a reference that directs you to these documents.

Along with internal verification, many larger firms audit a portion of their receivables portfolio. To do this, they send a representative cross section of their customers a letter showing the balance they owe and requesting verification. If customers respond saying they've never heard of your company, something is wrong.

Control Point 2: Invoicing

Invoices are the lifeblood of an A/R system. A primary control should be to verify that invoices leave the firm in a timely manner after the sale. The same day is acceptable. Anything longer than a day or so presents a problem, as the company is unnecessarily delaying its own payments. Monitoring the sale date, invoice date and A/R posting date ensures timely invoicing.

Control Point 3: A/R Posting

The receivables mechanism should provide proof that all invoices are correctly posted to the customer's account. Comparison of the daily invoice listing and the A/R posting entries by customer accomplishes this. So much the better if a department other than Accounts Receivable produces the daily invoice listing.

Someone independent of both the invoicing and receivables staff should be the one to verify that all invoices were posted to the A/R subledger. This procedure isn't necessarily required each day. Often random surprise reviews are just as effective and much less time-consuming.

Control Point 4: Receivables Reports

The A/R system should provide timely and accurate reports on the state of the portfolio. It answers questions like

- Which customers are delinquent?
- Which have purchased over their credit limit?
- How much is in each aging bucket?

These are not idle questions designed to create busywork. Delinquent customers won't pay unless they are contacted. We establish customer credit limits for a reason—to control the company's credit risk. If they're not followed, there should be a good reason. Documentation of the A/R portfolio's aging helps in collection. Additionally, if the portfolio serves as collateral for financing, the lender must periodically see its condition.

Control Point 5: Credit Entries

There are only two normal ways for the A/R system to credit customer's accounts:

- Payment of the amount owed • Credit memos

The most common method should be payment. However, the system must have the ability to relieve a customer's balance for things such as disputed interest charged, returned items, and errors. Do this with a credit memo.

Control Point 6: Agreement Among Ledgers

The A/R system consists of

- Detailed customer transaction records
- Subledger balances
- General ledger accounts receivable balance

All three parts of the system must agree. Any A/R system's routine maintenance procedures should include balancing the system's components among themselves. Here's how:

Customer detail to subledger balances

The sum of the customer balances equals the subledger balance. Verifying this equality can be complicated for companies operating a manual A/R system whose receivables portfolio is scattered among four or five aging buckets. This situation makes it more difficult to balance not only the total receivables number, but all the aging categories that make up that number.

Yet a good way to be sure the A/R system produces accurate aging reports is to list the balances in each aging category for all customers. Then total each category and match them to the A/R subledger. With a manual system you would total customer account cards and match them against the A/R subledger totals.

Figure 7-1 shows a simplified look at this reconciliation process.

Figure 7-1
Reconciliation of Customer Files to A/R Subledger

Customer Name and Account Number	Current	30 Days	60 Days	90 Days	120 Days	Over 120 Days	Customer Account Balance
#100 Jones	$400	$100	$50	$0	$0	$0	$550
#200 Andrew	300	400	600	340	0	100	1,740
#300 Tobby	0	0	0	0	0	600	600
#400 Maggie	1,000	500	25	75	0	0	1,600
Total customer balances	$1,700	$1,000	$675	$415	$0	$700	$4,490
Subledger balances	$1,700	$1,000	$675	$415	$0	$700	$4,490
Difference	$0	$0	$0	$0	$0	$0	$0

Notice how the customer account detail foots for each aging bucket and crossfoots for each customer's entire A/R balance. Had there been any difference, the customer account detail would not match to the receivables subledger.

Subledger to general ledger

The next step is to match the subledger totals to the general ledger. Again, these should be identical. If not, then there's a problem. Since the G/L doesn't have any aging detail, we reconcile against just one number: total receivables.

How could there be any difference? The answer is a failure to operate the system as designed. For example, a difference could arise from forgetting to post a receivables subledger batch to the general ledger. If you're running a manual system, perhaps there was a transcription error.

Automated systems sometimes have glitches. For example, data "burps" may occur in the middle of posting, resulting in some of the data being either lost entirely or garbled. Usually the system aborts during such episodes. However, the result is still an out-of-balance condition. The same thing can happen if there's a power surge on an unprotected computer or if power fails entirely.

> When using an automated system, always make sure that subledger batches are correctly posted to the general ledger by matching debits and credits transferred to the appropriate accounts.

MAKING ENTRIES

Entries into the accounts receivable system as designed above require three steps:

- Post each transaction to the individual customer account.
- Summarize customer account transactions and create an A/R subledger entry.
- Post subledger entries to accounts receivable in the general ledger and other offsetting accounts.

As we post each detail entry to the individual customer accounts, we also post it to the subledger summary. This posting shows which customers had which transactions. The subledger summary is then totaled to form the entry that goes to the general ledger. Figure 7-2 shows the flow of information.

Recording Sales

Sales information can come from several places depending on the sophistication of your overall accounting system. Often the order entry system produces the invoices and processes customer transaction information before handing it over to Accounts Receivable. This step may include updating the A/R customer transaction files or cards (if you're using a manual system).

Regardless of how Order Entry assists, use invoices to record sales. They contain all the vital information required:

- Customer name and account number • Date of transaction
- Amount • Items purchased • Payment terms

Figure 7-2
A/R Posting Information flow

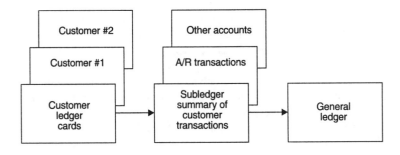

Follow the entry through the information flow described in Figure 7-2. First record the sale on the individual customer card. Automated systems process this entry automatically either at the order entry stage or when the invoice is cut. Alternatively, most automated systems allow manual entry of sales invoices to individual customer accounts.

Next, summarize the credit sales to the different sales accounts. The A/R subledger receives the offset. Finally, use summarized entries to accounts receivable and the sales accounts to post the batch to the general ledger. File the batch and all supporting documents for future retrieval.

Recording Payments

Payments most often come in the form of checks sent through the mail. Most small businesses route checks through their mail rooms to someone in the accounting department. Chapter 14, "Internal Accounting Control," explains why this isn't always such a good idea. However, at this point, let's assume that we deposited our checks and the control mechanism did its job.

Customers who send either a copy of the invoice or a payment stub make it easy to match their payment with their account in the A/R system. This information provides all the reference data needed to determine

- The identity of the person who sent the money
- What invoice is being paid
- Any amounts in dispute

Many companies make a copy of each check before sending it to the bank. This proves the payment amount. Others write the amount of the payment on the invoice copy or payment stub.

Control totals

The total payment amount going into the A/R system must match the amount deposited in the bank. Control totals provide that assurance. We use the bank deposit amount as one control total. Match that to the payment batch amount entered into the A/R system. They should be equal.

When recording the payments to customer files, make sure to record the amount to the cash account at the same time. This provides another control total against which the bank deposit should balance.

If the bank returns a check after it is posted to the A/R system, just reinstate the amount owed. Most computer systems allow manual entry of debit memo items. Alternatively, some provide for deletion of previously posted payments. However, the audit trail gets deleted at the same time. This can be a problem when trying to reconstruct a transaction. Still others allow posting of a zero-item invoice. This is a special invoice with the bounced check amount and nothing sold from inventory.

Recording Credit Memos

From an accounting standpoint, credit memos work just like payments. They reduce the customer's balance in the receivables subledger. A summary entry goes from the subledger to the general ledger. The entry credits A/R and debits the account hit during the original transaction.

If the credit memo resulted from returned merchandise, debit sales. If it came about as, say, withdrawal of an interest charge because the company was late in processing a payment, the debit goes to interest income (thus lowering it). The cause of the original debit usually isn't hard to find. More often than not the amount of the credit memo matches some transaction amount in the customer's transaction history.

Controlling credit memos

Credit memos are like cash to the A/R system. The best control over credit memos comes from authorization for their use. Company policy should prohibit credit memo entries to the receivables system without a completed and properly authorized credit memo form documenting the transaction. Further, many companies require that all credit memos be batched separately from the regular entries into the A/R system. Someone separated from the function reviews each batch. Match the credit memos against each entry.

Most companies require supporting documentation with their credit memos. These prove that the original transaction that produced a debit occurred. If the reason for the credit memo is a withdrawn interest charge or a sale incorrectly posted to the customer's account, include the transaction batch reference.

Recording Returned Merchandise

The majority of credit memos result from returned merchandise. Perhaps a manufacturer drop-shipped its customer too much of an item. The customer ships it back for credit to the receivable account. Frequently, sales agreements contain specific terms regarding return for credit. The garment industry works this way.

Clothing retailers often return unsold merchandise for credit. Booksellers work the same way. These are almost consignment industries.

Return of merchandise for credit requires verification that the items were indeed returned. For a small business, this procedure usually isn't difficult. However, companies receiving back items for credit at multiple locations have a risk. Employees accepting merchandise returns could credit a friend's account without any merchandise *actually* being returned.

Having someone independent of the transaction match the returned merchandise against the credit slip reduces that risk. From that point the credit slip, usually accompanied by the original sales slip or invoice, goes to Accounts Receivable. The process then becomes one of correcting the appropriate accounts:

- Reduce the account in the individual customer transaction ledger.
- Reduce the balance in the accounts receivable subledger.
- Reduce the general ledger accounts receivable and sales revenue accounts.
- Decrease the cost of goods sold account.
- Increase the inventory account.

Writing Off Bad Debts

Bad debts are a fact of life for most companies. There comes a time when customer receivables age beyond the point where they can reasonably be collected. Remove them from accounts receivable and record them as an expense. Usually the aging process takes 120 days or more before most companies write off a receivable as uncollectable. Many companies carry these aged receivables even after turning them over to a collection agency.

Bad debt write-off is a simple (but painful) entry. It flows through the receivable system just like a credit memo. However, instead of debiting sales or another income account, we debit the bad debt expense account.

Accruing for bad debts

Most companies know that they're going to have some bad debts. The FDIC requires banks to recognize a certain percentage of their loans as being bad— even before they go bad. Some small businesses with a long and consistent track record can predict the percentage of their credit customers who won't pay. Generally accepted accounting principles (GAAP) try to match income with expenses during the period in which they occur. Therefore, if you know that a portion of your receivables won't pay, GAAP requires accrual of the expense in the period in which the sales occurred based on a percentage of credit sales.

The entry to accrue for bad debt expense never touches accounts receivable. How could it? We don't know which receivables are bad. Further, we want to keep the A/R subledger exactly in balance with accounts receivable in the general ledger. The entry goes like this:

Bad Debt Expense	$1,000	
Reserve for Bad Debt Expense		$1,000
Records accrual for bad debts.		

Then, when a receivable defaults, you can take it out of the reserve for bad debts (thereby lowering it) and out of accounts receivable (lowering it also). Here's the entry to record a receivable write-off:

Reserve for Bad Debts	$1,000	
Accounts Receivable		$1,000
Records write-off of Jones's receivable.		

Of course, the subledger must also reflect the write-off. Accomplish this by removing the balance owed by the individual deadbeat customer from the subledger file. Many automated receivables systems provide for write-off at the subledger level. Debit the default account, reserve for bad debts, when posting to the general ledger. The posting routine flows up to the G/L just like any other A/R subledger entry. The subledger and general ledger remain exactly in balance throughout the transaction.

Reinstating previously written-off receivables

Sometimes companies write off a receivable, only to find later that the customer pays. This entry doesn't happen often. Nevertheless, should your company be the lucky one, here's how to do it.

1. Reverse the write-off entry to reinstate the receivable:

Accounts Receivable	$1,000	
Reserve for Bad Debts		$1,000
Reinstates Jones's receivable previously written off on July 6, 199X.		

2. Reverse the bad debt expense:

Reserve for Bad Debt	$1,000	
Bad Debt Expense		$1,000
Reverse bad debt expense on Jones's receivable previously written off on July 6, 199X.		

3. Record payment receipt:

Cash	$1,000	
Accounts Receivable		$1,000
Record Jones's payment.		

Note that step 2 is a matter of accounting policy. Some companies don't want their bad debt expense accrual to change just because a previously written-off account is paid. The entry still balances without this step.

TRACKING RECEIVABLES

Have you ever noticed that more people in a department, the more reports it generates? That's especially true of Accounts Receivable. This particular aspect of business lends itself very well to analytical work.

However, few small businesses have the luxury of producing volumes of analytical reports. Instead, focus on just those reports needed to track accounts receivable. If you run a manual A/R system, you'll have your hands full compiling these few reports.

Receivables Turnover

The faster a company collects its receivables, the faster they turn over. A rapid turnover of A/R means that the company converts its credit sales into disposable cash quickly. That's good. Compute A/R turnover as follows:

$$\text{A/R turnover} = \frac{\text{net credit sales}}{\text{average receivables}}$$

Most companies track both A/R turnover and the turnover of their accounts payable. They want to match these rates. It's even better if they can get the A/R turnover to exceed that of the payables portfolio. Then the vendors are financing the time it takes to collect on credit sales.

Liquidity

Lenders often look at the relative liquidity of a borrower's receivable portfolio. Banks using receivables as collateral for a loan want liquidity. The greater the liquidity, the higher the quality of the A/R portfolio. We measure liquidity by the number of days of sales tied up in A/R. Here's how to compute it:

$$\text{Days of sales in A/R} = \frac{365}{\text{net credit sales} \div \text{average A/R}}$$

Note that the denominator is the receivables turnover rate described above.

Aging Receivables

Most companies use their receivables system to generate an aging of the entire receivables portfolio. This practice shows the relative collectibility of each part of the portfolio. The theory is that the older a receivable, the less likely collection. Therefore, we want the receivables aging *front-loaded* in the younger buckets. Most companies use the following aging buckets:

- Current
- 30 days
- 60 days
- 90 days
- 120 + days

Tracking Customer Balances

Accounts receivable represents a significant asset. Early identification of problem accounts means a greater chance of collection. The best warning signs come from these reports:

- Aging
- Balance exceeds credit limit
- Largest balance
- Highest balance

The last three reports—balance exceeds credit limit, largest balance and highest balance—measure *elective risk,* the risk the firm *chose* to take from particular customers. The company didn't have to sell them an order whose value raised their receivable balance higher than ever before. The credit manager could have refused an order that pushed the customer over its established credit limit. So could have the sales person (fat chance). Instead, the customer's receivable balance grew.

That's not necessarily bad. Indeed, if the customer pays on time, it was a good decision. However, the receivables system must track these decisions and report how they affect company policy. Using this information, particular customers pop out as potential risks.

Perhaps the credit manager just needs an updated credit application. Maybe the customer's new balance sheet demonstrates an increased ability to pay. Perhaps there's a problem, though. An excessively aggressive sales force may try to circumvent the company's credit policies. This generates commissions, but it could prove costly in terms of bad debt expense.

In any case, reporting regularly not only the aging of the receivables portfolio but also those conspicuous customers whose balance exceeds their credit limit or is now larger than ever before is vital. Additionally, it's always useful to know who owes your five or ten largest receivables balances. You never know what you'll hear or read about them that might change your judgment and collection strategy.

Dunning Customers

The receivables tracking reports provide a good list of those customers who need to be reminded to pay. We call this *dunning*. It amounts to a request for payment. Dunning comes in various forms. The first stage is usually a letter. Persistent problem accounts get a phone call. For customers with larger balances who refuse to pay, legal action is the last resort.

Some companies find it embarrassing to dun their customers—especially long-standing customers. Nevertheless, it works. Customers who are strapped for cash won't pay unless they are specifically asked for payment.

Some companies send out different dunning letters for various stages of delinquency. These range in potency from "maybe you forgot" to "pay up or else." Many popular accounts receivable computer systems have dunning packages. Some allow for different letters depending on aging and balance owed.

Never make a hollow threat to a customer. Simply lay out the sequence of events the customer can expect. Be sure to follow through with these actions. Some customers are like children. They see you as an adversary drawing a line in the sand. They'll push you as far as you allow. The best strategy is to treat collections as something that is important to the company—it is. Don't tolerate payment delinquency. Take aggressive action.

ACCELERATING COLLECTIONS

Successfully accelerating collections is the result of work done on the *front end* of the sales transaction. Customers first must have the ability and the inclination to pay in accordance with the terms of sale. Given that, there won't be a collection problem.

Selling only to quality customers accelerates collections. The sales force determines the type of customer reviewed for credit standing. Many companies take this so seriously that they've changed their sales commission payment policy. No longer do they pay commissions on the gross sale. Instead, they pay based on the *collected* amount.

It doesn't make sense to sell to a customer and to pay a full commission on that sale if you can't collect within the contractual terms. It makes even less sense if the debt goes bad entirely.

Alternatively, some companies that can't change their commission computation dock their salespeople for delinquent customers. This puts another person (the sale person) in the collections loop talking about the problem with the customer. Further, it gets the sales staff's attention. They won't waste their time on customers who are currently delinquent.

Customer Statements

Make sure of two things about your customer statements:

- They go out on time every month. • They're accurate.

The saying, "out of sight, out of mind," applies to the world of collections. Customers that don't receive an invoice or a monthly statement of their account won't pay. Further, they won't pay on wrong invoices or incorrect statements either.

Once again, the receivables system provides a quick way of checking to make sure customer statements are correct. In the aging analysis introduced earlier, the balance owed for each customer was computed. Prior to mailing, pull a representative sample of customer statements. Compare the balance owed and the aging (if you use it) on the statement with the customer's balance on the aging report. If they don't match, the balance is wrong.

Additionally, when dunning customers for payment, be sure to find out if the balance is in dispute. That's a frequent cause of nonpayment. (It's also a habitually used excuse.) Too many disputed balances may point to a problem with the transaction recording process of your receivables system.

Collections Personnel

Most larger companies with a substantial investment in receivables have a professional collection staff. These people understand the art of collecting money from those who don't want to pay. Their approach includes

- Obtaining agreement on the amount owed

- Solving any problems associated with the delinquency
- Eliciting a promise to pay by a particular date
- Following up if payment isn't made

Small businesses may not have the resources for a dedicated collection department. Nevertheless, those people charged with the collection function should know what they're doing.

Ineffective collectors damage the company more than they help. First, they're expensive, and the firm doesn't receive an appropriate return on its investment. Second, when customers see a novice or an incompetent trying to collect their money, they conclude that the firm isn't serious about obtaining payment.

Collections Agencies

Don't hesitate to use a professional collection agency after your collectors have had a crack at the account. They are expensive. However, collecting *something* is better than the nothing you presently have.

Legal Remedies

When all else fails, sue. Don't be afraid of damaging a long-standing relationship. The customer did that when it decided to purchase goods it couldn't pay for. Most firms have a set minimum amount owed before it makes economic sense to bring in a lawyer. Nevertheless, filing suit or sometimes the mere threat of it is enough to make an otherwise recalcitrant customer pay.

PROCESSING PAYMENTS

Payment processing is more important for larger firms than for their smaller counterparts. For companies that receive hundreds of thousands in payments each day, unnecessary delay of even a few hours can be expensive.

Still, smaller companies can't afford to waste time dunning or going after delinquent customers only to find that they did pay—the company just hasn't received or processed the payment yet. Here are two easy ways for small businesses to accelerate payment processing:

- Include a return address envelope with the invoice.
- Include a payment stub in the payment envelope.

MANAGING TRADE CREDIT

Trade credit has two different meanings when associated with accounts receivable:

- The credit granted to customers that allows them to buy without paying immediately
- The discount offered by the company for early payment

Trade Credit for Sales

Trade credit granted to customers revolves around the following issues:

Sales Revenue

Credit Risk   Competition

Unnecessarily restrictive credit policies don't allow the company to compete. Policies that are too loose raise sales revenue, but they increase credit risk. Extended costs of carry for the receivables portfolio and increased bad debt expense eat up the added profits.

Use your receivables system and the aging reports to determine the appropriate level of trade credit. Make it a company policy. Determine procedures for evaluating customers seeking to buy using credit. Most important, *stick to your policies.*

The receivables system also assists in evaluation of requests for credit line increases. The detailed customer transaction records contain items such as

- High credit extended • Payment history
- Amount purchased year to date • Amount currently outstanding

Discounts for Early Payment

Many companies are so desperate for cash flow that they offer discounts on receivables balances for early payment. Usually this amounts to a full percentage point or two off the amount owed if payment is made within ten days of the invoice date. This is the most expensive financing a company can get.

Here's how to compute the annualized interest expense from offering a trade discount for early payment:

$$\frac{\text{Discount \%}}{\text{Due date} - \text{discount date}} \times 360 \text{ days} = \text{Interest expense}$$

On a discount of 1 percent if the invoice is paid within ten days (otherwise it's due in thirty days—1/10, net 30), the interest expense is 18 percent, computed as follows:

$$\frac{1\%}{30 - 10} \times 360 = 18\%$$

Unless your cost of funds exceeds 18 percent, don't offer early payment discounts on accounts receivable. If you need the money, borrow it at a lower rate.

PREDICTING CASH INFLOWS

Accurate aging reports help predict future cash inflow. As long as the variables that affect collections remain stable, the forecasts are fairly accurate. Variables that affect cash inflow from accounts receivable include

- Customer mix • Credit policies
- Location of the customer base • The economy

Here's an example of a monthly collection forecast using various percentages collected in each aging bucket throughout the month:

Current:	20%
30–60 days:	40%
60–90 days:	25%
90–120 days:	15%
	100%

Doobie Partners, Ltd.
Schedule of Receivables Aging

Total Sales	January Collections	Current Collections	February Collections	March Collections	April Collections
January sales	$20,000	$4,000	$8,000	$5,000	$3,000
February sales	30,000	0	6,000	12,000	7,500
March sales	40,000	0	0	8,000	16,000
April sales	50,000	0	0	0	10,000
Total	$140,000	$4,000	$14,000	$25,000	$36,500

This schedule forecasts cash inflow from collections for the upcoming months. Note three things many accountants include in this schedule:

1. The schedule begins in January. However, collections come from sales in previous months—in this case, in October, November, and December of the previous year. Include those cash inflows in analysis.

2. This cash inflow forecast does not provide a cushion for contingencies. Many conservative accountants who rely on such forecasts include a cushion for the unforeseen.

3. Bad debts aren't included. Every business has bad debts. Many accountants add this after the last aging bucket.

Finally, collections change just as your customer's payment habits change. Many companies compute their forecasts of cash inflows from receivables collection each month.

FINANCING ACCOUNTS RECEIVABLE

Accounts receivable are often used to collateralize bank loans. Indeed, some of the major money center banks have created derivative bonds out of their underlying credit card receivables. However, for accounts receivable to serve as collateral, the lender must have confidence in the borrower's system of receivables accounting and collections.

Factoring Receivables

Banks and finance companies act as factors. They purchase all or a portion of the receivables portfolio. The company actually transfers the assets to the factor. The factor advances funds to the company based on a discount to the receivables' face value. The discount is the factor's fee for taking the delinquency and bad debt risk plus profit.

Factoring with and without recourse

Companies selling their receivables *with recourse* remain liable for bad debts in the acquired portfolio. Those deals *without recourse* make the factor liable.

Invoice Discounting

This is similar to factoring except that the company's customer is unaware that the receivables were sold. The company still collects the amount originally owed. In that sense it's more expensive than factoring. However, it does provide advance funds faster than if the receivables rolled through the normal collection process.

Cautions about Receivables Financing

Most discounting or factoring arrangements cost more than conventional financing. They are usually a last resort for less creditworthy enterprises. Additionally, some customers may wonder about the financial stability of a company that needs cash so desperately that it must sell its accounts receivable. Finally, check the covenants and restrictions on any outstanding loans. Often they prohibit selling accounts receivable.

Chapter 8 moves us into establishing the accounts payable system.

Chapter 8

Accounts Payable

Overview

Chapter 8 sets up the accounts payable system. Here we'll record the payment obligations incurred by the company. This chapter demonstrates how to

- Set up an accounts payable system.
- Make entries to the A/P system.
- Track vendors owed.

We'll look at the A/P system first from the manual point of view. Most computerized payables systems employ the same theory as a manual system; they just use automated files instead of paper.

Additionally, Chapter 8 provides specific instructions on how to record

- Purchases • Payments to vendors • Vendor credits
- Merchandise returned to vendors
- Accruals for purchases made but not yet invoiced

We'll also generate a reporting mechanism that allows you to control disbursements coming from the A/P system. Using these methods, you remain in compliance with purchase terms and discount payment dates. That way you don't risk damage to your reputation with late payments, nor do you needlessly dribble away working capital by paying early. Further, you know just when to pay an invoice on which there's a discount for early payment.

Setting Up Accounts Payable

Think of the A/P system as just the reverse of the accounts receivable system. The mechanism works the same way, except that instead of taking in money, we disburse it. We take just as much care with accounts payable—sometimes even more, since money actually leaves the firm.

Accounts payable is another of the subledgers described throughout this book. Information flows into the A/P system from sources both inside and outside the company. It comes from the vendors and from the purchasing department. The A/P system processes this information, summarizes it, then sends it up to the general ledger for posting. The G/L lacks the capacity to detail the account balances for each vendor. That's the job of the A/P subledger.

The payables system does four things:

- Tracks the amount the company owes each vendor.
- Tells when to pay in accordance with the purchase terms and company policy.
- Pays vendors.
- Tallies the amounts paid to vendors throughout the year for reporting 1099 information.

It also has other uses. However, they're tangential to the above jobs of the A/P system.

Designing the Manual Payables System

Manual payables systems come in a variety of types depending on the company, its buying habits, and the way it pays vendors. However, any system must record each purchase, allocate it to the right expense account, and tell when to pay the vendor. When the firm buys a product and doesn't pay at the point of sale, the system records the payable as a liability. Conversely, when the firm pays for a previous purchase, the system removes the payable liability and deducts the amount paid from the cash balance.

The two components of the A/P system are

- Vendor ledgers • Accounts payable subledger

Vendor ledgers

In some manual A/P systems, transactions with each vendor are recorded in a card file—one card for each vendor. Each purchase and payment is recorded along with all other transactions. The cards are alphabetized for easy reference. The drawback comes if more than one person needs to work on the vendor cards at one time. Like the manual customer cards in the receivables system, backups for vendor ledger cards are out of date as soon as the cards are updated.

A/P subledger summary

The A/P system must have a way to summarize all transactions processed through the individual vendor cards. The manual method works best for companies without many vendors. Post the A/P transactions to a columnar page that has these column headings:

- Vendor
- Purchase description
- Date
- Amount
- Expense or asset accounts—these are the G/L accounts to which the purchases are posted
- Cash
- Accounts payable

The page serves as a summary of all vendor payable transactions. Additionally, it acts as a source document for posting to the general ledger. The accountant summarizes all the A/P transactions daily. Some companies post the summary transactions to the G/L daily; others wait until month-end or sometime in between.

Automated Payables Systems

Automated payables systems use these same steps. Instead of vendor cards and columnar sheets of paper for the subledger, however, they use electronic computer files. The advantages of using an automated payables system include the following:

- Identical information doesn't have to be entered twice, since computer files share data.
- The computer reports how much the company owes each vendor.
- The system tracks and reports payables automatically.
- The system automatically posts individual vendor transactions to A/P subledger files and to the general ledger.

Most automated systems have a menu that walks users through the procedures for recording payables transactions. During setup of the system, you'll establish these items:

- Vendor files
- A/P subledger files
- Default G/L files to which the payables system posts specific types of transactions, such as invoice receipts, vendor payments, and account adjustments

Transaction recording for an automated A/P system begins with the recording of a vendor invoice. The vendor history file records and saves each vendor transaction. If it's a purchase, record the following information:

- Date of transaction
- Vendor invoice number
- Items bought (optional, but sometimes a short memo line is provided to remind users of the purchase)
- Invoice amount
- Terms of payment, such as discount and due dates

The system summarizes all the individual vendor transactions, then sends them up to the A/P subledger. It creates a batch detailing all payables transactions by vendor. It also balances the batch according to the G/L accounts to which the subledger will be posted. The system flags wrong entries or out-of-balance batches for correction.

Most automated systems set up preestablished or default accounts, either for each vendor when entries are entered into the system or for particular types of purchases. When an invoice from a particular vendor comes up for recording, the system knows (because it was told) the probable G/L expense or asset account to debit. The system offers this default account for transaction posting. More often than not the user accepts this account. However, the system provides the option to change it manually for a particular transaction if you're purchasing something different.

Linking with inventory control

Often an automated system links the accounts payable system with Inventory Control. That way, when the warehouse receives goods into inventory, it automatically transfers the information over to the A/P system for recording in the subledger and then the general ledger.

Accruing accounts payable

Some companies that use the accrual basis of accounting choose to record significant expenses into the A/P system even if they have not received the invoice yet. A cash basis accounting system wouldn't have to recognize the expense. Indeed, cash basis systems don't have accounts payable, since the only transactions they recognize are cash related.

Nevertheless, accruing better matches the income and expenses incurred in any given accounting period. Here's how to do it:

1. Determine the amount of expenses incurred but not yet invoiced and entered into A/P for the period. Focus on *material* expense items. Don't make yourself crazy trying to identify every little expense item for which you haven't yet received an invoice. Further, don't do this every month unless you're in a regulated industry. These industries usually require monthly financial statements. If your firm undergoes a certified audit at year-end, your auditors will search for unrecorded liabilities as part of their audit routine. The expense accrual and offset to A/P should fall out from there.

2. Make a journal entry that debits the asset or expense account for the purchase and credits a special account for "accrued liabilities." We want to keep these separate from the regular *invoiced* accounts payable to avoid double counting.

3. When the invoice finally arrives, no asset or expense account is involved in the entry. We recorded the purchase last month. Instead, remove it from accrued liabilities with a debit and credit the regular accounts payable account.

The entry to accrue uninvoiced accounts payable goes looks like this:

Consultant's Expense	$10,000	
Accrued Liabilities		$10,000

Records accrued consultant's fees incurred during the month but not yet invoiced.

Then, when the invoice finally arrives, the entry to record the payable looks like this:

Accrued Liabilities	$10,000	
Accounts Payable		$10,000

Records invoice received for consultant's fees previously accrued.

MAKING ENTRIES

We usually take the following three steps when we make entries into the accounts payable system:

1. Post each transaction to the individual vendor account.
2. Summarize purchase transactions by vendor and create an entry to the A/P subledger.
3. Post subledger entries to accounts payable in the general ledger and other offsetting asset and expense accounts.

As we post each invoice to the individual vendor account, we also post it to the subledger summary. This action shows the vendors with which there were transactions. We then total the subledger summary to form the entry that goes to the general ledger. Figure 8-1 shows this flow of information.

Figure 8-1
A/P Information Flow

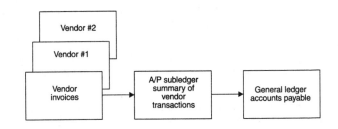

Recording Purchases

Purchase information usually comes from vendor invoices. However, the purchasing department may notify the A/P department that it has just placed a major order. If the invoice doesn't arrive before the month-end close of the accounting system, then accrue the expense. The inventory control system is another place purchase information might come from.

Regardless of where Accounts Payable gets its information, it updates the A/P vendor transaction files or cards (if you're using a manual system). Each vendor entry requires at least the following information:

- Vendor name • Amount
- Payment terms—particularly the payment due date

All of these items come from the invoice itself.

Follow the entry through the information flow described in Figure 8-1. First record the purchase on the individual vendor card. Most automated systems have prompt features which show the default asset or expense account information that's keyed to each vendor during the setup process. You can change this account manually at this time if you want.

Next, summarize the trade credit purchases to the different asset and expense accounts. The accounts payable account in the general ledger receives the offset. If you're on a manual system, use columnar paper to summarize each account.

Finally, summarize the entries to accounts payable and the expense accounts and post the batch to the general ledger. File the batch and all supporting documents for future retrieval.

Using a Manual System to Record Purchases

The manual system of recording accounts payable requires several checks and balances to be sure no transaction gets lost. Let's assume you've set up the vendor card system described above. Here are the steps to record the purchase of an item and liability for future payment:

1. Record the purchase transaction on the vendor card. Generally, the vendor's invoices communicate this to the A/P department.

2. Foot each individual vendor card to show a new balance after each day's entries.

3. Record the transactions from each card on the A/P subledger summary sheet. This shows entries to the various asset and expense accounts and to accounts payable. Make sure all debits to the asset and expense accounts equal the credit to A/P.

4. Post the A/P subledger summary sheet to the general ledger. Each asset or expense account affected gets posted along with accounts payable. All debits equal all credits.

Recording Payments

From a cash management standpoint, it makes sense to run accounts payable checks every day. That way, we're sure to pay invoices exactly when we should—not before and not after. Practically speaking, however, many small businesses find this difficult. The people who must approve and sign the checks are busy. Frequently they're out of the office earning the money to pay A/P in the first place.

Regardless of when you pay your vendors, the payment recording mechanism works the same way every time. The steps are as follows:

1. Identify those invoices paid during this check run.

2. Print the checks themselves.

3. Assemble the check approval/signature package for review.

4. Sign the checks.

5. Mail the checks.

6. File the supporting invoices in this batch for future reference.

7. Post the amount paid for each invoice to the individual vendor accounts.

8. Post to the A/P subledger.

9. Summarize the A/P subledger and post this to the general ledger.

Batch control totals

Be sure to match the amount in each check run against at least one other total, thus verifying that everything balances. The first such control total is the amount of all invoices from the individual vendor cards. As you go through the files identifying which invoices to pay, note on the A/P subledger the

- Vendor • Invoice number • Amount to pay

The total amount paid is the first control total. As you write the checks, tally the amounts on your check register. Computerized systems keep this running total automatically. At the end of the check writing process, you have the second control total: the amount subtracted from the checking account. Both control totals should agree. If they don't, then something is wrong.

Note that the asset and expense accounts do not concern us here. We debited these earlier when we first entered the invoice into the A/P system.

The third control total comes from the A/P subledger summary that posted to the general ledger. The debit to accounts payable should balance against the amount subtracted from the checking account. Again, if it doesn't, something is wrong.

Using a manual system

Many manual systems employ a tickler file that provides information on vendor pay dates. For some companies it's as simple as using an accordion file with a divider for each day of the month. Enter all invoices according to payment date. Note that the day the payment should come from the company interests us, not the due date. If we file invoices according to due date, they'll be late. Additionally, be sure to allow time for drafting the checks, review, signature and mailing. Some firms drag this process out a day or two. The steps needed to generate an A/P check run using a manual system are the same as those listed above. From this point, operation of a manual system for generating A/P checks is the same as that described above.

Recording Vendor Adjustments

Vendors issue their customers credits. The process works in your A/P system exactly the reverse of the way it does in accounts receivable for customer credits. Vendor credits result from such things as disputes, correction of errors, and returned merchandise.

Vendors also issue debits that *increase* customers' account balances. Recording interest charges on a delinquent account is one example. Vendors also document these debts and send them on to their customers.

As with adjustments in the receivable system, you should be careful when making adjustments to vendor payable accounts. Errors in credits don't place the company at financial risk. However, they make us look bad and might damage a valued vendor relationship.

If the A/P system doesn't have control over *increases* in its vendor balances, it is at risk. An employee might pay an inflated invoice (or a fictitious invoice) and cash the check. Then the actual payment would go to the vendor, with the employee pocketing the difference.

Make sure you require supporting documentation for any vendor adjustments made to the A/P system. Have someone independent of the disbursement system review these entries. Finally, summarize all adjusting entries periodically and vouch them against the vendor's monthly account statements to be sure the vendor actually received them.

TRACKING PAYABLES

Just as we carefully monitor our collection performance in the A/R system, we do the same thing with disbursements. We want to verify compliance with our payment policies. It makes little sense to determine when we want to pay vendors if the staff doesn't follow policy.

Payables Turnover

The faster a company pays its liabilities, the faster they turn over. A rapid payables turnover means that the company releases its cash quickly. Too large an A/P turnover can mean that the firm isn't taking advantage of trade credit offered by its vendors. Compute A/P turnover as follows:

$$\text{A/P turnover} = \frac{\text{annual expenses}}{\text{average A/P balance}}$$

The faster the A/P turnover, the more working capital is required to run the firm. As we saw in Chapter 7, receivables turnover ideally should match A/P turnover. Say, for example, that the average collection time for receivables is forty-five days. If payables also turn every forty-five days (or more), your vendors finance your inventory. In other words, you use none of your own working capital to pay for inventory.

Weighted Average Aging

Many companies have a policy regarding the aging of vendor invoices prior to payment—regardless of payment terms. The weighted average aging of the A/P portfolio tells the age of invoices before payment. Many industries have a customary average for vendor payments. For the dairy industry it's legally regulated at eleven days. In the garment industry it's less formal—whatever you can get away with.

Whether your firm uses an automated or a manual A/P system, there must be a conscious effort to set a payment date that will comply with both the company's A/P aging policy and the purchase terms.

Of course, policy can always be circumvented if a particular vendor demands payment or for any number of other good reasons. The weighted average aging computation identifies the firm's actual payment aging practices. Here's the equation for the weighted average aging of A/P:

Weighted average age of accounts payable = sum of (weighted average % of each aging bucket × # of days in each aging bucket)

Figure 8-2 shows one company's weighted average payables aging.

Figure 8-2
Computation of Weighted Average Payables

A/P Balances by Aging Bucket	Amount Owed by the Company	Weighting % in Aging Bucket	Weighting Factor in Days
Current	$5,000	4%	0 days
30 days	25,000	18%	6 days
60 days	75,000	55%	33 days
90 days	31,060	23%	21 days
120 days	0	0%	0 days
Total A/P	$136,060	100%	60 days

In this case the company pays its obligations in sixty days. The longer payables age, the more leverage we get from the company's vendors. Compare this with company policy and the industry standard. Some industries (bookselling, for example) do not consider this a slow-paying company (unless you're an author).

Computing the Average Payment Period

The average payment period illustrates the amount of trade credit the company uses. The higher the average payment period, the more money the company's vendors have invested in its accounts payable. We want this number to be as high as possible without damaging the creditworthiness of the company. Here's the equation:

$$\text{Average payment period} = \frac{\text{average accounts payable balance}}{\text{annual expenses} \div 360}$$

Let's run an example to see how one company takes advantage of vendors' trade credit:

Average A/P balance:	$750,000
Annual expenses:	$15,000,000

$$\text{Average payment period} = \frac{750,000}{15,000,000 \div 360}$$

Average payment period =   18 days

This may be too low in some industries, especially if the A/R collection period exceeds thirty days. This company might try stretching its payment aging policy. The tactic would bring the firm closer to industry custom and probably wouldn't damage its creditworthiness.

Balancing Favors

Many companies track those vendors who were paid either before or after the average payment period. Vendors paid prior to the average "owe" you something. If you chose to pay either before the due date or before the date indicated by industry custom, make sure those vendors know that this was a conscious decision of yours. They may be in a cash crunch themselves. Perhaps the treasurer called you to request payment by a certain date. Be sure they understand that there is a quid pro quo for early payment. Like the Mafia, good controllers don't do favors; instead, they collect debts.

Some negotiate a discount for the next purchase. Others request more lenient payment terms in the future. Regardless, your company should receive compensation in some way for paying before standard industry custom would indicate.

Tracking Tardy Payments

It's a good idea to track tardy payments that might jeopardize a valued relationship. You may want to correct the payment policy for those vendors. The cost of a terminated relationship usually outweighs any benefit from holding the cash owed.

Aging Payables

Report aging of the payables portfolio using the same techniques as for accounts receivable. The aging report shows the relative distribution of payment liabilities over a series of aging buckets. It gives us an indication of how our vendors perceive us as a credit risk. Additionally, it demonstrates how closely we're tracking against our aging targets.

Ideally, we'd like our A/P portfolio aging concentrated toward the aging payment policy time. Use these aging buckets:

- Current • 30 days • 60 days • 90 days • 120 + days

If you're on a manual system, prepare the aging analysis using the following steps:

1. Head a seven-column pad with "vendor name," the five aging buckets, and "vendor total."

2. Transfer the balance in each aging category from each vendor card to the columnar sheet.

3. Crossfoot each vendor row to be sure the total entered in the aging analysis matches the vendor card total.

4. Foot each aging bucket column.

5. Match the total accounts payable balance (in the lower right corner) with the total A/P subledger balance and the accounts payable balance in the general ledger. All three should be the same number. If they aren't, something is out of balance.

Most automated systems provide this report as a preprogrammed reporting option.

MANAGING DISBURSEMENTS

Most small businesses experience a cash crunch sometime during their lives. These are the times when your A/P system really earns its keep. Astutely managing disbursements when there's not enough money to pay all vendors keeps the wolf from the door.

The A/P system assists in allocating scarce funds for disbursement to vendors who can do the company the most good (or those who can cause it the most damage). Generally we pay those vendors who furnish critical items first. Next come vendors threatening serious action, such as a lawsuit.

Managing Late Payments

Treat vendors your company must pay late the way you would like to be treated when you face the same situation. Astute disbursement managers personally contact vendors they must pay late. They do this so that the problem doesn't compound itself by making vendors wonder about the company's financial stability.

Confront the issue honestly and with candor. Explain the nature of your firm's cash flow problem. Let vendors know the steps your firm is taking to solve the problem.

Vendors want an estimated payment date. Use the A/P system to help forecast cash flow. Put the vendors in a payment queue. Using this technique, tell your vendors when their payment date comes up. Once they understand the situation, most vendors will grudgingly accept the payment schedule. They have no choice.

Be sure to stick to your payment schedule. Late payment already damaged the company's credibility once. You've built it back up with honesty and a credible disbursement schedule. Vendors may grant you the benefit of the doubt once. But if you miss a second payment deadline, any lingering trust will dissolve immediately.

Controlling Purchase Terms

Purchase terms affect the speed with which funds leave the company through the A/P system. Terms most relevant to management of the A/P system include

- Payment date • Discount terms, including date and percentage
- Type of payment • Place of payment

Buyers usually focus more on the purchase price of products they're buying. That's important. However, if they ignore the four issues above, they could end up giving back the price concessions they worked so hard to win in the first place.

Educate the company's purchasers on the impact of payment term concessions. Compute the cost of giving something away, such as the lost float from payment by electronic funds transfer instead of a check. Changes in terms like these affect the total purchase price. Armed with this type of information, the firm is in a position to extract a concession to offset what it just gave away.

Dealing Directly with Vendors

Some purchasing agents want to be the vendor's best friend. Problems often get turned over to the A/P department, with the purchasing agent saying, "I don't know what's wrong. Why don't *you* talk with them?"

If your firm allows this sort of game playing, make sure to transfer the vendor to someone with authority. Additionally, make sure the financial people involved have sufficient information to make an informed decision on payment terms. This information should include

- The importance of the supplier to the company
- Competition for your business
- What kind of a customer you've been in the past
- Future needs for this vendor

Armed with this information, the payment decision can be made accurately. It also reduces the risk to the company if the vendor still goes away unhappy.

Payment Destination

Vendor companies are often proud of their cash management efforts. They make a splash with new lockbox systems and request that customers send payments to their new, more efficient location. "To better serve their customers," they say. The only real purpose is to accelerate payment clearing and improve cash flow.

Resistance to vendor requests that you use their lockbox system slows cash outflow. Many astute disbursement managers ignore these requests. Payment continues to go to the same old place. Some companies even send their payments to the vendor's salesperson. After all, often these are the people with authority to grant more favorable sales terms or even discount prices because you are such a good customer who pays the account promptly. Besides, it will probably be several days before the salesperson thinks to send the payment to the company, and it will probably still be sent to a location different from the lockbox payment processing center.

Remote Disbursement

Aggressive disbursement managers often use a bank located some distance from their vendors. For example, if most of your vendors are located on the east coast, a policy of remote disbursement calls for use of a *west coast* bank. This practice extends the clearing time. However, in this day of electronic clearinghouses, the chance of this having a material impact on the float of a small business is remote.

Even more aggressive managers take the idea of remote disbursement one step further. They use a remotely located country bank—one that does not belong to the Federal Reserve System. This further slows check clearing time. Some companies use certain banks in Waco, Texas, and South Carolina in this manner.

Most professionals agree that companies should use common sense when trying to slow disbursements. Small businesses don't usually employ the sophisticated cash management techniques used by large companies. Even when successful, these methods may gain you a day or two (at most) in float. That's important to a company disbursing millions a day. However, it's usually not worth the effort to a smaller company.

MANAGING TRADE DISCOUNTS

Most astute companies take advantage of all trade discounts offered. Here's the equation for determining the annualized income from a trade discount:

$$\frac{\text{Discount \%}}{\text{due date} - \text{discount date}} \times 360 \text{ days} = \begin{array}{l}\text{income from taking}\\ \text{advantage of a trade discount}\end{array}$$

If the payment terms were 1/10, net 30—that is, 1 percent discount if paid in ten days; otherwise the entire amount is due in thirty days—the income from taking advantage of the trade discount is 18 percent. Compute this as follows:

$$\frac{1\%}{30 - 10} \times 360 = 18\%$$

Unless the firm's cost of funds is over 18 percent, it doesn't make economic sense to pass up the discount offer.

PREDICTING CASH OUTFLOWS

Many companies get an interest-free loan simply by managing disbursement float. If they don't abuse the rules, there's little danger of overdrawing the checking account. There are three main opportunities for disbursement float:

- Mail float between the disbursing firm and the vendor
- Vendor's internal processing float • Bank system float

The first two, mail float and internal processing float, don't offer much opportunity. Our mail system is fairly efficient. There's not much benefit in trying to slow down the U.S. mail. We can't manage the vendor's internal processing float. Don't attempt the irritating tricks of not dating or not signing your checks. Don't try making the number amount disagree with the written amount, either. These ploys are transparent and just generate ill will.

Working Bank Float

Compute bank float. Use it to your own advantage. The computation consists of just three steps:

1. Track check release dates against the dates the checks clear the bank.

2. Compute the weighted average clearing time.

3. Compute book balance, bank balance, and payment capacity.

Disbursement float doesn't usually change unless there's a change in payment procedures. Changes in disbursement float might be caused by

- Increased use of electronic funds transfer payments
- Payees having installed a new lockbox system
- One company in the loop switching from a country disbursement bank to one that's a member of the Federal Reserve System

Figure 8-3 (page 136) shows how one fictitious company estimated and managed its disbursement float. (Figure 8-3 was reprinted by permission of the publisher, Prentice-Hall, a division of Simon & Schuster, Englewood Cliffs, NJ from *The Cash Management Handbook*, by Christopher R. Malburg, 1992.)

FUNDS OUTFLOW

We want to maintain control of outgoing funds for as long as possible. The information provided by A/P system's disbursement operation is useful for this purpose. If your firm has excess cash, the A/P system furnishes information on funds available for investing without danger of overdrawing the checking account.

The three types of disbursement control devices offered by banks are

- Presentment reporting • Sweep accounts • Balance reporting

Presentment Reporting

This refers to your notification of the amount of checks presented at your bank for clearing each day. This amount is the biggest unknown in managing the disbursement float. Presentment reporting services eliminate the guesswork. Here's how.

Separate disbursement account

The company establishes a separate checking account designated as the disbursement account. This is the account that pays out funds for the A/P system.

Figure 8-3
Tracking Float

T-D-O Corporation's cash manager has determined that the firm enjoys a weighted average float of 4 days from check disbursement to check clearing. The company now wishes to take advantage of this float. It tracks the float in its disbursements system along with the bank balance to incur negative balances in its general ledger cash account. The table below shows what the cash manager did:

T-D-O Corporation
Float Tracking System
($ in thousands)

Date	Begining Book Balance	Checks Mailed	Deposits	End Book Balance	Checks Cleared	Actual Bank Balance	Total Float	Payment Capacity
9-1	$200	$0	$0	$200	$0	$200	$0	$200
9-2	200	50	0	150	0	200	50	250
9-3	150	75	0	75	0	200	125	325
9-4	75	0	0	75	50	150	75	225
9-5	75	95	0	-20	0	150	170	320
9-6	-20	50	0	-70	75	75	145	220
9-7	-70	0	0	-70	0	75	145	220
9-8	-70	75	125	-20	95	105	125	230
9-9	-20	90	0	-110	50	55	165	220
9-10	-110	25	0	-135	0	55	190	245

Notice that the book balance goes negative on September 5 while the bank balance remains positive. The payment capacity continues to be a function of the actual bank balance and the total float. T-D-O's cash manager will have $75,000 in checks written on September 8 presented for clearing on September 11, thus producing an overdraft of $20,000. However, that day happens to correspond with the pay date by EFT direct debit of two customers. Funds inflow on September 11 will be $200,000. Because the bank does the EFT transaction first thing in the morning, there will be no overdraft. Indeed, the bank balance at the end of business that day will be $180,000.

Bank reporting services

The bank notifies the company early in the morning (before 11:00 a.m.) of the amount of checks *presented* for clearing that day. Subtracting that amount from the bank balance tells us the account's excess balance at the end of the day. Since we know this number early in the morning we can invest the excess money.

Investment

The investment watchwords for any company using its excess funds are *safety, liquidity,* and *yield.* Usually the vehicle of choice is an overnight repurchase agreement. It matures the next morning and the presentment reporting process begins again.

Sweep Accounts

This is an additional service that further enhances the value of presentment services. The bank automatically scans all disbursement accounts and *sweeps* any excess funds not needed for clearing checks that day into an interest-bearing account such as a money market fund.

If your company has several divisions, each with its own checking accounts, the bank can automatically perform the presentment and investment function for the corporate controller for all accounts. The bank determines the amount presented against each account for clearing that day. Early in the morning the bank subtracts the available balance from the amount scheduled for clearing and sweeps the excess into a corporate investment account.

Alternatively, if the firm has an outstanding line of credit, the sweep funds might be used to pay down the LOC rather than being invested.

Automated Balance Reporting

Many banks offer their corporate customers on-line computer access to their accounts using nothing more than a desktop personal computer. You can do most of the company's banking right from your office. The information and transactions most commonly offered include

- Line of credit draws and paydowns
- Transfer of lockbox deposits to a concentration account
- Account balance reporting and availability schedule
- Automated clearinghouse transactions

For international companies, some major money center banks offer worldwide account access from the same computer system.

In Chapter 9 we'll install the order entry component of your accounting system.

Chapter 9

Order Entry

Overview

Chapter 9 sets up the order entry system. It provides for the sharing of information between the people who take orders and the accounting system. Included in this chapter are issues such as granting of trade credit, review of payment history, and the method of recording the order into income as well as accounts receivable. We'll move farther along the accounting process by demonstrating how to remove the goods already sold from the inventory system and place unavailable goods on back order. Doing this at the time of order entry makes the information more current and reduces duplicate effort.

Information Flow

Order entry (O/E) acts as a bridge between the accounting system and inventory control. It processes orders coming in from the field sales force as well as directly from customers. Most order entry staffers earn their living on the phone. Many companies, even the smallest, have automated order entry systems.

An organized O/E system integrates these components of your accounting system:

- Inventory control • Back orders • Warehouse picking
- Accounts receivable • Sales processing and analysis
- Credit policy execution

Order Entry Responsibilities

Any time one part of your accounting system acts as a hub for information flowing to other parts, it has a myriad of tasks. Most of these cross departmental lines. For example, O/E's most basic job is to enter an order. However, this simple task becomes complicated, as the order entry mechanism draws information from other accounting departments just to process the order. Additionally, O/E distributes information to other accounting departments after completing order processing. Figure 9-1 lists the O/E department's responsibilities.

Figure 9-1
Order Entry Department Responsibilities

Responsibility	Description
Sales order processing	Receives orders from outside sales force and directly from customers. Generally done by telephone request.
Identifies inventory availability	Determines that items ordered are in stock. If the company has more than one warehouse, determines from which facility to ship.
Back order	Lists items not available for back order. Follows up on filling back orders when items finally arrive.
Executes company pricing policy	Uses pricing lists for inventory items. Often prices vary for types of customers and for the quantity purchased.
Executes company credit policy	Follows credit-granting guidelines for selling to customers. Uses credit authority granted by the company. Sends orders by customers exceeding that authority to the credit department for review.
Produces warehouse pick list	Sends pick list to warehouse for pulling the items ordered and shipment.
Processes shipping information	Determines method of shipment and cost. Adds this to the invoice. Separates shipping costs passed to customer from sales revenue.
Produces invoices	Generates an invoice for each order on a timely basis. Invoice is assigned to the customer, extended, and forwarded to accounting department.
Produces sales reports	Prints sales journals and recap reports.

Processing Information

This is what O/E does best. Most companies' O/E departments just receive orders. However, mail order operations combine the sales force with order entry. They train staff not only to run the order entry system but to sell as well.

Processing a sales order requires information from four sources:

- The customer or sales representative
- Accounts receivable
- Company policy
- Inventory control

Customer or sales representative

The first order of business is to determine what's being ordered. Easy, you say? Many customers don't have a current catalog. Sometimes the stock numbers of items in an earlier catalog don't agree with those currently in use. Often the prices have changed.

The O/E system must provide a mechanism for precisely describing what the customers wans, when the customers want it, and how they want it shipped. Additionally, customer location determines both sales taxes and shipping costs. Each of these items affects the final price.

Some of the more sophisticated computerized O/E systems have sales tax and shipping cost information already entered. O/E clerks automatically have the right answers fed them.

Drawing information from A/R

Most companies don't just blindly sell to any customer who happens to call and place an order. For repeat customers, it's nice to have an idea of their purchase and payment history prior to accepting a large order.

The best way to do this is by looking at the customer accounts receivable subledger transaction history. There, the O/E person can see the credit balances and when they were paid.

Company policies

Company policy determines the amount of credit granted any given customer. The customer's current outstanding balance is added to the amount now being purchased. The total must be less than the established credit limit. Otherwise, the order falls outside established O/E policy guidelines.

For customers who insist that their orders be processed even though they exceed established credit limits, company policy must provide O/E personnel with procedures that don't unnecessarily ruin otherwise good customer relationships. Generally these include transferring the order request to the company's credit officer. That person is better qualified to make a credit decision that isn't in accord with normal company policy. If the decision is favorable, Order Entry completes the transaction.

Terms of sale is another policy the company determines. Order entry personnel pass them on to customers at the time of the sale. Additionally, the invoice confirms the purchase terms. The most common purchase terms include

- Payment due date
- Trade discount for early payment—both percentage and the due date to earn it
- Shipping terms, such as F.O.B.
- Point of departure
- Insurance arrangements

Inventory control

Before processing a sale order, the O/E clerk must determine that the items are available. This determination doesn't present a problem for very small companies. Chances are that whoever takes the orders knows from memory what's available and what isn't.

However, larger companies often have several warehouses, each stocking different inventory items. They may have several order entry clerks working at the same time. These people probably don't know what's out there in the warehouses.

This situation necessitates either a current inventory listing by location or an automated connection between the inventory control system and the O/E system. Indeed, many computerized O/E systems flag out-of-stock inventory items when they are entered into the order menu.

The problem is compounded for companies whose warehouses serve multiple O/E facilities. Even if the clerks have an inventory list that shows that an item is currently in stock, it may have already been allocated to a customer by another O/E clerk. It still shows up as being in stock, and it is; however, shipment is imminent. Automated systems usually have some sort of mechanism that flags inventory items already allocated to orders even though they still appear on current listings.

The issue of *substitutability* arises for out-of-stock items as well. The inventory control system should provide the O/E people with some sort of cross-reference for items that are substitutes for one another. This information saves sales that might have gone to the competition for lack of availability.

Figure 9-2 shows a top-level view of the information flow in and out of order entry needed to process an order.

Figure 9-2
Order Entry Process Information Flow

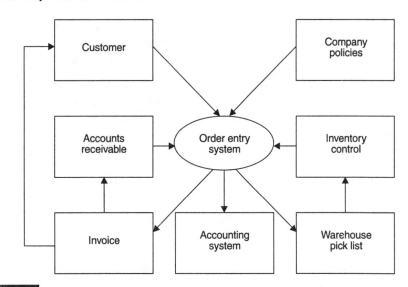

Information Flowing out of O/E

In Figure 9-2, you can see three information outflows:

- Invoices to the receivables system and to the customer
- Entries required by the accounting system to record transfers out of inventory and sales income
- Warehouse pick lists so that the items may be picked, packed, and shipped to the customers

Invoices

Many companies make Order Entry responsible for producing invoices for all sales. This practice makes sense, since no matter who makes the sale, it must run through O/E for processing, pricing, warehouse picking, and accounting.

What is the single most important attribute of any invoice produced by O/E? *Clarity!* Excessively complicated invoices extend the payment time. There are only five things that interest customers about an invoice:

- *What* did they buy? • *Whom* should they pay?
- *How much* should they pay? • *When* should they pay?
- *Where* should they send the payment?

Give customers clear descriptions of the items they bought. Make sure they can match them against the shipping advice. Some companies include a reference to their customer's purchase order number as well to further accelerate matching. When you format your invoices, keep these five critical pieces of information in mind. They'll help your customers pay you faster.

Some companies insist that invoices be sent out no later than a day or so after the sale. This is a good policy and one that your controller should support. An easy control mechanism to track this performance is to establish an *invoice backlog report.* This simply reports the invoices not yet sent, their dollar amount, and the date of sale. Large dollar amounts of sales that remain uninvoiced after the company's policy date are a problem that should involve top management.

Along with the purchase amounts, the invoice must include the sales tax computation and early payment discount terms, if applicable. Additionally, it should include any insurance, postage, or shipping charges for which the customer is responsible. There's usually no better place to compute these things than in the order entry department. After all, O/E usually generates the invoices.

Accounting entries

Most of the information required by the accounting department comes from the invoice. Entries to the general ledger summarized from the O/E sales journal include

- Cost of goods sold • Inventory • Sales income
- Accounts receivable

The O/E system must identify each item sold and provide the accounting system with the information needed to remove it from inventory. At the same time, the offset goes to cost of goods sold. Some companies track the sales revenue and costs of particular products or lines of products. This requires unique general ledger account numbers for each product's sales revenue and costs.

If you're using a manual order entry system, summarize your sales by whatever product or product line distinction you want. Then prepare a journal entry form to record the day's sales. Here are the entries going from O/E to the accounting department:

```
To record transfer of inventory:
    Cost of Goods Sold          $1,000
        Inventory                           $1,000


To record the sale in accounts receivable:
    Accounts Receivable         $1,500
        Sales                               $1,500
```

Notice that there's a difference between the amount moved from inventory and sales. That difference is profit.

The A/R system records its entries from invoices generated by the O/E system. First, it records all invoices in the customer subledgers. Then it summarizes the entries, posts them to the A/R subledger, and finally posts them to the general ledger accounts receivable and sales accounts.

Warehouse pick lists

Whether you're using a manual O/E system or one that's automated, somehow the warehouse has to be told what to take off the shelves and ship. Usually the responsibility for this communication falls to Order Entry. When you design your warehouse pick list format, here's a list of the items you might consider including:

- Order date
- Salesperson or O/E clerk who processed the order
- Warehouse location, if you have more than one
- Customer name and number
- Customer purchase order number
- Order number for referring back to the O/E system
- *Sold to* name and address
- *Ship to* name and address
- Shipping method
- Item numbers ordered
- Units
- Number of items ordered
- Warehouse location

Additionally, some pick sheets include a space for the warehouseman to note the number of items actually shipped and those placed on back order.

Commission

We try to keep the information generated for a particular transaction in the originating department. Since Order Entry generates the sales orders, it often computes sales commissions as well. After all, O/E has all the information needed to compute this important number:

- Salesperson • Amount of sale
- Items purchased in the event of special commissions on certain items

One caution, however: Ideally we want a good separation of duties between functions such as sales and computation of sales commissions. Therefore, from a control standpoint, many companies compute commissions at some place other than in a sales-related department. Often they assign this responsibility to a department within Accounting. The accounting department gets the invoices too. That means that they have all the information required for the computation, just as O/E does.

Sales performance reports

Again, Order Entry has all the information needed to generate most sales statistics. It makes sense to assign this responsibility to O/E rather than moving the data somewhere else. Some of the more useful reports generated by O/E include

- Daily and monthly sales recaps • Customer sales history
- Gross profit reports • Open sales orders • Back orders
- General ledger posting recap • Product sales reports
- Warehouse sales reports
- Territory, district, and region sales reports

You may want to include some or all of these reports in your system.

ESTABLISHING THE O/E MECHANISM

Whether you install a manual or an automated order entry system, the principles are the same. We want a mechanism that traps the sales information, formats it in a way that's useful, and sends it to the appropriate departments for further processing. This process entails just a few steps:

- Accepting the sales order • Recording the sales order
- Generating a warehouse pick list • Generating an invoice
- Forwarding sales information to the appropriate departments

Accepting the Sales Order

Acceptance is more a matter of the O/E person being satisfied that the customer meets the company's credit risk criteria. This requires an awareness of the

- Customer's current receivables balance

- Customer's credit limit
- Total amount of the proposed purchase

Manual systems

If you run a manual system, you need a current listing of the accounts receivable detail for each customer. Depending on the activity in your receivables subledger, you may have to update these lists weekly or even daily.

Additionally, you'll need a list showing each customer's credit limit. Find it in the A/R customer subledger. Company policy should require new purchases combined with an existing receivable balance not to exceed established credit limits. The receivable system should track customers with balances exceeding their credit limits. If there are any, you should cut them off from further purchases until the balances fall below their credit limits.

Automated systems

Most automated systems have an automatic linkage with the receivables system. This provides instant access to current balances owed by existing customers and their preset credit limits. These systems often will warn the order entry clerk if acceptance of the proposed order will put the customer over the limit.

Recording sales orders

Well-organized sales order input sheets provide a script for the order takers. Whether the input sheet is paper, as in a manual system, or on a computer screen, the information needed is much the same. Here's a list of the information you might find it useful to obtain and enter at the point of order:

Order number: For future reference, it's easier to look up sales order records if they are consecutively numbered. If you use a manual system, consider preprinting the sales order number on your order forms. Most computerized order entry systems automatically assign the next order number to each new order.

Order date: Customers frequently place similar orders throughout the year. Order dates and numbers distinguish identical orders to prevent miscounting or double counting.

Customer information: Your O/E system needs to know whom you're dealing with. Customer information should include

- Name
- Customer number
- Sold to address
- Ship to address
- Salesperson who made the order or O/E clerk who took it

Detailed order information: Here's a list of the rest of the information you need when processing an order through Order Entry:

- Shipping method
- Shipping terms
- Purchase terms
- Customer P.O. number

- Items purchased by item number and verbal description
- Number of items ordered • Unit price
- Number actually shipped • Number placed on back order
- Dollar amount extended for each item
- Subtotals for the items purchased • Applicable discounts
- Freight charged to customer • Sales tax
- Subtotal for entire order • Applicable customer deposit
- Total order amount

Most companies use preprinted order entry forms with spaces for all of the above information. Figure 9-3 shows a sample O/E form.

Figure 9-3
Sample Order Entry Form

Company Name
Company Address
Company Phone

Sold to   Order #
Address   Date
Phone   Salesperson

Ship to
Address
Phone

Customer P.O. #   Shipping terms   Purchase terms

Item #	Description	Units	# Ordered	# Shipped	# Back ordered	Price	Amount $

Net order   _____
Less discount   _____
Plus freight   _____
Plus sales tax   _____

Order total   _____
Less deposit   _____

Order balance   _____

Processing Sales Orders

Once you've completed the order entry sheet, it's time to finish processing the order. There are several more steps before the order is ready to go. Many automated systems provide the information necessary to continue right there on the O/E screen. Manual systems require you to check several places to verify this data.

Customer qualification with credit criteria

We need to be sure that the customer is in good standing with our accounts receivable department. This consists mainly of checking that

- The customer's account isn't delinquent.
- The proposed sale doesn't make the account exceed the customer's current credit limit.

Item availability

Next check the inventory list to be sure that each item ordered is currently in finished goods inventory and ready to ship. Put out-of-stock items on back order or remove them from the customer's order. This point is a good time to check an item substitute list for goods on hand that can be substituted for goods that are currently unavailable.

Once again, automated systems often suggest preprogrammed substitutes for goods that are out of stock.

Print warehouse pick list

The O/E department prints a warehouse pick list for each order. This is forwarded to the warehouse supervisor. The warehouse staff picks the items from finished goods inventory, packs them, and ships them.

Print invoices

The O/E department prints an invoice for each of the orders it processes. It then forwards these invoices to the accounting department for use in making entries into the sales journal and the A/R system. Often duplicate invoices go to the shipping department if it's the company's policy to include an invoice along with the packing slip that accompanies each order shipment.

Processing Back Orders

Disorganized back orders can be a nightmare. When back ordered items finally arrive in the warehouse or in finished goods inventory from the production line, match them against those orders requesting the items. However, the question is, how to match them?

That's the difficult part and the part we'll discuss now.

Manual systems

Different companies organize their back orders differently, depending on their needs and volumes. The best back order system is one that immediately matches items just received finished goods inventory with the orders waiting for them.

This is done with a back ordered item list. Format the list to include the items back ordered and a list of the order numbers that require each item.

Next, use an accordion file to keep the open sales orders organized. Some companies file them by inventory item needed. Others file them by sales order number. Once the back ordered items are pulled from inventory, match them with the missing items from the open sales orders. The sales orders already include all the information needed to generate an invoice. Enter the items just received from back order on a new invoice. All the customer information necessary comes from the original sales order. From this point the process is the same as that for a regular sales order. The system subtracts the items just shipped from inventory. The invoice goes to Accounting for journal entry processing.

Automated systems

Most of the top automated systems have a back order management module which is automatically linked with the inventory control system. When back ordered items arrive in inventory, they are flagged and matched with open orders. Warehouse pick sheets and invoices are printed automatically.

PRICE LISTS

Order Entry does not maintain the company's price lists. However, it *is* responsible for executing the most current pricing policies. Each O/E clerk needs the firm's price list and discount policy right there at his or her desk. Sound obvious? We've all seen order takers fumble around trying to find a current price list when taking customer orders over the phone. Sometimes they found it and sometimes they didn't. The result was that someone not even in the decision-making loop arbitrarily made a pricing determination that affected the company's gross margin.

Make sure each price list has the current revision date somewhere on it. If the price of even one item changes, print the list and distribute it again. Make sure all O/E staff use the most current price list.

Many companies anticipate price changes and use higher prices as a hook in their advertising. This sometimes confuses order takers. Just one price—the one they enter on the sales order in front of them—interests them.

Order Entry isn't usually the place to sell customers on buying items in anticipation of future price increases anyway. The sales force or your company's advertising does that.

TRADE CREDIT DECISIONS

Order entry staffers are on the firing line when it comes to implementing the company's credit policy. Often customers place orders knowing full well that these orders put them over their credit limit. The best credit decisions made at the O/E level are those with black or white answers.

O/E clerks take orders over the telephone and pass them on to the warehouse and to Accounting. They don't usually sell (except in mail order operations). They don't always do credit either. The decision rules that work best regarding credit include the following:

- Orders that place customers over their credit limits are declined.
- Orders from customers that are currently delinquent are declined.
- In special circumstances, orders outside established credit guidelines may be placed on hold, pending credit review.

Unless specifically allowed to do so by company policy, the O/E clerks aren't authorized to accept orders in these three categories. Those that do are subject to termination. That may sound like a tough policy. However, companies work hard devising their credit policies. Those polices are based on experience and knowledge of their customers' payment behavior. Generally they work.

You don't want your O/E clerks circumventing those policies on their own. If you give them discretion, allow them to refer the sale to a credit supervisor who reviews the case. We'd rather lose the 5 or 10 percent net profit on an order than potentially thousands on a bad debt—especially one we had the opportunity to avoid in the first place.

Granting Credit

Reduce decisions regarding trade credit to just one question: Can the customer pay the bill? Some automated O/E systems give the clerk a great deal of latitude. If a proposed order places the customer's account over the credit limit or if there's a past due balance, a special screen flashes, interrupting the normal order-taking process.

The O/E clerk sees that the proposed sale exceeds the credit limit. In addition, the screen presents the customer's A/R aging record. The amount delinquent in the various aging buckets shows up as well. Some of the more sophisticated systems give an entire credit history, including

- Date of last activity • Date of last payment
- Last payment amount • Date of last statement
- Highest credit balance • Date of last finance charge
- Unpaid finance charges

With all this information available, the O/E clerk can make limited credit decisions. Many small businesses allow such decisions within certain guidelines, such as those described in Figure 9-4.

Under these circumstances, a clerk may override the O/E system's warning screen on an overlimit customer and accept the order. However, it's an excellent idea to make management aware of all orders accepted that fall into these categories.

Required Information

Granting trade credit is a complicated process. It's part science and part art. We can analyze a customer's balance sheet and past credit history all we want. However, in the final analysis, it still comes down to the question we posed earlier: Will this customer pay the bill?

Some companies combine the credit department's duties with those of the order entry group. Most separate the two duties and designate one person as the

Figure 9-4
Sample Credit-Granting Criteria

China Diggers, Ltd.
Order Entry Staff
Trade Credit Guidelines

Order entry staff may grant trade credit exceeding credit limits or to delinquent accounts *only* under the following circumstances:

1. *Amount over credit limit:* If the existing A/R balance plus all unbilled open orders plus the proposed order does not exceed the credit limit by $100.

2. *Delinquent accounts:* Accept sales on accounts with $500 or less in the thirty-day bucket. Decline without exception orders by customers with balances aged more than thirty days.

3. *Finance charges:* Decline sales on accounts with unpaid finance charges.

When in doubt, place an order on credit hold and refer it to the credit manager.

---

chief credit officer. Even if the person in your O/E department knows nothing of credit evaluation, there's no time like the present to learn. There are many excellent books on managing trade credit. There are magazines published by professional credit managers' trade groups. Indeed, many industry groups hold instructional seminars dealing specifically with credit assessment.

Learn to use the credit management tools professionals use. They provide a written audit trail on why the credit officer granted credit to a particular customer. If the credit goes bad, you can look at the credit decision and figure out where you made a mistake. That's how you learn to avoid similar problems in the future.

Further, even if your credit-granting decisions aren't as sophisticated as those of some organizations, asking for these things gives customers the chance to think twice before stiffing you. Here are the things commonly used to evaluate a customer's trade creditworthiness:

- Payment history from your company's A/R system
- Professional credit report such as Dun & Bradstreet or TRW
- Credit references in the industry
- Customer's financial statements
- Bank references

Credit policies

You need established credit policies to run an effective credit screening operation. Put them in writing. Make sure those responsible for administering your credit function follow them. After all, it isn't their money that's at risk.

Credit policies should cover at least these points:

- Documentation required for making credit decisions.
- Minimum net worth levels for each level of credit limit.
- Minimum bank balances.
- Number of derogatory reports from credit rating agencies and other credit references before the application is rejected—often it takes just one.
- Your own company's credit history with the customer—good customers with a history of prompt payment are usually granted more latitude.
- Future benefit of the customer to your company. We don't work in a vacuum. Sometimes companies accept marginal credit risks in order to gain strategic market penetration.
- Effect of customer location. It may be that a customer's geographic area depends on just one industry—and it's declining.

Hierarchy of authority

Authority to grant trade credit rises up the executive ladder as the dollar amount at risk increases. However, we want to keep credit-granting authority as low as possible so that the decision is truly worth the time of the person making it. Too many small-business owners retain a death grip on credit-granting authority—at any limit and create bottlenecks in the process. Often these people have much larger dollar decisions pending than a $100 credit approval. Consequently, they get shoved off and delayed.

Use a *stratified* credit-granting authority hierarchy. Figure 9-5 shows an example of what we mean.

Figure 9-5
Credit Authority Hierarchy

Approval required	<$500	$500-$1000	$1000-$5000	$5000-$10,000	>$10,000
Order entry clerk	X	X	X	X	X
Assistant credit manager		X	X	X	X
Credit manager		X	X	X	X
Controller			X	X	X
Chief financial officer				X	X
President					X

It makes sense to spread the risk of the vast majority of credit decisions among more people. The potential loss is less than for the comparatively fewer credit sales reviewed by the firm's senior executives. Further, it's a good idea to review a representative sample of everyone's credit decisions periodically. We want to be sure the company's policies are followed.

Impact on Accounts Receivable

Credit policies and the company's credit-granting criteria affect both sales and cash flow. Bad credit decisions made today will haunt you until write-off. Customers see trade credit as part of the terms of sale. All things being equal, vendors with more lenient trade credit policies get the business.

Here are the three things that happen financially if you have excessively generous credit policies:

1. *Decrease in cash sales*: It's suddenly cheaper for customers to have you finance their purchases. They buy using trade credit instead of cash.

2. *Increase in accounts receivable*: More customers take advantage of liberal credit guidelines. Accounts receivable balloons in all aging buckets. With it, so do working capital requirements.

3. *Increase in bad debt expense*: Customers normally rejected find their way into the A/R system, thus increasing bad debt expense.

Preapproved Credit Lines

Some companies conduct all their credit-granting reviews at one time and predesignate a line of credit for major customers, usually at the beginning of the year. That way, when the busy season rolls around, there's no time-consuming credit decision to make.

Preapproval often starts with the bidding on a sale. The credit department gets involved to make the terms of purchase part of the bid. This procedure may differentiate your company from the competitors who didn't think to add this often important selling point.

Chapter 10 adds the inventory control system to our accounting system.

Chapter 10

Inventory Control

OVERVIEW

Most manufacturers have three kinds of inventory: raw material, work in process, and finished goods. Chapter 10 sets up a simple inventory control mechanism. It identifies the special accounting treatments associated with inventory throughout the production and sales process. Additionally, the chapter demonstrates techniques of maintaining a physical inventory count and the role it plays in the computation of cost of goods sold and internal control.

FEATURES OF THE INVENTORY CONTROL SYSTEM

The inventory control systems that operate most successfully in small businesses have just three objectives:

- Track inventory as it progresses through the manufacturing process.
- Maintain a perpetual count of finished goods available for sale.
- Assist in computing cost of goods sold.

Controlling inventory isn't a difficult task. However, several complicating factors enter into the process. First, companies often have many inventory items—sometimes hundreds. As with anything else, the more things there are to manage, the more complicated the process.

Second, there's usually rapid movement of items throughout the inventory system. Items come into the raw materials inventory. The system processes them and eventually puts them into finished goods.

Items move out of the system too. Customers order inventory. Some goods are drop-shipped from the warehouse to customers. Items return to inventory for credit. Some items sold require back ordering because the warehouse is out of stock.

Each of these transactions, though simple by itself, when combined and repeated as often as the inventory control system requires, complicates the whole process.

Tracking Inventory through the Firm

Inventory control (I/C) monitors each inventory item as it moves through production. From a financial standpoint, inventory is the most valuable asset of many small businesses. For purposes of valuation, financial statements usually separate the three components of inventory: raw material, work in process, and finished goods.

This separation also aids in maintaining control over cost of goods sold. The accounting system builds production costs into inventory from the time items enter as raw materials. As we add other raw materials, subassemblies, and labor, the costs accumulate in work in process inventory. When the item is completed, we transfer it to finished goods. There the order entry staff can see items available for shipment.

Inventory Valuation

Inventory control maintains a count of the company's inventory, recording changes to inventory. This way, we have a count of each inventory item both in units and in dollar value. When we close the books at month-end, the balance sheet reports the dollar value.

Inventory value interests owners and investors. They have a vested financial interest in the inventory items in the warehouse and on the production line. Additionally, lenders whose loans are collateralized by inventory are *very* interested in this value as reported each month.

The company's production control people want to know the amount of each item on hand for ordering purposes. They match this with their material requirements plan and decide when and how much to order.

From a control standpoint, the inventory balance reported on the books should match the actual physical count. If it doesn't, there's a problem. More often than not, it's an accounting problem. However, inventory sometimes has a habit of walking out of the warehouse. The inventory control system serves as a deterrent against pilferage.

Compute Cost of Goods Sold

The ending inventory number is part of the equation used to compute cost of goods sold. Without accurate values for beginning and ending inventory and purchases, we cannot compute the cost of the items sold. The accounting system cannot compute profit without knowing the cost of goods sold.

Linking with Other Systems

Inventory control sends information to and receives it from several other parts of the accounting system. These include

- Order entry • General ledger • Purchase order processing
- Accounts payable • Cost accounting • Bill of materials
- Work order processing

Anything in the financial system that involves inventory starts in I/C. Records of transactions, costs, or transfers of items flow throughout the accounting system from inventory control.

FLOW OF INVENTORY

The I/C system we'll design in this chapter tracks inventory items from the time they come into the firm as raw materials, subassemblies, or finished goods ready to ship. It's a simple matter to track the flow of these items as they make their way through the system into the finished goods warehouse. Figure 10-1 shows the process of transfer through I/C.

Figure 10-1
Inventory Information Flow

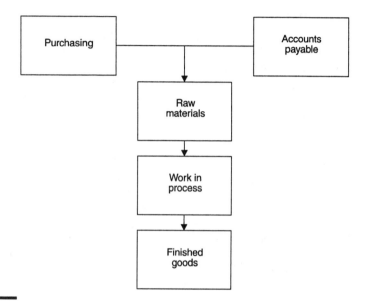

Raw Materials

The production plan indicates the amount of raw materials and subassemblies required to produce the goods scheduled. From this, the purchasing department generates purchase orders, orders the items, and informs Accounts Payable of the transaction. When the invoices arrive, Purchasing approves them and forwards them to A/P for inclusion in the payment queue.

When the warehouse receives the items ordered, I/C records them into raw materials inventory. Generally we make this entry both in units and in dollars. The production department uses the unit measure, and Accounting uses the dollars. The raw material sits in the warehouse until it is needed by the production line. Then it enters work in process inventory.

Work in Process

The production line transfers items from raw materials inventory to work in process (WIP) inventory. WIP inventory accumulates the costs of raw materials, subassemblies, and labor for each item in process by means of the cost accounting system. However, at any point in time we can look at WIP inventory and see all the value added in the production process.

Finished Goods

Upon completion of the production process, Inventory Control transfers the items from WIP into finished goods inventory. This count is what interests the order entry staff and the sales force. Make the entry on both a unit and a dollar basis.

FLOW OF INFORMATION

We just saw the way inventory flows through the I/C system. Now we'll identify the information required to generate those changes in inventory balances. Our objective is to have an accurate *perpetual* inventory balance—one that is accurate at any point in time.

Contrast this with the *periodic* method of inventory valuation. This system records inventory only periodically—at month-end and at year-end. Most small businesses don't use the periodic method unless a perpetual system just isn't feasible.

Receiving Raw Materials

The first involvement of the inventory control system comes when raw materials arrive. Once checked in, they're transferred to the raw materials stores area. A shipper document usually accompanies the items. Often shippers are nothing more than blind copies of the purchase order issued when the items were bought.

For inventory control purposes, the shipper, packing slip, and purchase order copy go to I/C for recording in the subledger. I/C records the number of units received and their costs.

The transactions for the day are tallied in the inventory subledger and summarized for entry to the general ledger.

Transferring Raw Materials to Work in Process

Many companies that manufacture custom items or equipment assign each item a work order number, thereby linking the manufacturing process with the customer's sales order. Other companies produce a line of items for entry into finished goods and *then* sell them.

Either way, the inventory control system tracks the progress of manufacture. Goods move from raw material stores to the production line. The cost accounting system adds the labor needed to combine different raw materials and subassemblies. Overhead is added to WIP items. As all these costs are added to WIP, they get posted to a production record.

The I/C records this movement through the cost accounting system. When finished, raw materials and WIP have both been updated with each day's transactions.

Completing Production

Once the items come out of WIP, they're transferred to finished goods inventory. The production tracking sheet simply closes out the work in process item, allocates overhead and any other costs not already included in WIP, and moves it over to finished goods inventory.

The entry appears on the inventory control system as a credit to WIP and a debit to finished goods. Inventory Control summarizes the day's transactions. Then it prepares a journal entry for recording in the general ledger.

Updating the Inventory List

Posting the items from WIP to finished goods inventory automatically updates the inventory listing. At this point the sales staff and order entry clerks can get a list of items available for sale and shipment. Additionally, the system fills back orders for sales already written.

SETTING UP THE I/C SYSTEM

Manual inventory control systems consist mostly of individual records of each inventory item. Automated systems employ the same method. However, they use computer files and transfer data from one to another.

The inventory control system includes a subledger for each of the three inventory types: raw material, work in process, and finished goods.

Manual System

For each item, create an inventory transaction record. Make transaction records for all the raw material items. As raw materials move into WIP, make an inventory transaction record for each item in WIP. When the manufacturing process is completed, move the WIP items to transaction records for each item in the finished goods inventory.

Probably the simplest method of recording inventory transactions is with card files. Each inventory item has its own card. The status of each item in any of the three inventory categories appears on its transaction card.

Using this method, we see a complete history of each inventory item. Figure 10-2 (page 158) illustrates a sample inventory transaction card.

Inventory transaction record

Chances are that the person who moves inventory around the warehouse and production line doesn't record each transaction on the inventory cards. Instead, the people on the shop floor record inventory movement using a transaction record. This document tells the I/C clerk what items went to which inventory account. They usually contain the following data:

- Date • Person responsible • Item number • Number of items
- Moved from • Moved to • Comments

Automated systems

Setting up an automated inventory control system, like the process of I/C itself, is easy. The complicating factor is the sheer volume of items many companies have. Additionally, the more sophisticated the system, the more options users have and the more questions they must answer during initial installation.

Figure 10-2
Inventory Transaction Card

MTH Partners, Ltd.
Raw Materials Inventory
Transaction Card

Item number: 123
Description: #112 Box subassembly
Warehouse location: Downtown

Dates	Description	Quantity	Unit	Cost/Unit	Extension
4-6-9X	Receive from supplier	110	Box	$5.50	$605.00
4-7-9X	Move to WIP—order #456	25	Box	5.50	137.50
Balance on hand after transactions		85			$467.50

MTH Partners, Ltd.
Work in Process Inventory
Transaction Card

Item number: Work order #456
Description: Johnson computer chassis
Production location: Downtown

Dates	Description	Quantity	Unit	Cost/Unit	Extension
4-7-9X	Receive box #123	25	Box	$5.50	$137.50
4-7-9X	Add PC board #567	25	Brd	55.50	1387.50
Balance after transactions					$1525.00
4-8-9X	Transfer to finished goods	10	Chassis	61.00	610.00
Balance after transactions					$915.00

MTH Partners, Ltd.
Finished Goods Inventory
Transaction Card

Item number: Work order #456
Description: Johnson computer chassis
Finished goods inventory warehouse: Downtown

Dates	Description	Quantity	Unit	Cost/Unit	Extension
4-8-9X	Receive order #456	10	Chassis	$61.00	$610.00
Balance after transactions		10			$610.00

Here are some of the questions often asked by automated I/C systems when they're first set up:

- How many warehouses?
- Default to which warehouse?
- Decimal places in price entry
- Decimal places in cost entry
- Set up inventory item code format
- Calendar months or fiscal period?
- Include quantity on back order in quantity available?
- Retain transaction history for each item?
- Integrate I/C with any other accounting systems such as order entry, general ledger, job cost?
- Specify general ledger account numbers for:
  - Inventory
  - Cost of goods sold
  - Sales income
  - Sales returns
  - Purchases clearing

The list goes on for every brand of automated I/C system. However, once you've established the system, actually entering your initial items into inventory is a clerical task.

One caution, however: Once you've finished entering all your inventory items, run a complete inventory listing. If you're converting, make sure the unit count for each item exactly equals the unit count from your old system. Additionally, make sure the dollar amount on hand for each item equals the old system's dollar amount on hand. Finally, the total inventory dollar balance in the new system should exactly equal the dollar balance in the old system.

Make sure you do these checks prior to transferring the new inventory balance to the general ledger.

Accounting Entries

Accounting entries flow from the I/C subledger summary to the general ledger. The process is similar to the one we used for the receivables and payables subledgers. We post individual activity each inventory transaction card to an I/C control recap sheet. This step summarizes all inventory transactions and is used to make the journal entry for posting to the general ledger.

Inventory Control Recap Sheet

The I/C recap sheet identifies each transaction and allocates it to the proper inventory account classification and the right location. It provides an audit trail straight back to the individual inventory subledger cards.

The control recap sheets separate inventory transfers from one location to another from sales and purchases. Thus the G/L entry shows intracompany transactions as well as sales and inventory purchases.

The transactions in Figure 10-3 illustrate one way to set up the inventory control recap sheets:

Figure 10-3
Inventory Control Recap

Date	Item #	Name	Transaction	Debit	Credit
6-7-9X	123-001 3456	Inventory Chassis	East coast Transfer		$456.78
	G/L acct.		Total		$456.78
6-7-9X	123-002 3456	Inventory Chassis	West coast Receipt	$456.78	
	G/L acct.		Total	$456.78	
Total	Postings			$456.78	$456.78

Notice how the inventory control recap sheet lists each transaction. In the example, the transaction was a warehouse transfer between the east and west coast warehouses. The example shows the general ledger account numbers and the individual inventory item number. The system updates all inventory balances to record the transfer. Additionally, the recap serves as a journal entry form for posting to the general ledger.

However, when used as a journal entry form, the recap sheet must contain an identifying number. Many firms just use an increasing number stamp to stamp each form. Some use prenumbered forms. Enter the recap form number into the G/L transaction entry to preserve the audit trail started by the inventory recap sheet. If there's a question on the entry, the G/L shows where the entry came from. Now we can trace a transaction back to the individual inventory subledger card if necessary.

ACCOUNTING POLICIES

The most significant accounting policies regarding inventory for small businesses are those that involve cost recognition. If your company undergoes a certified audit, issues of inventory costing may crop up. The main thing to remember is that whatever method you choose must be

- Logical considering your industry and the way business is conducted
- Consistently applied

Let's first define inventory. Accounting Research Bulletin (ARB) 43, Chapter 4 identifies inventory as

Items of tangible personal property that (1) are held for sale in the ordinary course of operations as finished goods, (2) goods in the process of production as work-in-process, or (3) raw material and supplies which are to be currently consumed directly or indirectly in the manufacturing process.

Sound familiar? That's the way we set up our inventory control system. It's also the way we treat the flow of inventory through the production cycle.

Process Contracts

Many small businesses custom-produce inventory for specific customers under contract. We account for the costs of production as the work is completed on each contract. Therefore, we use a separate cost of goods sold account for each contract in the production process.

Further, the firm accrues earnings each year for the progress made toward completion of each contract. We're really estimating earnings applicable to undelivered items on a fixed-price contract. The income and expenses most often attached to such process contracts include

- Accrued earnings
- Labor by contract
- Material
- Variable manufacturing
- Fixed manufacturing
- Delivery

A good example would be a home builder who has custom homes under construction throughout the year. Some of the process contracts are still in production at year-end. However, the "inventory" has already been sold under the terms of the contract. Therefore, we accrue and recognize a portion of the expected income to match the costs and expenses incurred during the period.

Inventory Costing Methods

Your choice of inventory costing method usually depends on the nature of your business. Generally your controller or independent CPA can recommend the most appropriate method for reporting purposes. We base the choice on four criteria:

1. Which method maximizes the firm's net income?
2. Which method minimizes the firm's income tax liability?
3. Which method provides the most information considering the nature of the company
4. Which method is least likely to be abused?

Regardless of the inventory costing method used, it's imperative that it be *consistently* applied. Don't switch from one method to another without good reason. Additionally, never change in the middle of an accounting period regardless of the reason. The four most common inventory costing methods are

- Last-in, first-out (LIFO)
- First-in, first-out (FIFO)
- Lower of cost or market (LCM)
- Average costing

LIFO

LIFO assumes that goods enter cost of goods sold in *reverse* order of their entry into inventory. Therefore, LIFO sells the newest goods first. The older goods remain in inventory longer. Industries selling perishables *would not* logically use LIFO for costing their inventory.

What happens during periods of rising prices? The LIFO method increases cost of goods sold. Higher-cost goods go out to customers first, leaving the older and lower-priced goods in inventory. Taxwise, this can be advantageous. Cost of goods sold is higher, making net income lower than under the other inventory costing methods.

During periods of falling prices, LIFO yields a lower cost of goods sold and a higher ending inventory valuation. This means a higher current ratio (current assets ÷ current liabilities = current ratio).

Investors and lenders see excessively large current ratios as a negative. The company uses long-term liabilities such as debt or owners' equity to finance current assets. Assuming that longer-term financing is more expensive than short-term, this practice cuts into profit margins.

FIFO

First-in, first-out assumes sale of the oldest goods first. Industries concerned with spoilage or obsolescence employ the FIFO costing method. They want to sell the oldest goods first.

When prices rise, FIFO provides a lower cost of goods sold, thus increasing net income and the consequent income tax liability.

Lower of cost or market (LCM)

This is one of the more conservative approaches to inventory valuation. The results are usually close to those from FIFO except in periods of rapid price change. With this method, ending inventory is valued at the lower of what the company purchased (or produced) the goods for or their current market value.

Some accountants argue that this method more closely approximates the true value of inventory and that it's less likely to overstate this major asset. Items best valued using LCM costing include

- Precious metals • Publicly traded securities with a ready market
- Commodities

Notice that the values of these types of items can change rapidly. Additionally, we can easily ascertain and verify the current value.

Average costing

Automated inventory control systems often use this method. It attempts to remove the peaks and valleys of inventory costs throughout the year. It does so by recomputing inventory costs after each purchase or production run. That way there's always a fairly constant average cost per unit that reflects pricing *trends* rather than actual changes.

Unless you're using an automated I/C system offering this option, don't try to employ this cost system.

Influences on inventory valuation

In addition to changing prices, three other factors can influence the income effects of inventory valuation:

1. Year-to-year changes in inventory quantity

2. If there was a liquidation, the amount that was actually liquidated relative to the quantity of goods sold

3. If there was a liquidation, the spread between inventory cost and average LIFO layers related to the increase in price from the preceding year

Figure 10-4 summarizes how each factor influences income under various pricing trends.

Figure 10-4
Inventory Method Income Summary

Current price is:	Greater than last year	Equal to last year	Lower than last year
...and ending inventory is:			
1. Equal to beginning inventory	LIFO income < FIFO income	LIFO income = FIFO income	LIFO income > FIFO income
2. Greater than beginning inventory	LIFO income < FIFO income	LIFO income = FIFO income	LIFO income > FIFO income
3. Less than beginning inventory	LIFO income > FIFO income	LIFO income = FIFO income	LIFO income > FIFO income

---

PHYSICAL INVENTORY

Many small-business owners and managers consider physical inventory a real pain. It's laborious, its tedious, it comes at the very beginning of the new year, and it always creates problems. Nevertheless, physical inventory is an important component of your inventory control system. Not only does it assist in computing cost of goods sold, but it also provides an important internal control function.

Conducting a Physical Inventory

Ideally, the warehouse shuts down during a physical inventory. However, for many small businesses that just isn't practical. Loss of even one shipping day means disaster for the bottom line. If you must keep the warehouse open, section off those parts that cannot be disturbed until inventory is counted. Some firms actually rope those sections off. Others tape around the entire area.

The counting team must consist of at least two people. Each is responsible for counting particular sections of the warehouse. When they have finished, each checks the other's work. The following is a short list of the steps taken in a physical inventory:

1. Draw a map of the warehouse and designate each section by inventory item numbers.

2. Assign particular sections to each member of the counting team.

3. Generate a complete list of the entire inventory being counted. Some companies leave out the perpetual inventory balance for fear it may bias the counters.

4. Count the inventory. Check off the map sections already counted.

5. Check-count samples of the inventory.

6. Reconcile the physical count with that appearing on the perpetual inventory records.

Reconciling the Physical Count

There should be no difference between the inventory value from the physical count and that from the inventory records. However, that's rarely the case. Sometimes counters miss items. Sometimes items aren't costed correctly in the inventory records, resulting in a different value for the number on hand. Other times, if the warehouse remains open, items are added to or removed from inventory before they're counted.

There's one more explanation: pilferage. That's part of the reason we conduct a physical inventory. Deterrents work best if everyone knows that the company can find a thief. Differences in inventory values attributed to theft point to warehouse control problems.

Once the reconciliation is complete, a journal entry is probably necessary. The book balance must match the physical inventory. The difference may go to an expense account such as cost of goods sold.

COMPUTING COST OF GOODS SOLD

This is the largest expense for most companies. Both the beginning and ending inventory balances figure in the computation of cost of goods sold.

There are two different ways to arrive at cost of goods sold depending on the inventory method used.

Periodic Inventory Method

This method assumes a physical count of inventory at the end of the accounting period. Compute cost of goods sold as follows:

CGS = Beginning inventory + purchases – ending inventory

This method poses two problems for the company:

- Cost of goods sold, and therefore gross margin, cannot be computed before the end of the operating period.
- It requires a physical inventory.

Not knowing the gross margin until the end of the operating period hides problems in production costs and selling prices. By the time we compute cost of goods sold, it's too late. Further, physical inventories are costly and time-consuming.

Perpetual Inventory Method

This method computes cost of goods sold using a transaction-oriented basis. Whether the perpetual system uses FIFO, LIFO, or average cost, it computes CGS as the items are produced. That way we can have gross margin figures for every single sale if we want them. Problems associated with sales prices or production costs pop out when we look at the gross margin.

INTERNAL CONTROL

Physical counts of inventory and its value are one way of controlling warehouse inventory. A way to increase the effectiveness of this deterrent is to make the warehouse manager responsible for losses from inventory. Make this part of the job description. Give the manager the tools needed to make sure the actual count matches the company's I/C records.

Additionally, maintain records of the physical inventory reconciliation with the accounting records. Spot trends quickly and correct them. If the firm finds it has suffered a loss each time it conducts a physical inventory, there's a problem. Sometimes this results in personnel leaving the firm. In some cases, criminal prosecutions result.

Uncomplementary Duties

There are some warehouse jobs that cannot be done by the same person or by two people who are related parties. For example, the person responsible for receiving inventory into the warehouse should not be the same person who enters it into the inventory control system. Additionally, the person who conducts the physical inventory count should not check items into the warehouse.

Control of inventory requires at least two independent people who oversee the stock as it comes into the company, as it sits in the warehouse awaiting processing or sale, and as it leaves. The objective is to make collusion necessary for a misappropriation to occur. The probability that two or more people will conspire to defraud the company is much less than the probability that just one person will do so. One isn't impossible—just less likely.

Securing Inventory

Be aware of the value of your inventory. If you see a sudden increase in either its value or its liquidity, review your security measures. For example, Lapin Company maintains and sells an inventory of jewelry boxes. However, Lapin has begun inventorying and selling precious gemstones as well. The inventory value has soared. So has its liquidity. It's easier to sell a diamond than ten wooden jewelry boxes. Suddenly Lapin's inventory presents a more profitable target—for insiders as well as outsiders.

Some insurance companies have security professionals on staff or work with consultants who specialize in physical plant security. Sometimes just placing a deadbolt lock on the back door is sufficient. Often a specialized alarm system in parts of the warehouse is required.

Preventive measures taken to maintain internal control of inventory are usually far less expensive than losses from unexplained shrinkage or theft.

Ordering Controls

Inventory systems require control over the amount of stock ordered. You don't want to order too many or too few goods. Further, you want to take advantage of price discounts by ordering in large quantities. However, the cost of carrying inventory eats into profit margins.

How do you monitor the inventory ordering process? Even the smallest companies use two equations to help determine the amount to order and how much excess stock to keep on hand. These are the *economic order quantity* and *safety stock* equations.

Economic order quantity (EOQ)

EOQ represents the order size for an inventory item that provides the lowest possible overall cost to the company. Here's the EOQ equation:

$$EQQ = \sqrt{\frac{2ap}{sz}}$$

where a is the annual quantity of the item used, in units

p is the purchase order cost

s is the annual direct and indirect carrying cost of a unit of inventory

z is the purchase price of the inventory item

Assume the following for Lapin Company, the manufacturer of jewelry boxes and now a seller of precious gemstones:

- Annual demand for box lids is 200,000 units.
- Lapin's cost to issue a purchase order, receive the goods, and stock the warehouse is $200.
- Annual cost of carrying inventory is 10 percent.
- The cost of each box lid in quantities between 5,000 and 10,000 is $3.00.

$$EOQ = \frac{\sqrt{2 \times (200{,}000 \times \$200)}}{10\% \times \$3.00}$$

$$EOQ = 16{,}3330 \text{ units per order}$$

If Lapin needs 200,000 units annually, it must issue about 12 orders (200,000 ÷ 16,330 = 12.25) during the year. If it issues more than that, it won't use the lids in time to justify carrying them. If it issues fewer than that, it isn't taking advantage of costs and its warehouse capacity.

Safety stock

Safety stock provides a cushion to prevent running out of raw materials and subassemblies. Running out of stock isn't only embarrassing. It creates costly disruptions to production runs. The manufacturing staff likes a large safety stock. So does the sales staff. Their livelihoods depend on there being sufficient finished goods inventory to fill orders.

However, excessively large safety stocks often hide sloppy inventory control methods. There's a balance between safety stocks being adequate for production requirements and not being so large that they unnecessarily eat into valuable working capital. The trick is to marry the production department's need for emergency stock with the controller's objective—a small inventory that turns quickly. Here's the equation to compute optimum safety stock:

> Probability of stockout at a given level of safety stock × stockout cost × number of orders per year (demand ÷ EOQ) = expected stockout cost + carrying cost of safety stock = total inventory carrying cost

It's easiest if you set up the safety stock computation in tabular form. The lowest total cost is the best answer. Figure 10-5 gives an example.

Figure 10-5
Computation of Inventory Safety Stock

Units of Saftey Stock	Probability of Stockout	Cost of Stockout	Number of Orders per Year	Stockout Cost (A)	Carrying Cost (B)	Total Cost (C)
60	60%	100	15	$900	$300	$1200
70	40%	100	15	600	350	950
80	35%	100	15	525	400	925
90	33%	100	15	495	450	945

A. Compute stockout cost as the probability of stockout × cost of stockout multiplied by number of orders per year (EOQ).

B. Compute carrying cost as the cost of holding one unit per year (assumed to be $5.00) × safety stock. Carrying costs include such things as financing, space, handling, security, and insurance. All are associated with the cost of keeping an item of inventory on the warehouse floor. Often carrying costs run as high as 25 to 35 percent of an item's acquisition cost.

C. Compute total cost as stockout cost + carrying cost.

In this example, the optimum level of safety stock is 80 units. When planning inventory purchases, make sure to consult other departments concerning order levels. The manufacturing department might know of a risk to a steady supplier. That would justify increasing inventory well beyond any levels required by safety stock considerations. Anticipated cost increases also justify expanded inventories. The production department wants to maintain its cost plan. So it stockpiles low-cost inventory. In effect, the company trades commodity futures. Instead of just buying an option to hedge against a possible price increase, it has taken delivery—a very risky enterprise.

TRACKING INVENTORY PERFORMANCE

Setting up the inventory control system isn't enough. We need a mechanism to track its performance. Inventory is too expensive an asset for us to just assume it's being managed expertly. Just a few quick computations reveal how closely inventory tracks with common sense, company objectives, and needs.

Inventory Turnover

It seems that everyone wants to know the speed with which a company converts its inventory investment into sales. Inventory turnover tells us that. Here's the equation:

$$\text{Inventory turnover} = \frac{\text{annual CGS}}{\text{average inventory balance}}$$

The more times inventory turns over, the faster it flows out of the warehouse to customers. The faster inventory turns, the less working capital companies have tied up in slow-moving stock. Slowly turning inventory means a buildup of stock. Conversely, an accelerating turnover rate means a reduction in inventory stockpiles.

Smart managers *anticipate* changes in inventory turnover. They adjust the firm's stock purchases accordingly. After the turnover rate actually changes, it's too late. Purchases have already been made for goods that won't be sold at the pace for which the order was placed.

Gross Margin per Inventory Turn

Fast inventory turnover increases liquidity. Investment in inventory turns into sales and eventually cash. However, some companies reduce their profit margin for the sake of accelerating inventory outflow. Computing gross margin per inventory turn monitors this tendency. Figure 10-6 shows how.

Notice how fast inventory turned in the second year—10 times compared to just 5 times in the prior year. Additionally, the days of sales tied up in inventory fell from 73 to just 37 days. Both changes make the inventory more liquid. Everybody in the production and shipping areas is working harder. However, Applebee is working harder for *less profit*. Gross margin per inventory turn has dropped by over 70 percent. Uncontrolled price discounts just to move inventory could have caused this profit erosion. So could a jump in production costs. Whatever the cause, Applebee sacrificed profit for cash flow and liquidity—not a smart thing to do.

Figure 10-6
Gross Margin per Inventory Turn

Applebee Manufacturing Corporation
For the year ended December 31, 19X2

	19X1	19X2
Cost of goods sold	$40,000,000	$40,000,000
Average inventory of finished goods	$8,000,000	$4,000,000
Inventory turnover	5 times	10 times
Days of sales in inventory (360 days / turnover)	73 days	37 days
Gross margin	$17,000,000	$9,500,000
Gross margin per turnover	$3,400,000	$950,000

Average Investment Period

This index tells the number of days of inventory on hand at the current sales level. A rising average investment period signals a buildup of inventory which slows turnover and eats into working capital. Compute average investment period like this:

$$\text{Average investment period} = \frac{\text{present inventory balance}}{\text{annual cost of goods sold} \div 360}$$

Days of Inventory on Hand

Here's a quick way to tell how well the investment in inventory matches demand. The equation is

$$\text{Days of inventory} = \frac{\text{total inventory}}{\text{daily demand}}$$

Most companies want enough inventory to meet the daily demand. They also want a large enough stock to last until the next delivery. Many inventory managers add a reserve for delayed delivery and a safety stock in the event demand increases. Figure 10-6 used days of inventory as a reference point. As inventory turnover increased, the number of sales days of inventory on hand fell.

Estimating Ending Inventory

Estimate ending inventory to test the reasonableness of ending inventory numbers. Additionally, once you know the estimated ending inventory, you can also estimate profits and cash flow. The two ways of estimating ending inventories are the

- Gross margin method
- Retail method

Gross margin method

Manufacturing companies producing or assembling finished goods inventory use this method. Here's an example of how it works:

Waffles Enterprises
Estimated Ending Inventory
Gross Margin Method
December 31, 199X

Beginning inventory balance at cost		$10,000,000
Plus inventory purchases at cost		30,000,000
Cost of inventory available for sale		$40,000,000
Less computation of estimated CGS:		
Sales:	$50,000,000	
Gross margin @ 35%	17,500,000	
Estimated Cost of goods sold		(32,500,000)
Estimated ending inventory as of December 31, 199X		$7,500,000

If Waffles's actual ending inventory was substantially different from this estimate, there could be a problem. Perhaps the perpetual inventory system miscalculated. Perhaps the physical count was off. Either way, the estimate provides a test of reasonableness.

Retail method

For retail companies, there's a similar method for estimating ending inventory.

Harvey's Gourmet Shops, Inc.
Estimated Ending Inventory
Retail Method
December 31, 199X

	Cost	Retail Price
Beginning inventory balance	$10,000,000	$17,000,000
Purchases	5,000,000	8,500,000
Freight in	1,000,000	0
Cost of goods sold		
@ 40% gross margin	5,000,000	8,500,000
Estimated ending inventory	$11,000,000	$17,000,000

Balancing Inventory

Many small companies allow inventory balances to eat into profits because they fail to balance purchases with sales. Certainly, we don't want inventory to greatly exceed our planned sales, wasting working capital. Here are two inventory balancing equations commonly used.

1. Beginning inventory + planned production = projected sales + target ending inventory

2. Target ending inventory = normal inventory balance + growth stock (if any) + safety stock

Notice how both equations work together to balance the aspects of inventory covered earlier.

Chapter 11 moves on to establishing the cost accounting system.

Chapter 11

Cost Accounting

OVERVIEW

Most people think of cost accounting as just for manufacturing operations. However, many different types of companies use at least some cost accounting methods to monitor and control their profit-making process. Even if your company doesn't manufacture anything, look over this chapter. Chances are you'll see something that's of use in another part of your small-business accounting system.

Chapter 11 creates a simple mechanism to account for the production costs of a small business. Once installed, the cost accounting system tracks production costs for profit control purposes. We'll explain the mechanics of transferring inventory during the various stages of production. Additionally, we'll demonstrate how this simple accounting system enters labor into the product manufacturing costs.

Just as important as setting up the cost accounting system is its use. Chapter 11 identifies the various ways cost information assists in monitoring profitability and identifying problem areas.

PURPOSE OF THE COST ACCOUNTING SYSTEM

Cost accounting systems have one purpose: To accumulate the costs of production and assign them to the items produced. The manufacturing process combines different materials and some already partially assembled components. Doing that takes labor on the production shop floor. Materials and manufacturing labor are the *direct costs* associated with making a product.

There are two other types of costs the cost accounting system identifies:

- *Indirectly identified* costs • *Arbitrarily allocated* costs

These costs do not specifically arise from the process of manufacturing any particular item. However, we know that the products benefited from them. Therefore, the cost accounting system allocates portions of these costs to each item produced.

The accounting system traces all these costs from their source and accumulates them in cost accounts for the products your company manufactures. That's how we compute the all-important *cost of goods sold*. Indeed, that's one purpose of the cost accounting system—to maintain a running tally of production costs.

Another equally important purpose of the cost accounting system is to control production costs. We do this by identifying what the standard production cost *should* be. Then the system accumulates all *actual* production costs. With these two pieces of information—the standard costs and the actual costs—it's easy to tell where favorable and unfavorable cost variances occur.

Tracking the Flow of Inventory and Other Costs

In Chapter 3 we described the flow of information through the accounting system. Part of that flow was the transfer of inventory from raw materials to work in process and finally to finished goods. The cost accounting system we're creating executes that transfer of information. It also tracks the labor used on the production floor and all the indirect costs allocated to each item produced.

Figure 11-1 shows how the accounting system tracks production costs.

Figure 11-1
Production Cost Flow

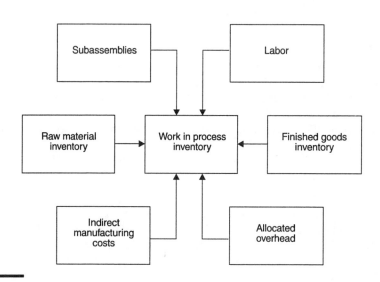

The cost accounting system draws its information from five sources:

- Raw materials • Subassemblies • Labor • Indirect costs
- Allocated overhead

It feeds this information into the work in process inventory accounts as the items proceed through the production line. Eventually, upon completion of production, all costs are recorded. The system then transfers all production costs to finished goods inventory. At that point we know the cost of goods sold.

Tracing Service Costs

What about businesses without inventory? Such businesses are often in service industries. Walk-in medical clinics, auto repair garages, professional businesses, and real estate operators are good examples. These businesses still need to trace service delivery costs for decision-making purposes.

For example, let's take a hotel that provides a room service menu. Often it tacks on a delivery charge or some sort of compensation for taking the food to the customer. That charge is a direct reflection of certain cost accounting information the hotel has derived. It adds one delivery charge rather than adding a certain amount pro rata to each menu item. That's because it costs as much to send up a waiter carrying a single piece of pie as it does a four-course meal.

TYPES OF COST SYSTEMS

Different businesses use different cost accounting methods to track their production. The most common cost accounting systems are

- Job order • Process • Full cost
- Costing joint products and byproducts

Job Order Cost Systems

Many businesses that manufacture custom made-products use a job order cost accounting system. This system attaches specific costs of production to *each* unit produced. Custom cabinet shops and builders of custom homes use job order cost systems. Additionally, certain service providers, such as engineers, architects, and consultants, use some job order techniques to track the specific costs of each project.

The key to job order costing is that each product is unique and has specific costs allocated to it.

Job order by lots

A variation on the straight job order cost system is to produce a batch of identical products for a customer. Private-label manufacturers cost jobs for their customers by the lot. For example, a production run of 250 pairs of shoes for a private-label retailer lends itself to job order costing. We allocate the costs for each pair of shoes and compute the profit.

Further, as the job goes through our production line, we'll compare actual costs with those we estimated when we bid the contract. Variances that pop up can be corrected while there's still time. That's the real benefit of any cost accounting system—control.

Process Cost Systems

Typically process cost systems are appropriate for businesses that produce large quantities of one or a few identical products. There's usually no need to distinguish among the items produced—they're homogenous. The system accumulates costs for the entire production run. It then computes unit costs by dividing the total production cost by the number of units produced.

Process cost focuses on the *operation* that produces an entire batch of similar goods. Contrast this with the job order cost system described above, which focuses on the production cost of a single unit. Often the production process goes through a series of steps to produce the final product. Each process is costed separately, since at any point different products can branch off the same process.

Firms that use a process cost system include mills, textile manufacturers, canners, food processors, glass and metal manufacturers, and paper processors.

Petrochemicals cost their products like this too. In the beginning all products go through the same processes. As the plant refines the crude oil, it branches off into different products—automotive gasoline, aviation fuel, kerosene, and alcohol.

Reporting process manufacturing costs

Process cost systems report the cost of production for each stage or department. They then average these costs over the equivalent units produced for a given period of time. Process reporting for small business accounting systems usually consists of

- Total units transferred from one process department to the next
- Material, labor, and overhead added by each process department
- Total costs converted to unit or equivalent unit costs for each process department
- Identification of the costs accumulated in the various stages of work in process
- Total costs accumulated at the very end of the production process, converted to unit or equivalent unit costs, and transferred to finished goods inventory

Valuing inventory

The method of inventory valuation, discussed in Chapter 10, "Inventory Control," enters into the cost accounting system. Costs are accumulated during each process. The ending costs for one process become the beginning costs for the next. Most firms use either average costing or FIFO costing.

Average costing uses the costs of the inventory at the beginning of the period, then adds the costs incurred during production. We determine unit costs simply by dividing total costs for the period by the number of units produced. Ending inventory is transferred to the next process step as one cumulative number.

FIFO, on the other hand, separates products involving beginning work in process inventory from those products started and finished in the same accounting period. FIFO first takes WIP at the beginning of the period and adds the cost of completing the production process. FIFO also separately accumulates the costs of products begun but not finished.

Next FIFO determines the cost for items begun and completed in the current accounting period. It transfers these to the next step at a cost separate from the cost of those items that were in WIP inventory at the beginning of the period.

However, the next department averages out these inventory costs anyway, losing much of the value given by FIFO accounting.

Full-Cost Systems

Full-cost accounting systems seek to allocate every cost associated with manufacturing an item. These include all costs directly traceable to each item and those that are indirectly related. Small businesses carefully allocate indirect costs in their accounting systems. This is the area where your lunch gets eaten.

Overhead and other costs that are not directly traceable to production can get out of hand quickly if they do not get frequent attention. By allocating them to production for standard (planned) costs as well as those actually incurred, the cost accounting system tracks overhead. We understand what these costs should have been for each item. Excess indirect costs show up as unfavorable variances that get investigated and corrected.

Costing Joint Products

Many process manufacturers make several products from the same process. For example, a dairy processes raw milk. From this process come the joint products whole milk, skim milk, low-fat milk, and buttermilk. However, these *joint products* all emanate from the original process.

How do we allocate the costs of the original process to these joint products? The usual method is similar to the way we allocate some overhead items—by volume.

Let's continue with Maggie's Dairy Corporation to illustrate how the cost accounting system allocates joint product costs. Assume that Maggie processes milk for a series of private labels sold in grocery stores. Figure 11-2 shows the joint processing costs shared by three of Maggie's products—whole milk, skim milk, and low-fat milk.

Figure 11-2
Allocating Costs to Joint Products

Homogenizing process	Whole milk
	45,000 gallons, $81,000
	Low-fat milk
100,000 gallons, $180,000	33,000 gallons, $59,400
	Skim milk
	22,000 gallons, $39,600

The allocation of the homogenizing process used the percentage of each joint product that was derived from the joint costs of the process. This isn't complicated. If you use a process cost system, the entry that records these costs is similar to the entries for other production costs.

One issue that sometimes confuses people is *when* to record the joint product cost. The answer is, *at the split-off point.* This is the point at which the joint products become separately identifiable.

Costing Byproducts

Many manufacturing processes actually create one or more secondary products that have some value. We call these *byproducts.* Generally byproducts have only a minor residual value compared to the primary product. Take, for example, the production of applesauce. Part of the process is to core and seed the apples. The residual cores and seeds are byproducts that have a ready market.

Some firms can sell their byproducts in the original form. Other byproducts require some work. The meatpacking industry is a good example. It produces many byproducts along with primary cuts of meat. Packers sometimes grind these and encase them for hot dogs. Or they add gelatin for head cheese. Though the result is not appealing to some (me included), this does present a cost allocation issue.

Most companies use one of three methods to account for byproducts:

1. Recognize byproduct revenue on the income statement in a separate category, such as "other income."

2. Deduct revenue from byproduct sales (less costs for any additional work) from the costs of the main product.

3. Treat the byproduct as if it were a normal production item and allocate all joint production costs.

ORGANIZING THE GENERAL LEDGER

The cost system we're setting up adds accounts to the general ledger. By design these separate specific costs, assign them to the appropriate inventory, and identify areas of responsibility. Figure 11-3 shows the list of additional accounts the G/L needs for the cost accounting system.

As a rule, include an account for all the critical costs associated with the production area you want to track. We've identified most of the important ones above—materials, labor, overhead, and maintenance. Your company probably has others. Be sure to include them.

General Ledger Account Numbers

Adding cost centers can quickly increase the number of accounts in your general ledger. The first step is to think about the way you want these costs reported. Most companies want to identify particular costs with specific items manufactured. Therefore, they create one main G/L account for each type of cost and add a suffix to identify the item manufactured. That way the accounting system can report in four ways:

- All the manufacturing costs for all products

Figure 11-3
Cost Accounts Used in the G/L

Raw materials inventory
Work in process inventory
Finished goods inventory
Direct materials
Spoilage expense
Supplies
Labor:
    Direct labor
    Indirect labor
    Supervisory labor
    Idle labor
    Manufacturing overtime
Overhead allocations to manufacturing costs:
    Depreciation of manufacturing machinery
    Supplies
    Utilities
    Supervisory costs
    Equipment repair
    Repair parts
    Repair labor
    Production department's share of general administrative expense
Specific manufacturing department expenses

- Just one manufacturing cost for all products
- All manufacturing costs for a particular product
- One manufacturing cost for a particular product

Using the account numbering scheme XXX-XX provides this information. The first three characters identify the G/L account, and the last two identify the cost center. For example, identify the manufacturing costs as follows:

Material:	200
Labor:	300
Overhead:	400

Identify the products for which the accounting system accumulates these production costs. For example, a luggage manufacturer might number its products like this:

Suit case:	10
Brief case:	20
Garment bag:	30

Entries in the cost system to record labor for the briefcase go to account number 300-20.

Using Cost Centers

Our cost accounting system assigns responsibility for managing production costs to those best able to control them. This requires separating costs by areas of responsibility. For example, many companies that have distinct areas of the manufacturing process form a cost center for each area. In the example used earlier, cost centers for the production process of Maggie's Dairy could have included

- Homogenizing department
- Vat cleaning and sterilization department • Whole milk
- Skim milk • Low-fat milk • Testing and quality control
- Container filling • Shipping • Receiving

Each cost center has its own suffix number attached to the G/L number. That way the firm identifies all costs associated with each cost center. The account number now looks like this: XXX-XX-XXX. The first three characters identify the cost, the next two designate the product, and the last three show the cost center.

For example, say we want to record the costs of the latches used by the fastener department (cost center 300) on the suitcase. The entry goes to account 200-10-300.

Using this account numbering scheme, our cost system can tell us each individual cost added by each production department to each product.

Integrating Cost Accounting with Other Accounting Subsystems

The cost accounting system provides a ready source of information needed by several accounting subsystems. If you're using an automated accounting system that provides for electronic transfer of transactions, you'll find much of your cost accounting work done for you. Here are the accounting subsystems that transfer cost data back and forth.

General ledger

The G/L receives all inventory transfers and production costs *from* the cost accounting system. The more frequently we post cost information and transfer it to the G/L, the more accurate the cost reporting at any point in time. Indeed, that's the point of using a cost accounting system. We want up-to-date reporting to track actual costs while there's still time during the month to fix any problems identified.

Inventory control

The cost accounting system constantly transfers inventory around. The entries move raw materials to work in process and into finished goods upon completion. These transactions flow directly into the inventory control system as well. Often in more sophisticated computerized accounting systems, a single entry made in Cost automatically moves to the inventory control system.

Accounts payable

The payables system records expenses from invoices it receives and moves them to the cost accounting system, which allocates them. Invoice information moves from the A/P system to the various jobs, processes, or products for tracking by the cost system. Often these include not only raw materials purchased, but sub assemblies and subcontractor fees as well.

Accounts receivable

Many firms that manufacture custom products on fixed contracts do progress billing. As the project moves along, the manufacturer bills its customer based on the portion completed. Often this includes time and materials, direct costs, allocation of indirect costs, and a percentage of the estimated profit.

The cost system records these invoices against the products or projects in WIP. Then the amount billed is transferred over to the A/R system for tracking and collection.

Payroll

Once we process payroll, the labor expense allocation moves over to the cost accounting system. Often the time and cost of one employee is allocated to several projects or products in process.

Purchasing

Purchase orders often belong to specific projects being tracked by the cost system. Many companies record receipt of goods and receipt of invoice to the cost accounting system. This process allocates the direct expenses to the job being controlled by the cost system. Further, some companies also record open purchase orders and trace them to particular jobs on the production floor. That way they can always tell the purchase commitments outstanding for any given production job.

Journal Entries

Cost accounting systems require up-to-date information to provide value. Very small businesses with just a few people don't usually have the time to run a complete cost accounting system. They often don't pay much attention to the movement of material around the shop floor. They may not track the amount of labor going into each item. They don't know exactly what it costs to produce their products. Consequently, their profit margins are fuzzy.

Running an effective cost accounting system requires some effort. Shop floor personnel must record all production transactions in a timely and accurate way. The most frequently entered costs record

- Movement of raw material into work in process inventory (WIP)
- Addition of direct labor into WIP
- Addition of indirect and overhead costs into WIP
- Transfer of completed WIP to finished goods inventory

Here's how each of these entries looks on the general ledger:

Movement of raw material into WIP:

Work in Process Inventory	$5,000	
Raw Material Inventory		$5,000

Addition of direct labor:

Step 1: Record Labor Costs:

Direct Labor Expense	1,500	
Wages Payable		1,500

Step 2: Allocate labor costs to WIP:

Work in Process Inventory	1,500	
Direct Labor Expense		1,500

Addition of indirect expense allocation:

Step 1: Allocate overhead to the particular WIP inventory in question. Say the overhead item in question is the production shop's electrical expense of $1,000. Also say that the production item we're allocating accounts for 25 percent of total production. The allocation of electrical expense is $250 ($1,000 × 25% = $250). Record the total electricity expense:

Electricity Expense	$1,000	
Accounts Payable		$1,000

Step 2: Make the entry to allocate electricity costs:

Work in Process Inventory	$250	
Electrical Expense		$250

Transfer completed production items out of WIP and into finished goods inventory:

Finished Goods Inventory	$6,750	
Work in Process Inventory		$6,750

The WIP account accumulated production costs throughout the manufacturing process. Upon completion, the item included these costs:

Raw materials	$5,000
Direct labor	1,500
Electricity allocation	250
Total costs transferred	$6,750

The entries above cover the theory behind most cost accounting transactions. Some are more complicated owing to allocations of indirect costs, joint costs, identification of split-off points, and byproducts. However, every entry comes down to recording these debits and credits.

Capturing Cost Information

The cost accounting system records production costs for each unit or batch of units on the production line. It does this using detailed cost records. These records show everything that's put into the goods produced. In practice, we usually pre-print detailed cost record sheets showing all the materials and labor that *should* go to the product. The detailed cost record accounts for these costs as the production process progresses.

All the costs accumulate in the work in process inventory accounts. Later a journal entry transfers them into the general ledger.

Detailed cost record

The best detailed cost records are those that provide all the costs and the general ledger account numbers to which they're posted. We want to make the transfer of data as simple as possible. Often cost information comes in units, pounds, or hours worked, not in dollars. Therefore, the detailed cost record extends these various units of measure by their unit costs. Figure 11-4 shows a sample detailed cost record

Figure 11-4
Detailed Cost Record

Autumn Manufacturing, Inc.
Cost Record Detail

Product: Plastic carry basket #348

Cost Description	G/L Account #	Units	Number of Units	Cost per Unit	Extension	Date Entered	Person
Polyurethane	100-45	lbs	3	$0.25	$0.75	4-6-9X	JB
Metal handles	100-45	ea.	2	1.50	3.00	4-7-9X	RS
Rubber feet	100-45	ea.	4	0.25	0.25	4-7-9X	JR
Direct labor	200-45	hours	1	15.00	15.00	4-8-9X	MC
Indirect labor	300-45	hours	0.25	20.00	4.00	4-8-9X	ES
Fastening machine	400-45	hours	0.25	10.00	2.50	4-9-9X	MC
Overhead allocation	500-45	units	2	10.00	20.00	4-9-9X	CR
				Total cost	$45.50		

Note that the raw materials all contain the same general ledger account number. This makes it easy to remove them from raw materials inventory and transfer them to WIP for this product. The *cost system* wants to know how much of each raw material goes into the product, not the general ledger system.

Additionally, notice that all the G/L account numbers end with the suffix 45. That designates the particular inventory item: the plastic carry basket #348. Using this G/L suffix designation, we can identify all the costs associated with this item throughout its manufacturing process.

Summarizing the detailed cost record

Detailed cost records accompany each job or production run as it makes its way through the manufacturing process. As much as practicable the people on the production floor record the items added to each cost record. Then periodically the cost records are transferred to someone responsible for cost accounting, who extends the costs, summarizes the changes, and prepares the journal entry for the general ledger.

Some companies summarize the detailed cost records once a month—usually at the end to record inventory and cost changes that have occurred since the last financial reporting period. Others do it more frequently—often every day. The more often the cost system receives updated information, the more help it provides in controlling production costs.

We want our summarization of the production costs to accomplish two things:

- Provide a journal entry form for recording cost changes in the general ledger.
- Provide a comparative report for tracking actual costs against standard costs.

Figure 11-5 shows a sample cost summary record.

Figure 11-5
Summary Cost Record

Autumn Manufacturing, Inc.
Summary Cost Record

Product: Plastic carry basket #348

Description	G/L Acct #	Debit	Credit	Standard Costs	Variance
Polyurethane	100-45		$0.75	$0.80	$0.05
Metal handles	100-45		3.00	3.10	0.10
Rubber feet	100-45		0.25	0.20	-0.05
Direct labor	200-45		15.00	13.00	-2.00
Indirect labor	300-45		4.00	5.00	1.00
Fastening machine	400-45		2.50	2.50	—
Overhead allocation	500-45		20.00	20.00	—
WIP inventory	150-45	$45.50			
Total entry		$45.50	$45.50	$44.60	-$0.90

Just as in the accounts receivable system, each product has its own individual record. If you're using a manual system, keep the different records on separate cards. Computer systems maintain separate files for each item produced. Using these summary records you can make the journal entries to record production costs into WIP inventory. Additionally, each card maintains a tally of actual production costs compared to standard costs. The difference—a negative cost variance in the example above—shows up on the summary as well. If management has enough advance warning, it can take action to correct production problems. *That's* the value of maintaining a cost accounting system.

ORGANIZING STANDARD COSTS

Standardizing costs incorporates an element of planning and control into the accounting system. We want to know what each item *should* cost to produce. Then the cost accounting system compares this with the actual costs as in Figure 11-5. We use standard costs for

- Budgeting • Cost control • Reporting cost of goods sold
- Assigning costs to raw material, work in process, and finished goods inventories
- Establishing selling prices and formulating bids

Larger companies have an army of cost analysts who perform time and motion studies. The labor usage determined by this work goes into the standard costs for each item. Along with this information, the exact amount of raw materials and subassemblies for each item are included. Results from standard cost studies go to a document similar to the detailed cost record shown in Figure 11-5.

Smaller companies don't usually have the personnel to perform complicated standard cost studies. Still, you should have some idea of the cost to make each product. Without that control, production expenses have a habit of rising, eating into your profit margin.

Standard costing works best in companies that have stable production technology and manufacture similar items. Standard costs are less useful in more rapidly changing environments where each item made is unique.

Establishing Standard Costs

The method we'll use here is simple—purposely so. Professional cost accountants may criticize it as being somewhat inaccurate. This is true. However, as their cost accounting systems become more useful, the effort companies expend gathering accurate standard costs increases.

Determination of standard costs requires nothing more than common sense. Here are the steps to take for each product your company makes:

1. List all the raw materials that go into *one* unit of each product.
2. List all the subassemblies that go into *one* unit of each product.
3. List the amount of labor time that goes into each unit. Where labor rates differ, separate each labor step that has a different rate.
4. List all the shop machinery and equipment used in the production of each unit. Identify a separate cost for each *machinery usage hour.*
5. Assign a cost to each item in the steps above and extend by the number of units, labor hours, or machinery usage hours (or fractions).
6. Determine the overhead costs that are associated with manufacturing but not assigned to any particular production item. Assign a proportionate

percentage to each of the production items. For example, if Item A usually comprises 40 percent of total production, allocate 40 percent of the manufacturing overhead. If that normally amounts to $10,000 and production for Item A was 100,000 units, then allocate $0.10 for standard overhead to each unit of Item A produced.

7. Add up all the standard cost. The sum equals the standard cost to produce one item.

Tracking Variances

Many companies rely on their standard costs to compute cost of goods sold. They just assume that the standard costs are correct. However, they track actual costs and compare them with the standards. Then they adjust the cost of goods sold number to account for variances in the materials, labor, machinery, and overhead used in the production process. The entries to record these variances are

Cost of Goods Sold	X	
Materials Price Variance		X
Materials Usage Variance		X
Labor Price Variance		X
Labor Usage Variance		X
Machine Usage Variance		X
Machine Rate Variance		X
Overhead		X

This provides an excellent record of where the production problems lay. Notice that these entries treat all variances as negative (a debit to cost of goods sold *increases* production costs). However, they could just as easily have gone the other way (with a credit to CGS a and debit to the variance account), thus showing a favorable variance.

COSTING PAYROLL EXPENSES

Production payroll expenses involve three categories of labor:

- Direct manufacturing labor
- Indirect labor (production supervision)
- Overhead (allocation of executive salaries)

Most often these people are paid a fixed salary, by the hour, or by the unit produced (piecework). The payroll module of the accounting system records payroll expense. Then the cost accounting department (or person) allocates production labor expense from salary and wage expense to cost of goods sold.

Treating Labor Costs

The accounting system treats all salaries and wages the same way regardless of whether or not the employees are affiliated with the production operation. At the payroll level, there's no allocation to production labor. The cost accounting department does this. Figure 11-6 shows the flow of labor cost information.

Fgure 11-6
Capture and Distribution of Labor Costs

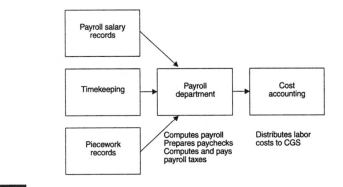

Allocating Indirect Labor and Overhead

Allocate indirect labor and overhead salaries just like any other overhead cost. For example, we can't allocate the production supervisor's salary to any particular item manufactured. All items benefit from his or her involvement. Therefore, many firms just allocate that salary pro rata among the items produced. Often we base the allocation on the percentage of total production represented by each item manufactured.

Vacation time for production people is an overhead expense too. It gets allocated to work in process as one of the normal costs associated with production.

ALLOCATING OVERHEAD

Production department heads bristle at overhead allocations. They often see front office activities as an unwanted intrusion on their task. Allocating part of the costs of this intrusion to production just adds insult to injury.

Nevertheless, most cost accounting systems allocate overhead associated with the production operation and the nonproducing entities (such as Accounting) to the manufacturing area. Small businesses don't usually perform the extensive analysis done by larger firms. After all, cash flow is what most concerns small businesses. Allocating overhead expenses simply assigns cash outflow from one pocket to another.

Allocate indirect costs and overhead using the same pro rata formula identified earlier. Some of the overhead items your cost system may allocate include

- Rent • Power • Utilities • Repairs
- Employee overhead, such as health insurance

- Purchasing department • Executive and officer salaries
- Warehouse operations

USING COST INFORMATION

The most valuable function of the cost accounting system is its ability to identify production problems. Use the variance reports that track actual costs versus standard or planned costs. Companies that maintain up-to-date work in process records at various stages of the production process can correct manufacturing problems while there's still time.

For example, say the quality control declines at a subassembly manufacturer. This decline could cause rework or negative material usage variances for customers who use the subassembly in *their* manufacturing operations. The cost accounting system catches these types of problems before they reach the customers' shops.

Many small businesses capture and compute cost data at various stages of the production process. Often these correspond to

- Critical inspection points • Breaks in the type of labor used
- Changeover to a different production line or machine
- Split-off point for joint products and byproducts

Regardless of where you accumulate production costs, be sure to review them at various stages of the process. Then act on the information provided.

Cost-Volume-Profit Analysis

How much do we need to sell in order to break even? Use the cost accounting system to find the answer. Three basic computations that provide the solution are

- Contribution margin • Break-even point in units and dollars
- Sales needed to achieve a targeted profit

Contribution margin

Contribution margin is that portion of sales that *contributes* to the coverage of fixed costs and profits. We usually measure this either in units sold or in sales dollar revenues. Contribution margin is generally expressed as a percentage. Here's the equation:

$$\text{Contribution margin} = \frac{\text{total sales - total variable costs}}{\text{total sales}}$$

Say that Tobby Corporation sells each dog collar it makes for $10.00. Variable costs for each unit of production are $4.25. Contribution margin for each unit is 58 percent [($10.00 - $4.25) ÷ $10.00 = 58%)]. Therefore, each collar sold at $10 contributes $5.80 to fixed costs and profits.

Break-even point

Now that we've computed the contribution margin, we're ready to calculate the break-even point. Again, we usually compute break-even either in units sold or in sales revenue. Use this equation:

$$\text{Break-even} = \frac{\text{fixed costs}}{\text{contribution margin}}$$

Figure 11-7 shows the break-even point in a graph.

Figure 11-7
Break-Even Point

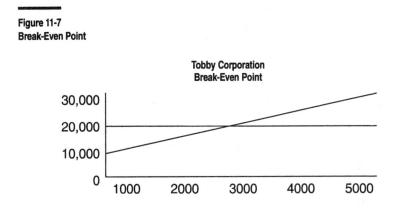

The horizontal line shows Tobby's fixed costs. The line running through it is the unit sales. For Tobby Corporation, the break-even point of 3,478 units assumes fixed costs of $20,000 per month. We computed this as

$$\text{Break-even} = \frac{\$20,000}{\$10.00 - \$4.25}$$

$$\text{Break-even} = \$34,783$$

We can also compute the revenue break-even using the contribution margin *percentage*:

$$\text{Break-even} = \frac{\$20,000}{(\$10.00 - \$4.25) \div \$10.00}$$

$$\text{Break-even} = \$34,783$$

We can prove the accuracy by multiplying the break-even units sold by the sales price. The answer is the break-even sales revenue.

Sales to Achieve Specific Profit Levels

If we want a particular profit level over the fixed costs, in calculating the break-even point, we simply add the desired profit to the numerator. Say Tobby wants a $5,000 profit *over* his fixed costs. Find the level of sales revenue that earns that profit:

$$\text{Required sales revenue} = \frac{\$20,000 + \$5,000}{(\$10.00 - \$4.25) \div \$10.00}$$

Required sales revenue = $43,478

Chapter 12 sets up the payroll system.

Chapter 12

Payroll

Overview

Chapter 12 steps you through the decision-making process to determine the cost-effectiveness of using a payroll service. Regardless of your choice, every company conducts specific procedures associated with payroll. Chapter 12 describes how to set up a payroll system. It demonstrates the various types of payroll computations likely encountered for salaries, bonuses, hourly wage earners and piecework payees.

Additionally, we'll identify the tax liabilities associated with payroll. We'll describe the various monthly, quarterly, and annual reporting requirements of a payroll system. Finally, Chapter 12 shows how to set up the accounting system for such employee benefits as vacation accrual and sick time.

Using a Payroll Service

Many small businesses wouldn't think of doing payroll themselves. Still others find the costs associated with a commercial payroll service exorbitant—especially when their in-house accountant can do the job and gets paid the same amount regardless who does payroll.

Deciding to purchase the services of a commercial payroll service is similar to any other decision to purchase an outside service. The answer reduces to

- Cost for the service compared to costs if done in-house
- Availability of time and adequate expertise of in-house personnel

Cost versus Benefit

Most payroll services charge a set-up fee and then a specified amount for each employee. Some offer discounts depending on the number of employees on the payroll system. Do the computation on a per employee basis, since that's what so many of the payroll services quote. Because we're comparing the service's cost with the cost of having our own employees payroll, compute the total *annual* cost.

For example, say that LP's Payroll Service charges $300 to set up a twenty-five-person company plus $5 per person to process each payroll. Add to that the time it takes for the client company's controller to gather the necessary payroll information and phone it in to LP.

Assume that the controller spends thirty minutes on each bimonthly payroll. The controller gets paid $50,000 per year (about $25 per hour). Total cost of LP's service the first year is $3,600 {[(25 × $5) × 24] + $300 + ($12.50 × 24) = $3,600}.

Assume that the controller has the expertise to do the payroll. The controller figures that it takes about two hours per pay period. However, the firm needs a backup payroll person in case the controller is gone on a payday. Compute the costs of doing payroll in-house as follows:

Controller's involvement: ($25 × 2) × 24 =	$1,200
Add controller's increased time preparing quarterly and annual government reporting: $25 × 10 hours =	250
Add involvement of backup person at $10 per hour: $10 × 20 hours =	200
Total in-house costs:	$1,650

Therefore, it costs about $1,950 more per year for this company to hire LP's Payroll Service than to do it themselves. This margin decreases as in-house personnel spend more time doing payroll. Further, some would argue that thirty minutes of the controller's time is an irrelevant cost since it's spent on payroll regardless of who processes it. This increases the cost differential between the commercial service and in-house processing.

To compete against the lower cost for in-house processing, LP would have to reduce charges per employee to about $1.75. If you're negotiating with a commercial payroll service, that's a number you need to know. It approximates your point of indifference between buying a payroll service and doing it in-house.

Time Factor

The big advantage payroll services offer over in-house personnel is time. People with the background and reliability necessary for payroll hold responsible positions in small businesses. Often they don't have the time to process payroll. They could be doing other things that would earn the company much more than the minor cost differential over the course of a year. The same holds true for the lead payroll person's backup.

Profit Motive for Payroll Services

People often ask, How can a payroll service afford to do the work for so little money? Indeed, many payroll services appear to receive very little for their efforts. Most payroll services just break even on their processing fees. Their profit comes in the form of *float*. The payroll service's contract has very specific language regarding timing requirements for clients funding their payroll checking accounts.

Usually the money hits the account well ahead of the payment date. Then there are the withholding payments along and all the other governmental payments that are paid through payroll. Usually these don't leave the checking account for days, weeks, or even months (in the case of quarterly payments). The payroll service has the use of the company's funds for all that time. That's why so many banks run payroll services for their customers.

ESTABLISHING YOUR PAYROLL SYSTEM

The payroll system involves a lot of record-keeping. Many small companies don't have the systems or the personnel to run an effective payroll system—that's the reason for the success of the commercial payroll industry.

Whether it pays 5 people or 500, your payroll system has to perform the following eight tasks:

1. Gather all timekeeping and piecework records.
2. Gather all records concerning sales commissions and bonuses.
3. Process all payroll changes, such as rate increases, new hires, and terminations.
4. Compute all payroll deductions.
5. Compute the payroll and draft checks to employees and government agencies.
6. Maintain the payroll journal.
7. Make journal entries from the payroll journal to the general ledger.
8. Maintain a system of accounting for the accumulation and use of sick leave, family leave, and vacation time.

Figure 12-1 shows how the information required to produce a payroll enters the system.

Figure 12-1
Flow of Information into the Payroll System

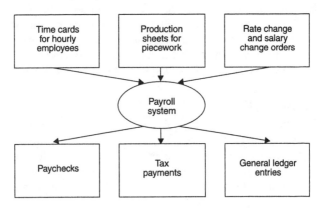

Gathering Payroll Information for Hourly Employees

Most small businesses pay at least some of their employees on an hourly basis. Time cards and a time clock provide an effective way of capturing time information. Use these three rules regarding time cards:

1. Company policy requires time cards on all employees who wish a pay check. No time card, no pay check.

2. Employees may stamp only their own time cards. Employees stamping time cards other than their own are subject to termination.

3. The supervisor is responsible for the accuracy of all subordinates' time cards. Time cards are not valid without the supervisor's signature.

Responsibility for accurate time reporting is placed where it belongs—on those closest to the situation.

The payroll department usually computes overtime pay rates and holiday pay rates based on established multipliers. Pay for hours over the standard work week or hours worked on a holiday receive the special pay rate. The payroll department identifies these from the time cards submitted by employees.

Gathering Piecework Information

Calculating payment on a piecework basis is similar to calculating it on a time basis. However, the unit of measure by which the firm computes payroll is *production*.

Most small companies use a production card or sheet. It identifies

- The employee • The pay period • Each day in the pay period
- Each item that was produced each day

Some companies pay different rates for different production items. That's why we identify each type of item produced. The supervisor reviews each employee's production sheet and signs it.

Paying Sales Commissions

Every payroll system establishes a routine method of gathering sales commission information from the sales department. Some small businesses have the sales department compute commissions, then transfer that information to Payroll in the form of gross pay. Other firms simply gather sales information from the sales department. The payroll department then computes commissions.

Decisions regarding commissions

Setting up a payroll system to pay sales commissions requires several decisions up front. The first is the basis of commissions. Most firms pay based on gross sales. However, the more profit-oriented companies pay based on the *net collected sales*. This encourages sales staff not to waste time booking sales to customers who don't pay. Other firms pay on gross sales, but deduct commissions paid on uncollected balances.

The easiest way to compute sales commissions is to use a percentage of whatever sales figure (gross or net) becomes the basis. However, some companies get fancy with this too. They provide commission incentives for sales of particular products. Using this method, the commission rate changes depending on which products were sold.

Variable commission rates practically guarantee that the sales department computes commissions. The logistics of communicating this information to Payroll are difficult. Further, such a system makes deducting commissions already paid on uncollectable balances difficult. In order to deduct paid commissions, the payroll clerk must know the commission rate in effect *for the item(s) purchased during that period of time.*

Paying Bonuses

Most bonus payments fall into the category of *nonroutine*. They don't happen regularly, and they're usually not based solely on something the payroll department computes. For the payroll system we're designing, simply use a memo from whoever decides the bonuses to the payroll department. All the regular withholding and other deductions come out of the bonus's gross just as if it were an ordinary paycheck.

Monthly Salaries

Salaries are the easiest type of payroll to compute. They're constant throughout the year until they're raised. In most small businesses, the payroll department assumes that regular salaried employees receive a paycheck from every payroll unless it is told differently.

Document changes to salaried employees (raises and terminations, for instance) in a memo to the payroll department. Time taken for sick leave, family leave, or vacation doesn't change the amount paid salaried employees. However, it does change the *accumulated* time granted each employee under company benefits policy.

Data Required to Set Up the Payroll System

Payroll systems appear complicated because they require so much information. However, you can be sure that at some time during the course of the payroll year, they will use all of it. You need the following information to set up your payroll system:

- A list of all employees with quarter-to-date and year-to-date earnings
- Each employee's quarter-to-date and year-to-date federal, state, and local tax contributions
- Form W-4 for each employee
- Social security number for each employee
- Wage rate, piece rate, or salary rate for each employee
- Employer's federal, state, and local tax ID numbers
- Tax tables for federal, state, and local taxes
- All benefits accrued year-to-date

Additionally, you'll need to add some general ledger accounts to receive entries from the payroll system. Figure 12-2 lists the general ledger information required by our small business payroll system.

Figure 12-2
General Ledger Accounts Needed for the Payroll System

- Payroll cash account
- Federal withholding (FIT)
- State withholding (SIT)
- State disability insurance (SDI)
- State unemployment insurance (SUI)
- Local disability insurance (LDI)
- Employee FICA
- Employer FICA expense
- Employee MEDIC
- Employer MEDIC expense
- Elective insurance deductions
- Union dues deductions
- Garnishments and other withholding

Documentation Required for the Payroll System

We'll establish three documents for the payroll system:

- Employee payroll record card • Payroll ledger
- Journal entry to general ledger

Each records a particular level of the payroll process, then each gets totaled and the total is posted to the next document.

Employee payroll record card

Set up a separate payroll record card for each employee. This is similar in concept to the customer cards used in the accounts receivable system and the inventory item cards used in Inventory Control. Each employee payroll record card contains these items:

- Name, address, phone number, social security number
- Department • Start and termination dates
- Deductions taken from Form W-4 • Pay rate
- Pay method • Salary rate per pay period if applicable
- All quarter- and year-to-date payroll deductions

Most of these items are entered on the employee payroll card just once. Most large stationery stores carry preprinted payroll registers containing these items.

Automated payroll systems prompt users for most of them. Commercial payroll services request this information during initial setup.

Payroll ledger

The payroll ledger records and summarizes the payroll entered for each employee using time cards, production sheets, or the payroll record cards for salaried employees. The payroll ledger includes columns headed

- Pay period date • Employee
- Regular hours worked, if applicable
- Overtime or holiday hours worked, if applicable
- Number of pieces produced, if applicable • Salary, if applicable
- Gross pay • Separate columns for each payroll deduction
- Net pay • Check number

We total gross pay, all the tax liabilities, and net pay for the entire payroll using the payroll ledger. Automated payroll systems and commercial payroll services do this for users.

Journal entry to the general ledger

Once completed, the payroll entries transfer to the general ledger accounts. The source of all payroll entries is the totaled payroll ledger. Use the same journal entry form as for any normal journal entry. Include the entire payroll entry on one form.

Payroll entries usually look like this going into the general ledger:

Salary Expense	X	
Employer-paid payroll tax	X	
All payroll deductions payable		X
Cash		X

When the company actually pays the taxing authorities, the entry looks like this:

All payroll deductions payable	X	
Cash		X

Most payroll deductions go directly to the taxing authorities on the payroll date.

If you're using a commercial payroll service, the entry omits payroll deductions. The service sends payroll deduction deposits to the taxing authorities on your behalf. In this case, the entry would be

Salary Expense	X	
Employer's Payroll Tax Expense	X	
Cash		X

Costing Payroll

Payroll costs don't end with gross salary expenses. Other costs include benefits and the employer's payment to the taxing authorities. Total labor costs include gross salary expense plus

- Employer-paid FICA • Federal unemployment taxes (FUTA)
- State unemployment taxes (SUTA) • Compensation insurance
- Employer contributions to employee pension plan • Vacation pay
- Sick pay • Family leave pay

Adding about 25 percent to gross salary approximates total labor costs. This doesn't include the human resources consultants many businesses retain just to keep them out of employee lawsuits. Nor does it contain worker's compensation insurance premiums.

Withholding Taxes

Federal and state withholding taxes sometimes confound payroll preparers. The actual computation is simple. Here's the step-by-step method for arriving at federal and state withholding:

1. Obtain the federal and state withholding tables for the *correct year*. Users of automated systems usually receive an update from the manufacturer each time these tables change or at the beginning of each new year.

2. For each employee, find the weekly, biweekly, semimonthly, or monthly gross pay.

3. Read across the columns to the withholding allowances claimed. The point of intersection is the withholding tax.

4. If the gross pay for the payroll period exceeds the maximum in the table, use the alternative tables at the back.

Federal Withholding Payments

Strict federal laws prohibit keeping payroll withholding payments beyond statutory time limits. These time limits depend on the frequency of your payroll and the amount of the deposit. The rules appear on the inside cover of your federal and state withholding tax tables. You can't go wrong if you make the deposit on payday.

However, larger firms with significant payroll withholding deposits often elect to stretch payment of the deposit until the last minute. Commercial payroll service companies do this. Use of their customers' funds is a big part of their profit.

Reporting Requirements

There are reporting requirements for virtually everything associated with payroll. For example, the federal and state tax deposits require a payment card identifying the nature of the deposit.

Quarterly payroll tax reports summarize tax payments and deposits made to date. If you faithfully make each withholding and tax deposit after every payroll, quarterly reports usually verify payment of all taxes. Additionally, they compute the employer's contribution to unemployment tax—usually a small percentage of total payroll.

Annual payroll tax reports include Forms W-2 sent to each employee. That's why employers must retain complete payroll records on each employee who worked for the company during the year. The information that goes on the W-2s includes

- Employee's name
- Employee social security number or taxpayer ID number
- Gross earnings
- Amount withheld for federal tax purposes
- Amount withheld for state tax purposes
- Amount withheld for local tax purposes

What happens if you send a W-2 to an employee and the post office returns it because the person moved and left no forwarding address? Keep the form and the post office's notification that it was undeliverable. At least this provides a written record that you, the employer, attempted to comply with the law.

SPECIAL CIRCUMSTANCES

Every company seems to have a peculiarity that complicates its payroll. For some it may be tips; others have employees in different states with varying state withholding rules and rates.

Reporting Tips

The law requires employees to report tips as regular income. The taxing authority's preferred way is for the employee to report cash tips to the employer. These go into payroll tax computations as an *addition* to the gross income paid by the employer.

Tipping and the minimum wage

Tipping is customary in many industries. Some firms use tips to apply tips toward the minimum wage they must pay by law. Often tips bring employees' wages up to the minimum. If they don't, the employer must make up the difference in the employee's hourly rate.

Allocating tips

Some companies require employees to put their tips into one large pool for all employees. An example would be a catering company that automatically adds its tip to the final bill. The company then allocates tips to each eligible employee through the payroll system. These allocated tips become part of each employee's gross wages on which the firm computes payroll taxes.

Exempt Salaried Employees

We said earlier that it's usually easiest to compute payroll for salaried employees. That's because their gross pay rarely changes. However, sometimes it does, such as when a salaried employee takes vacation days exceeding those accrued. The company docks the salaried employee. Here's an example.

Assume the company paid Tobby $4,000 for a normal 80-hour pay period. However, Tobby took an extra two days of vacation that had not been accrued. Tobby agreed with that the company should dock his pay for the next period. The computation is

$$\text{Hourly rate} = \frac{\$4,000}{80} = \$50 \text{ per hour}$$

$$\text{Gross pay} = \$50 \times (80 \text{ hours - 16 hours})$$

$$\text{Gross pay} = \$3,200$$

For this pay period only, Tobby's salary is $3,200. Thereafter, it reverts back to the normal $4,000.

Changing Pay Rates

Sometimes pay rates for hourly employees change. Overtime rates and holiday rates are good examples. For piecework employees, the rate may change for different production items.

These factors complicate the payroll computation. Calculate gross pay for each pay rate. Here's an example:

Maggie works as a surgical nurse at a walk-in urgent care clinic. Her normal hourly rate is $30. In one two-week period she worked 90 hours, 8 of which were on Easter Sunday. Compute her gross pay as follows:

Standard hourly pay: $30 \times 80 =$	$2,400
Regular time and a half overtime:	
$(90 - 80 - 8) \times (\$30 \times 1.5) =$	90
Holiday double time: $8 \times (\$30 \times 2) =$	480
Total gross pay	$2,970

Multistate Payroll

Some companies have employees in more than one state. Each state has its own payroll tax withholding rules and rates. For each state in which your company has employees, find out the rules and the rates. Then include a separate column for each state in the payroll ledger. Additionally, many firms add a state tax withholding account in the general ledger for each state in which they have employees. This helps keep the amount owed to each state separate. The amount owed for state withholding taxes appears both in the payroll ledger and as a credit balance in each state's *accrued state withholding tax* account in the general ledger.

Earned Income Credit (EIC)

This is a special credit allowed by the federal government to employees earning less than the minimum wage. The EIC effectively brings each employee *up to* the minimum wage. Here's how it works in most payroll systems: Subtract the employee's gross pay from the statutory minimum wage. Include the difference in the employee's payroll as a *negative deduction*—an addition, in other words. This brings the employee's gross pay up to the minimum wage.

If you have employees falling into this category, be sure to investigate how your own state treats the EIC.

TRACKING BENEFITS

By default the payroll system usually tracks employee benefits. These include

- Vacation time • Sick time • Personal time off • Family leave

The benefits system is like a separate accounting system *within* the payroll system. Instead of dollars, it accounts for hours. The mission of the benefits tracking system is twofold:

- To accrue each month the amount of time granted by the company for each benefit category
- To deduct time used by each employee

Setting Up the Benefits Tracking System

You'll want an easy method of accruing and updating benefits. If you use a commercial payroll service or an automated payroll system, it probably does this for you. However, if you want to do it yourself or if you run a manual payroll system, follow these steps.

Determining the accrual amount

First identify the accrual amount for each month and for each benefit. Some firms accrue at different rates for salaried and for hourly workers. Others just identify a percentage to accrue for both. One easy way is to designate the number of hours an employee can accrue per year for each benefit. Determine the accrual rate using this equation:

$$\text{Accrual rate} = \frac{\text{benefit hours per year}}{\text{total hours in a work year}}$$

For example, suppose we accrue vacation time at a rate of 4 percent for employees having less than five years of service, 6 percent for employees having less than ten years of service, and 8 percent for employees having more than ten years of service. This yields annual vacation time of ten days, fifteen days, and twenty days, respectively, for the different service levels. A normal eighty-hour pay period for an employee with less than five years service yields accrued vacation time of 3.2 hours (80 hours × 4% = 3.2 hours).

Post to the Benefits Accrual Schedule

Each pay period the number of hours accrued for all the employee benefits is added. Figure 12-3 shows an example of a benefits accrual sheet.

Figure 12-3
Benefits Accrual Schedule

Employee name: _____

	Vacation				Sick Leave		
Pay Period	Hours Worked	Accrual Rate	Hours Accrued		Hours Worked	Accrual Rate	Hours Worked

Each pay period, transfer the number of hours worked from the payroll system to each employee's benefits accrual sheet. Then multiply by the accrual percentage to arrive at the hours accrued. When an employee uses accrued time, deduct the hours from the hours accrued column.

Account for time carried over

Some companies allow carryover of benefits time from year to year. Though that's not the point of having benefits, there's a way to allow for it. At the beginning of each year, the first entry on each employee's benefits accrual schedule is the amount of time carried over from the prior year.

Many companies have a policy regarding maximum vacation time carried over. That's to ensure that people take their vacations according to company policy. From an internal control standpoint, this is good policy. If that's the case at your company, it's a good idea to periodically remind people of their accrued benefit time and the firm's policies regarding carryover. Be aware, however, that this creates an urgency at year end to "use it or lose it."

Carryover of sick time is another issue. Many companies believe that employees should accrue all the sick time they earn over the years without penalty of losing it. Therefore, they have no restriction on carryover from one year to the next. This actually encourages people to stay healthy. Their sick time is like money in the bank should they ever have a serious illness that keeps them from working for long periods of time.

Chapter 13 establishes the fixed asset accounting system.

Chapter 13

Fixed Asset Accounting

OVERVIEW

Even at small companies, fixed assets generally include

- Cars • Trucks • Manufacturing machinery and equipment
- Furniture and fixtures • Building improvements and real estate

Chapter 13 installs a foolproof system that categorizes fixed assets by type and economic life for easy computation of depreciation expense. This system also helps control the identification and location of valuable assets. Further, fixed asset accounting assists in assessing property tax liability in districts that have a personal property tax as well as a real property tax.

SETTING UP THE FIXED ASSET SYSTEM

We want our fixed asset system to do just two things:

- Identify and categorize fixed assets
- Compute depreciation and amortization expense

This system isn't nearly as complicated as some of the other accounting subsystems we've already created. Fixed assets aren't as volatile as, say, accounts receivable. Transactions don't usually hit the fixed asset accounts more than once a month unless there's an acquisition or disposition. Further, most of the depreciation and amortization expense entries remain the same from one month to the next.

Even small businesses have a number of fixed assets they need to track. Each month depreciation and amortization expense flows from the fixed asset system. Often companies buy new assets or sell old ones. Sometimes they retire them; or simply abandon them. In each instance particular accounting entries hit the fixed asset subledger and flow up to the general ledger.

Like most of our other subledgers, the fixed asset system begins with a detailed ledger sheet describing each asset. The ledger sheet summarizes all entries for each asset and tracks accumulated depreciation or amortization. Journal entries document the transaction flow from the detailed ledger sheets to the general ledger.

Contents of the Fixed Asset Ledger

Some companies keep their fixed asset ledgers on individual cards, one card for each asset. This is similar to the way customer cards are used in the accounts receivable system. Other firms use multicolumn paper that lists the assets down the left and the various items of information across the top.

Regardless of how you choose to keep the fixed asset ledger, include these items of information:

- Fixed asset number • Description of the asset
- Serial number, if applicable • Location of the asset
- Date placed in service • Cost or basis • Estimated economic life
- Depreciation or amortization method
- Monthly depreciation or amortization expense
- Accumulated depreciation • Asset book value

Figure 13-1 (page 204) shows a sample fixed asset subledger.

Some small businesses without huge numbers of fixed assets include both the fixed asset accounts and the corresponding accumulated depreciation accounts in the general ledger. Do this only if you have very few fixed assets. Otherwise it clutters the G/L with a lot of detailed accounts that should be in a subledger. Further, these accounts probably get reported on the firm's balance sheet. We don't need that much detail on the balance sheet.

CATEGORIZING FIXED ASSETS

Categorizing fixed assets makes computation of depreciation and amortization that much easier. Further, it adds a level of organization that is often lacking in small business accounting systems. We don't want to leaf through hundreds of records trying to find the details of a particular asset. With proper categorization, we can quickly narrow the search and often go right to the property in question.

Separating Tangible Assets from Intangibles

The first cut in categorizing fixed assets is the separation of hard assets from the so-called soft assets. We treat the two differently. Hard assets—the tangibles—include such things as machinery and equipment. These incur a depreciation expense each month.

Soft assets include items of personal property that are physically untouchable, such as goodwill, patents, and copyrights. Each month these incur an amortization expense. Particular rules apply to tangibles that don't apply to intangibles, and vice versa. That's why we separate them.

Goodwill

Many small businesses have some sort of intangible assets they could amortize. The expense provides some income tax relief without actually incurring a cash outflow. If you purchased your company, chances are you bought some intangible assets as well.

Figure 13-1
Fixed Asset Subledger

Asset Tag Number	Des- cription	Serial Number	Location	Service Date	Cost or Basis	Economic Life	Depre- ciation Method	Monthly Depre- ciation Expense	Accum- ulated Depre- ciation	Book Value

For example, usually buried somewhere in the purchase price is *goodwill*. This is simply the price paid in excess of the fair market value of the assets purchased. Goodwill is a payment for future excess earnings of the company. Here's an equation the IRS recommended in Revenue Ruling 68-609 for valuation of goodwill:

$$G = D - \frac{(R \times C)}{I}$$

where D is the expected future earnings of the company

R is the constant rate of return typically earned in the industry

C is the capital of the firm—the purchase price

I is the capitalization rate of the company's goodwill

Let's say we purchased a plastic molding company for $2,000,000 ($C$ in the equation). We expect the first year's earnings to be $400,000 ($D$ in the equation). The annual return in the plastic molding industry is about 15 percent (R in the equation). We capitalize goodwill at 20 percent (I in the equation). Our goodwill in the acquisition of this company is

$$\text{Goodwill} = \frac{\$400{,}000 - (0.15 \times \$2{,}000{,}000)}{0.20}$$

$$\text{Goodwill} = \$500{,}000$$

Other Intangibles

Small companies, especially those involved in high-technology industries, often have other valuable intangible assets. Patents count as intangibles. Copyrights count as well. When the company was first started, it incurred some specific organization costs, such as corporate filing fees, attorney's fees, and accountants' fees. Classify these as *organization costs*. Trade marks and trade names purchased by companies incur amortization as intangible assets.

Tangible Fixed Assets

Categorize durable assets with an economic life exceeding one year that are not intended for resale in the regular course of business as fixed assets. All tangible assets have a physical existence. Include in this category such assets as

- Land • Buildings • Leasehold improvements
- Motor vehicles • Machinery and equipment
- Furniture and fixtures • Farm animals • Crops growing on land

Companies having a variety of fixed assets classify them using major asset headings such as those listed above. Individual assets go under each heading on the fixed asset subledger. Using this system of classification, it's easy to quickly find any particular asset.

DEPRECIATION AND AMORTIZATION

One major function of the fixed asset accounting system is the computation of regular depreciation and amortization expenses. The Internal Revenue Code fills over 500 pages with the rules governing depreciation and amortization expenses. That's beyond the scope of this book and is better left to your tax professional. However, we do want to show you how to compute depreciation and amortization using some of the more common methods.

To compute depreciation and amortization, you need to know just two numbers:

- Cost or basis of the asset • Economic life

Cost and Basis of an Asset

In most cases an asset's cost is straightforward. However, sometimes it gets complicated. Say that we lease office space. Next, we install a special Halon fire suppression system in our computer room. This is a depreciable asset. The system's cost includes the actual equipment and hardware associated with the fire system. However, it also includes installation. Such systems are very sophisticated and require professionals to install, test and maintain the system. Therefore, we can *capitalize* (depreciate as a capital asset) the cost of the system and its installation.

Costing intangible assets

Intangible assets carry a cost for developing. However, we don't amortize the costs of intangibles *internally developed at the firm*. Instead, we expense them in the year they are incurred. For example, say an engineering company spends $10,000 in research expenses to develop and patent a machine. We don't know how the costs relate to future benefits from the machine. Therefore, we just expense these development costs. From a tax standpoint, that's better anyway—it reduces taxable income and, therefore, tax liability sooner. Amortization, on the other hand, requires us to spread the tax benefits over a period of years.

All assets, both tangible and intangible, purchased from another party count as capital assets. The purchase price is the cost of the asset. Depreciate or amortize these as you would any fixed asset.

Basis of transferred assets

Frequently partners give the firm an asset instead of money as their capital contribution. For example, say a new partner gave the firm a warehouse he owned as his capital contribution. The value of the warehouse on the fixed asset subledger is the new partner's *basis* in the warehouse prior to transfer. This is also the value placed on the new partner's capital account. The firm and the partner do not recognize a gain or loss until sale of the asset. At that time, the new partner's capital account increases (or decreases) to reflect the gain (or loss) and the company recognizes a gain (or loss) on sale of the asset. The gain (or loss) flows through to the contributing partner to the extent that the property's fair market value at the time of contribution exceeded (or was less than) his basis. The partners share any gain above (or loss below) that amount according to allocations stated in the partnership agreement.

Economic Life

Computation of depreciation and amortization expense usually requires an estimate of an asset's economic life—that is, the amount of time the firm expects to benefit from the asset. Economic lives vary for different classes of assets. The IRS, under its MACRS system of recording depreciation expense, assigns blanket economic lives to various types of assets and directs taxpayers to use these in calculating depreciation.

For our purposes, the economic life is simply the amount time you expect to use the asset. Cars, for example, are usually used for three years. Trucks may last longer. In the earlier example of a fire suppression system on a leasehold, the economic life is the remaining life of the lease. After all, the company probably won't tear out the system when the lease expires and the company moves. However, be careful with leaseholds. Options and extension clauses in the lease often influence the economic life.

Economic life of intangibles

Use these criteria to logically arrive at the economic life of intangible assets such as goodwill:

1. What legal, contractual, or regulatory restrictions influence the asset's life?
2. How do obsolescence, demand, or other economic factors change its useful life?
3. Can the asset be renewed or extended to change its useful life?
4. Does the asset's life depend on the parallel service of some other asset? If so, that may be a limiting factor.

Some classes of intangible assets enjoy statutory protection. For example, the U.S. Patent Office grants patents for seventeen years. That's a patent's economic life. Copyrights generally run for seventy-five years. Practically speaking, however, it's rare for such assets to maintain their economic value for the entire duration of the statutory protection period. Therefore, the economic life is usually much less.

Organization costs are amortized over a period not to exceed sixty months. Goodwill amortization cannot exceed a period of forty years. Indeed, Opinion #17 of the Accounting Principles Board specified that goodwill be amortized over the maximum forty year period.

Computing Depreciation and Amortization

Compute depreciation and amortization expense using the method most appropriate for the asset. Again, for tax purposes, these methods and their economic lives must follow IRS guidelines—usually associated with MACRS.

Straight line

This is the simplest method of computing depreciation. Further, it's the only standard method used in computing amortization. It assumes that an asset's economic value declines by an equal amount each year. Compute straight-line depreciation using the following equation:

$$\text{Annual depreciation} = \frac{\text{asset cost or basis - estimated salvage value}}{\text{estimated economic life}}$$

For example, assume that Maggie Corporation bought a computer-controlled drill press. The cost installed was $200,000. It should last about five years. At the end of that time, its value should be about $40,000. Monthly depreciation expense is

$$\text{Monthly depreciation} = \frac{\$200,000 - \$40,000}{60 \text{ months}}$$

$$\text{Monthly depreciation} = \$2,667$$

Sum-of-the-years'-digits

The first method of *accelerated* depreciation is sum-of-the-years'-digits (SYOD). Like all accelerated methods, SYOD assumes that the asset's value declines more rapidly in the earlier years of service. The SYOD depreciation rate uses the years remaining in the asset's service life divided by the sum of all the years in the service life. For example, the depreciation fraction for the first year of a 5-year asset is 5/15 (5+4+3+2+1=15). Figure 13-2 continues the example of Maggie's drill press using SYOD.

Figure 13-2
Maggie's Drill Press Using SYOD

Year	Cost - Salvage	Remaining Years	Fraction	Annual Depreciation
1	$160,000	5	5/15	$53,333
2	$160,000	4	4/15	42,667
3	$160,000	3	3/15	32,000
4	$160,000	2	2/15	21,333
5	$160,000	1	1/15	10,667
				$160,000

Notice how the annual depreciation of Maggie's drill press falls less rapidly the farther out in its economic life it goes. This is typical of all accelerated methods. If we graph this depreciation schedule, the result looks like Figure 13-3.

Figure 13-3
SYOD Depreciation Curve

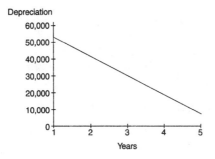

Declining balance

The declining-balance method uses a multiple of the straight-line rate. However, it has two differences from other depreciation methods:

• The depreciated value is cost, not cost less salvage value.

• The depreciable balance each year declines by the amount of the prior year's depreciation expense.

Figure 13-4 shows Maggie's drill press depreciated using the 200 percent declining-balance method—double the straight-line rate.

Figure 13-4
Double-Declining-Balance Method

Year	Book Value	Depreciating Rate	Depreciating Expense
1	$200,000	40%	$80,000
2	120,000	40%	48,000
3	72,000	40%	28,800
4	43,200	40%	17,280
5	25,920	40%	25,920
			$200,000

In reality, Maggie would switch depreciation methods from double-declining-balance to straight-line at the time straight-line exceeds DDB depreciation expense. That happens in the fourth year. At that time we depreciate the remaining book value of $43,200 at $21,600 for each of years four and five.

RECORDING DEPRECIATION EXPENSE

Now that we know how the fixed asset system computes depreciation expense, we must record it on the fixed asset record card for each asset. Using this method, we have a ready reference for the book value and accumulated depreciation of each asset in the system.

You're going to need balance sheet accounts for each *major* type of fixed asset. Use the following as a guide for major asset categories:

- Land • Buildings and improvements • Equipment
- Furniture and fixtures • Intangible assets

The cost or basis before depreciation or amortization of the assets goes in these accounts. Now you need a place to record both depreciation expense and accumulated depreciation (as a credit balance asset). This gets transferred from the detailed fixed asset ledger cards to the general ledger. Add these accounts to the G/L:

- Accumulated depreciation—buildings and improvements
- Accumulated depreciation—equipment
- Accumulated depreciation—furniture and fixtures
- Accumulated amortization—intangibles
- Depreciation expense—buildings and improvements
- Depreciation expense—equipment
- Depreciation expense—furniture and fixtures
- Amortization expense—intangibles

Notice that using these accounts, we can compute book value (asset cost - accumulated depreciation) for any given class of asset. The balance sheet usually summarizes such detail for reporting purposes. However, by using these accounts in the general ledger, we preserve the audit trail from the fixed asset system to the general ledger.

Monthly Journal Entries

Recording depreciation and amortization expense is easy. We take the monthly expense computed on the fixed asset subledger, then debit the expense account for each asset and credit the accumulated depreciation account for each asset. Figure 13-5 shows what the entry looks like.

Recording Sales of Fixed Assets

Businesses replace worn-out assets or upgrade items with newer and better equipment. The fixed asset system we've established records the sale and the gain

Figure 13-5
Journal Entry for Monthly Depreciation and Amortization

	Debit	Credit
Depreciation expense—buildings and improvements	X	
Depreciation expense—equipment	X	
Depreciation expense—furniture and fixtures	X	
Amortization expense—intangibles	X	
Accumulated depreciation—buildings and improvements		X
Accumulated depreciation—equipment		X
Accumulated depreciation—furniture and fixtures		X
Accumulated amortization—intangibles		X

or loss and removes the asset from the system. Then the entry is transferred to the general ledger for recording.

Assume that Maggie Corporation sells the automated drill press it purchased in the earlier example. The controller was depreciating it using the declining balance table in Figure 13-4. The press is sold at the beginning of the third year for a price of $80,000. Here are the entries to remove the asset and record the sale:

Cash	$ 80,000	
Accumulated Depreciation—		
Machinery	128,000 (1)	
Machinery		$200,000
Gain on Sale of Assets		8,000 (2)

1. The accumulated depreciation at the beginning of the third year was the sum of the first two years' depreciation: $80,000 + $48,000 = $128,000.

2. The gain on sale was the sale price less book value at the time of sale. Book value was

Purchase cost	$200,000
Less accumulated depreciation	(128,000)
	$72,000

The gain on sale was $8,000 ($80,000 - $72,000 = $8,000).

Notice how this entry wipes out the asset value and the accumulated depreciation accounts by taking their entire balances and entering an offsetting debit or credit. The balance sheet shows only what's left—cash and a gain on sale that makes its way into owners' equity.

Recording Abandonment of Fixed Assets

Often completely used fixed assets have no resale or salvage value. The company essentially abandons them. The entry works like the sale of a fixed asset in the sense that we want to wipe out accumulated depreciation and the cost of the asset on the firm's books.

Assume that Maggie's automated drill press turns out to be less than the stellar performer Maggie anticipated. It had no further utility or value by the beginning of the third year, Maggie had to plead with a salver to haul it away. Here's the entry:

Accumulated Depreciation—		
Machinery	$128,000	
Loss on Abandonment of		
Drill Press	72,000	
Machinery		$200,000

The loss Maggie incurred is actually the book value at the time of abandonment.

IDENTIFYING FIXED ASSETS

A well-maintained fixed asset accounting system provides an inventory listing of all fixed assets owned by the company and their locations. Additionally, it gives a physical description and each item's serial number, if applicable.

Companies often add a tag number to each inventory item. These preprinted tags physically adhere to the asset and match the tag numbers in the fixed asset subledger. When taking a physical inventory of fixed assets, matching each asset tag with the tag number and physical description listed in the fixed asset system guarantees the existence of the inventory items listed.

In practice, few small businesses actually tag their fixed assets. Usually, each fixed asset is obvious. However, if you have large numbers of expensive assets that all look alike—such as desktop computers—tag numbers are a good idea.

INVENTORYING FIXED ASSETS

Just as with a warehouse inventory, conducting periodic fixed asset inventories assures management that expensive items aren't walking out the back door. Follow these guidelines when conducting a fixed asset inventory:

1. Those responsible for maintaining and recording the fixed assets *do not* take part in the inventory.

2. Spot check the work of those counting fixed assets.

3. Match the physical count with the fixed asset subledger. If they don't balance, there's a problem.

4. Follow up any discrepancies between what the physical count says exists and what the fixed asset system says should be there.

PERSONAL PROPERTY TAXES

More often than you'd think, property tax authorities mistakenly lump items of personal property into the assessment of real property. This artificially raises the assessed value of the real estate. Such inflation of the assessed value of real property catches companies unawares. It is not in accord with the taxing district's statutory assessment authority. Even worse, most companies just sit by and watch it happen.

Look at your property tax bill closely. If your tax assessment district charges taxes on personal property items, they usually appear separately on the bill. It shows assessed value along with the tax percentage. Compare that with the items in your fixed asset system. If the values don't match, you may have an opportunity to appeal the assessment of personal property taxes.

Check the assessed value of the land and buildings that appears on your property tax bill. If the assessor mistakenly included personal property items as part of the real estate, the value should appear excessive. You may have to demand that the assessor's office show you its computation of the real property components.

During your review of the assessor's computation, keep these definitions in mind:

Real property: Land and those immobile and tangible things attached to it, such as buildings and roads. Real property has any one or all of these three characteristics:

- It can't be removed from the premises.
- It was built or adapted specifically for a certain site.
- It was intended to stay a part of the property permanently.

Personal property: Transportable items not meant to stay with the real estate, such as the furniture in the buildings.

If the assessor included personal property with the real property and the tax district does not allow taxation of personal property, you may have a case. Every year astute owners successfully appeal millions of dollars of incorrect or illegal property taxes.

Chapter 14 establishes the system of internal accounting controls.

Chapter 14

Internal Accounting Controls

OVERVIEW

If company owners did everything themselves, there would be little need for a system of internal controls. But they don't. By its nature, running even a small business involves a number of different people. The company is subject to the risk of

- Unauthorized conversion of assets
- Inaccurate transaction reporting
- Loss or theft of vital documents
- Entry of bogus documents into the accounting system to disguise fraud and embezzlement
- Disregard for management policies that eases the perpetration of illegal acts

Chapter 14 identifies the characteristics of an effective internal control system designed especially for small businesses. The emphasis is on cost-effectiveness. We'll target the areas of the firm that are most vulnerable to risk:

- Sales • Accounts receivable • Accounts payable • Inventory
- Cash

Chapter 14 demonstrates how to establish a testing mechanism that provides reasonable assurance that the company's internal controls work and that employees comply with them. Finally, it's not enough to simply design and operate a system of internal accounting controls. As with a lock, if someone really wants to get in, they will. Chapter 14 ends with a checklist you can use to judge the effectiveness of controls at your own company.

PURPOSE OF INTERNAL CONTROL

Certainly reducing the threat of theft or fraud on the part of employees and others is one purpose of establishing an effective system of internal accounting controls. However, most business owners and managers agree that *preventive* controls work better than methods designed to merely detect the occurrence of a problem after the fact. Detecting fraud after it has occurred is like closing the barn door after the horses are gone.

Deterrence

Effective systems of internal controls act like a lock on a door. Honest people won't try to beat the mechanism, and those inclined to steal will go to an easier target. Nevertheless, every company needs to understand that if people really want to steal, they will. Internal controls, no matter how effective, won't stop them. The best control systems make it harder to steal, increase the risk of being caught, and decrease the amount taken in each fraudulent transaction.

The deterrence internal controls provide is that perpetrators have to assume more risk than the take would net them. Given that, all but the very stupid or desperate don't even try.

Reliance on Reporting

The internal control system is also responsible for maintaining the accuracy of transaction reporting. Companies that do not place a premium on accurate financial reporting leave themselves open to fraud and embezzlement. Such actions are difficult to detect in any case. However, a low risk of discovery further diminishes a control system's deterrent effect.

Records Control

An important component of control is the records involved in the company's business transactions. Without an ability to retrieve the records that can reconstruct a transaction, companies open the door to such problems as

- Payment of invoices from vendors for work that was never done
- Payment to fictitious vendors or employees
- Sales without the proper recording of a receivable—a sure way never to be paid by your customers
- Investments being improperly recorded and transferred to someone else
- Incorrect reporting of cash deposits—which provides a big assist to those pocketing customer payments
- Improper inventory counts masking pilferage or outright theft

COMPONENTS OF THE INTERNAL CONTROL SYSTEM

There are three elements to the system of internal controls:

- The control environment
- The accounting system
- Control procedures

Each works with the others to safeguard the firm's assets and record transactions in accordance with management policies.

The Control Environment

This is the overall environment for control created by management's attitude, awareness, and actions. It runs through the entire company: the owners, board of directors, senior officers, and employees.

Three factors that influence the control environment are

- Assignments for monitoring control responsibilities
- Personnel policies and practices
- External requirements, such as regulatory reporting and independent audits

An effective control environment makes overriding of management policies and procedures the exception rather than the rule. Managers seek approval from an established authority hierarchy when they must circumvent policies or procedures. Such adherence to the rules makes everyone aware of how serious the company is about internal control. The attitude of adherence to internal control begins with senior management and works its way through the entire organization.

Accounting System

This provides the means and method of identifying, classifying, recording, reporting, and determining accountability for the company's assets and liabilities. The accounting system and those who run it should have a high level of credibility. The department should have an attitude of accuracy over expediency. Its well-trained personnel should have experience consistent with their responsibilities.

All this may sound obvious. But it isn't always practiced. Companies must either retrain, reassign or terminate employees unqualified for the demands of their jobs.

The hardware and software that form the company's books of original entry should be adequate for the job. It makes no sense to require convoluted procedures whose complexity invites error just to keep an antiquated accounting system limping along. Most efficient accounting systems return their costs in timely and accurate information used for management decisions that increase profits.

Accounting controls

The most common controls found in the accounting system revolve around transaction recording. There, the risk of error or losing vital documents is usually of greater concern than theft. Single isolated violations of accounting controls may be nothing. However, a consistent pattern of abuse should warn you that your company is risking fraud and embezzlement.

Control Procedures

Management establishes and maintains control procedures. For example, let's say the controller is responsible for investing the company's excess cash but is frequently out of the office in the morning. In the controller's absence, the senior accountant fills in and executes that day's investments.

On paper, executing and recording of transactions are done by two separate people. Actually, however, the senior accountant not only records all investment activity, but often makes the investments as well. This arrangement invites problems.

Everyone involved in internal control should share management's attitude of taking it seriously. One step that promotes this attitude is regular review of control points to verify compliance. Taking this one step further, those reviewing the controls should be independent of them.

When the business changes, control procedures must change with it. When people leave the firm, change controls such as passwords, keys, and combinations to locks. Additionally, update authorized signatures at the bank and any other place they are used.

RESPONSIBILITY FOR INTERNAL CONTROLS

In most small businesses, the accounting department designs and implements the system of internal controls. This includes protecting the firm's most easily convertible liquid assets: cash and its equivalents. Additionally, the accounting department controls the recording of liquid asset transactions. Failure of controls in areas involving access to assets and recording of transactions involving them creates the potential for fraud that could go undiscovered for some time.

Take the case of Adam, who had just taken over as general manager for a small label-making company. After hearing how unsophisticated almost all the company's systems were, his auditor suggested an internal control review. "It never hurts to find out what you're up against at the beginning of your watch," said the auditor. "That way if there's a problem you come out a hero for finding it."

"No problem here," said Adam. "The controller has been with the company for ten years. She's so dedicated she refuses to take her vacations. Why, I practically have to push her out the door at night. A control review would insult her as well as wasting everyone's time."

Six months later Adam's auditor discovered that the trusted controller had embezzled $50,000 over a five-year period. She ran the payables system, printed the checks, signed the checks, *and* reconciled the checking account. The company lacked any control over its cash.

DESIGN OF THE INTERNAL CONTROL SYSTEM

Large firms have experts in the controller's and treasurer's departments or on the internal audit staff who design, implement, and monitor internal controls. However, at smaller companies, managers may have little or no experience in designing a system of internal controls. If the risk is severe enough, small companies often hire outside consultants or their independent auditors to design control systems.

Experts designing internal control systems always include these five things:

- A plan for the segregation of functional responsibilities
- Separation of operations and custodianship of assets from record keeping
- A system of authorization and recording procedures
- Sound policies and procedures
- Personnel whose ability is commensurate with their responsibilities

Of these, separation of duties is often the most effective deterrent to employee fraud. Two or more parties would need to work together to perpetrate a successful theft. The chance that this will happen is less than the chance that one person will do so.

Figure 14-1 illustrates the different areas of control that small businesses try to separate.

Figure 14-1
Separation of Duties

Recording	Custodianship
1. Recording of transactions in the general ledger, and the accounts receivable and accounts payable subledgers, and of fixed assets transactions such as depreciation and inventory control	1. Holding or getting funds used to finance operations
2. Invoicing customers	2. Maintaining the capital structure required to meet the needs of the business plan
3. Personnel timekeeping	3. Holding and managing cash and other liquid assets of the firm
4. Payroll preparation	4. Approval of payment checks and acting as signatory on checks
5. Management reporting	5. Reconciliation of checking accounts
6. Business planning direction	6. Managing the credit function
7. Performing tax computations	7. Acting as cashier
8. Recording investment transactions and reconciliating the company investment account at brokerage firms	8. Executing short-term investment of excess cash on behalf of the company
	9. Implementing company policy related to trade discounts and receivables aging policies
	10. Implementing company policy with regard to vendor payments

Make sure that no single person does both the things listed in the left column and those listed in the right. That's part of the purpose of a successful system of internal accounting controls.

DELEGATION OF RESPONSIBILITY

As Figure 14-1 shows, smart management delegates responsibilities in such a way that no single person has complete control over a specific function. Take, for example, check payment. The controller (or his or her staff) posts invoices to the accounts payable subledger. This step includes printing payment checks. However, the controller doesn't have signature authority over the checks, thus making it more difficult (though not impossible) to issue a check without proper authorization. Further, after signing, the signatory, not the check writer, mails the checks. Therefore, there's less chance of a valid and correctly signed check being fraudulently altered.

Notice the simplicity and common sense of these controls. Most internal accounting controls work like that. Rarely do they become complicated. However, to install and monitor effective controls, business owners have to think like a thief—that's the hard part.

Collusion and Sabotage

Ugly words, aren't they? Yet creating the necessity for collusion is the objective of an effective system of internal control. That's right. Properly designed controls require that in order to perpetrate a fraud or defalcation, at least two unrelated people (preferably in different departments) will have to work together. The chances of this happening are more remote than if just one person is allowed complete access to a control point.

Designing a system that requires collusion to subvert a control prevents more than just fraud and theft. For example, disgruntled employees (and former employees) can sabotage the company. A good system of checks and balances makes sabotage by a single unsupervised individual less likely.

Many nonfinancial parts of companies use similar two-party controls. Computer systems are one such area. These are vulnerable to attack from computer viruses and logic bombs. At one aerospace company a discontented programmer installed such a retaliatory software device. Each day it searched for the programmer's name on the payroll list. When he was terminated, the company scratched his name from the list of active employees. The computer didn't find his name on the list, and the logic bomb erased engineering data valued in six figures.

Maintenance of Internal Control Systems

Internal control systems must be flexible and should change with the company. For example, let's say that the accounts payable supervisor who runs the checks and the person who signs the checks and acts as custodian of the signature plate are unrelated to each other. No problem so far. There's a solid separation of duties. Neither employee is related to the other. However, the backup person for the A/P supervisor just married the check signer's brother. Now these two are in-laws—related parties.

Smoothly functioning systems of internal control discover such changes *before* they occur and signal the implications. It's a matter of being aware of the situation, knowing your employees, and anticipating possible compromises to the company's accounting system.

In this case steps would be taken to either replace the backup person or implement another type of control, reducing the risk of collusion among family members. Of course, some may argue that a sister-in-law relationship is far enough removed to present little risk. Perhaps. This is a judgment call. Maybe the two people involved hate each other. But maybe they don't.

Another example is the person who has responsibility for investing excess cash. The company should have knowledge of the individual's personal financial situation. If the person is in bankruptcy or even teetering on its edge, the responsibility may not be appropriate right now. The point is that the control system must identify the potential weakness quickly and present possible solutions before a problem occurs.

Cost versus Benefit

Every control procedure has a cost. We want to keep that in mind when designing the system of internal accounting controls. The cost may be the time it takes to generate a report or to review a document for approval. It may be a real dollar cost, or it may be the cost of whatever else that person could be doing to earn the firm money. Regardless, the control procedure should never cost more than the loss it is trying to prevent. There comes a point where the cost of control isn't justified by the risk.

Certain assets represent hot buttons for management. Frequently, their controls are disproportionate to the risk or even the value of the asset being protected. Petty cash is often a case in point. Later, in the cash section of this chapter, we'll address petty cash controls that make sense.

Money is a common yardstick used to determine the effectiveness of controls. Here are the three questions you should ask when evaluating a control procedure:

1. Of what value is it in terms of preventing or detecting errors, sloppiness, defalcations, or other problems?

2. What is the expected frequency and cost of an occurrence without the control?

3. What is the cost of the control procedure?

Here's how one firm quantifies the value of a control:

Problem: The Lapin Development Group has a backlog in the sales invoicing department. This has delayed sending invoices to customers. One solution under consideration is to establish a daily sales invoice backlog report. The cash manager and receivables manager would both review the report. The invoicing manager estimates that the cost of producing the report would be $50 per day, or $13,500 per year.

Expected value of loss: Lapin computed the value of possible loss without this control. It assumed that an average invoice is $500. The maximum backlog is two full days of invoices at 100 invoices per day without the control. Lapin's cost of funds is 10 percent. Therefore, the cost of the backlog if ignored for an entire year is $10,000, computed as follows:

$$[(\$500 \times 100 \text{ invoices per day}) \times 2 \text{ days}] \times 10\% = \$10,000$$

Conclusion: Implementation of the control would actually cost the firm $3,500 ($13,500 - $10,000 = $3,500).

In this case the control does not make economic sense the way Lapin designed it. However, an astute manager might look at this problem and try to find a way to reduce the cost without compromising the control's effectiveness. For example, why not decrease the report frequency to weekly rather than daily? Another possibility would be to prepare a streamlined version each day, but distribute it only if the backlog exceeds a predetermined level. That's called an exception report.

PERSONNEL

Of all the internal controls available, both the best and the worst is people. Employees to whom the responsibility of maintaining control procedures is delegated can either make them work or cause exposure to actually increase. The best way to ensure proper maintenance of the control system is to emphasize its importance. Some companies even include specific control objectives in employee job descriptions and as part of their performance reviews.

Competency

All employees assigned to do a particular job must demonstrate the ability to execute that job. This may sound obvious, but it is a rule that is often broken. I've seen the president of a client company hire the children of his largest clients. The parents suddenly thrust the kids into jobs for which they had no training. However, they were given the salary and authority appropriate as if they had that training.

Nobody was happy—not the kids, nor their client/parents, nor the other employees who had to work their way up without the benefit of such nepotism. The president's theory was that the parents were such good clients that they would make up whatever loss the kids created.

Unqualified employees represent a risk even though they may not steal from the company. They know so little that they won't be of any use in maintaining the firm's system of internal accounting control. They represent a weak link just begging to be exploited.

Education and Training

Many positions require specific levels of education and training. Most companies establish the education and training levels for specific positions. The hiring process should verify that candidates indeed have the education and backgrounds they claim.

Some managers feel that it's an insult to request college transcripts, talk with prior employers, and ask candidates technical questions to verify their command of the skills required on the job. However, not doing so breaches the manager's responsibility to the employer. Law enforcement professionals frequently cite such failure as reasons their next victims hire repeat offenders.

Experience

Here's another obvious but often overlooked fact: People assigned the oversight of any control procedure must

- Understand the nature of the procedure.
- Know how the control works.
- Realize the most likely ways to perpetrate abuses.

People responsible for maintaining particular controls need to watch for abuses. Internal controls and those who maintain them must be one step ahead of those who may try to subvert the system. Awareness of potential abuses comes only with experience. Employees with little or no experience can be taken advantage of by others possessing greater familiarity with the system.

Check each candidate's employment record carefully. Record the results of these reviews and keep them in the employee's personnel file. Probe into any unexplained gaps. The candidate might be trying to hide a termination for cause or even a prison stretch for embezzlement.

Authorization Control

Authority to approve company transactions is a symbol of one's status in the organization. It says that the company trusts you and your judgment. The higher the dollar amount of someone's authorization limit, the greater the status.

Yet this control won't work unless you maintain an up-to-date list of employees' authorization responsibilities and limits. Verify all transactions against the documents reviewed before you give authorization. This ensures that the control is working. Some companies require formal control of authorization procedures. They list all personnel who authorize specific transactions, their dollar limits, and specimen signatures. As people leave the firm or the authorities change, update the list. Make sure those responsible for checking proper authorizations know of any changes.

As a final check, these control-conscious companies make spot reviews of transactions requiring authorization. They verify that the right person made the authorization and appropriately reviewed the transaction.

Bonding

Many jobs—particularly in the finance area—either involve handling money or provide an opportunity to handle money. Carrying a fidelity bond on each employee who has access to the firm's liquid assets provides insurance against theft, negligence, and other compromises that could place the firm at risk of loss. Some companies get a group rate on their fidelity bonds. They often don't bond particular individuals—instead, they bond all employees.

CONTROLLING SALES

Sales is the first aspect of internal accounting control most people think of. After all, we're dealing with cash. If we're selling on account, the system must properly record the sale and establish an asset (the receivable) to be paid at a future date. The three issues our control system focuses on are

- Unrecorded sales • Unissued sales receipts • Credit vouchers

Unrecorded Sales

Owners of retail establishments have nightmares about unrecorded sales. That's why they put in so many hours—to create a presence of authority. They're right. Management supervision is probably the best deterrent to an employee's failing to record a sale and pocketing the money. Another, less exhaustive way is to match cash register totals with totals from prenumbered sales tickets and the daily cash count.

If inventory suddenly drops at a rate that is inconsistent with recorded sales, there may be some *unrecorded* sales. "Shoppers" are another method larger companies use to track point-of-sale performance. These are employees of the firm who make purchases only to look for violations of company policy.

Today, a company doesn't even have to be all that large to employ shoppers. Several "shopping" companies will shop your stores for you and submit performance reports. A less expensive alternative is to hire someone whom you know (but who is unknown to your sales clerks) to perform this service.

Unissued Sales Receipts

Why would clerks deliberately fail to issue a sales ticket or receipt with a purchase? They don't record the *next* sale but can give a valid sales ticket to the customer and pocket the money. The sale never took place according to company records. The customer is happy because he or she received a valid sales slip.

The best defense against unissued sales tickets is the customers themselves. Most demand a receipt with their purchases in case they have to return an item. Place signs at the store's sales counter reminding customers:

- It's company policy to provide a sales slip with each purchase.
- Refunds or returns require a sales slip.

Another safeguard is to use prenumbered consecutive sales tickets in duplicate. The original goes to the customer, and the copy goes in the daily sales report (you *do* have a daily sales report, don't you?). Someone other than the sales staff audits the sales tickets to verify that the numbers are in sequence and that any missing tickets are properly accounted for.

Returning stolen merchandise

Anyone owning a retail establishment understands the cost and headaches associated with shoplifters. If that isn't enough, how about *buying back* your own stolen merchandise for cash? Valid sales slips in the hands of shoplifters provide the vehicle. The perpetrators bring back the stolen merchandise with a completed sales slip. The store exchanges cash for the stolen merchandise.

Credit Vouchers

Also called credit memos, these are valuable slips of paper. Both retail stores and companies that run a receivables system use these documents to credit a customer's account, or sometimes to issue a refund check. Most companies require approval by an authorized signatory depending on the size of the credit granted.

Separate the custodians and writers of credit memos from the check-writing function and from posting accounts receivable. That way defrauding the company requires collusion.

Additionally, consecutively number the credit vouchers themselves. Make a third party responsible for tracking any missing numbers.

Accounts Receivable

Three things concern management regarding control of accounts receivable:

- The receivable assets are properly recorded.
- Payments are properly recorded.
- The receivables actually exist.

Recording Accounts Receivable

One of the best ways to ensure proper recording of receivables is to separate the sales function from accounting. Without such separation, an inside party can "sell" merchandise to someone outside the firm and not record the sale or the receivable.

Invoicing is the primary control over receivables. Track the mechanism that converts sales information to an invoice and transfers that to the accounts receivable subledger, then to the general ledger. Make sure duties are adequately separated.

Additionally, compute total daily sales. That balance should be exactly equal to

- Cash sales
- Plus customer credit purchases (debits) to accounts receivables
- Less credit memos to accounts receivables

Another control over receivables is periodic reporting to management. Review such reports for things like

- Excessive aging
- Growth beyond the company's working capital projections
- Shrinkage beyond the bank's collateral requirement
- Excessive write-offs

Receiving Payments

Create a solid separation of duties between those who receive customer payments and those who post them to the accounts receivable ledger. Many firms route mail containing customer payments directly to someone outside accounting. That person

- Logs the checks received • Prepares the bank deposit
- Copies the checks (optional, though many firms insist on it)
- Prepares a package for Accounts Receivable that contains the invoice stubs, check copies, and check receipt log

With this method, bank deposit of payment checks isn't slowed by the more time-consuming accounting operations. Further, there's less chance that someone will misappropriate a customer payment and not record it in the accounts receivable ledger.

Lapping Checks

Check lapping is a common way of embezzling customer payments going into accounts receivable. Here's how it works:

- A/R clerk misappropriates customer A's payment.
- When the embezzler receives customer B's payment, he or she applies it to the balance in customer A's account.
- When customer C's payment is received, it gets applied to the balance in customer B's account, and on and on.

How do we control lapping? Conduct spot checks of account balances for customers you know have paid. If the transaction history doesn't reflect the payment, something may be wrong.

Don't make the existence of a control mechanism a secret. It's part of the deterrent. However, don't make the actual control procedures common knowledge either. For every control there's always someone with enough time and cleverness to circumvent it.

Verifying existence of receivables

Banks have a particular interest in verifying the existence of accounts receivable. Often companies use receivables for collateral. Someone independent of the A/R function should conduct this control. This person selects a representative sample of the receivables customers. The customers chosen for the test receive a written request for verification that the balance stated in the confirming letter is indeed the correct balance they owe.

Too many responses claiming an amount different from what appears on the company's books signal an internal control problem. It may not necessarily be fraud or unauthorized conversion of assets. The answer may be something simple (but irritating) like a delay in processing customer payment receipts through the A/R system.

By the way, make sure the responses *don't* go back to someone in the A/R department.

Balancing ledgers

Make sure the receivables subledger matches the accounts receivable balance in the general ledger. If it doesn't, at minimum you have an accounting problem. A good policy is to post all transactions in each subledger to the general ledger every day. Then take a balance of both the G/L accounts and the subledgers and make sure they agree.

That way, if there's a problem, you can isolate it immediately and probably identify the incorrect batch.

PAYROLL

Fictitious employees provide one method of breaching payroll system controls. Another is the time paid hourly employees. Most common breaches of payroll occur when a naive company designs its control system in such a way as to make collusion unnecessary to pay a fictitious employee.

The best control procedures for payroll involve common sense. Here are a few of them.

Reviewing the Payroll List

Someone independent of payroll but who knows each employee reviews every payroll list. The reviewer identifies any employees he or she doesn't know.

Reviewing the Timekeeping and Piecework Reports

Someone with knowledge of who worked what hours reviews the timekeeping reports. The firm determines hourly payroll from this record. The reviewer looks for employees with incorrect hours worked. Companies that pay for piecework conduct the same type of review from the production records. Match these against the computations for individuals receiving piecework payment.

Tracking Payroll

Another control is to reconcile the total payroll amount from one payroll period to another. Explain changes resulting from terminations, vacations, overtime, bonuses, and new hires. If changes can't be explained, it is possible that someone is receiving a paycheck who shouldn't be.

ACCOUNTS PAYABLE

The A/P system should be one of the most closely monitored areas of the company from a control standpoint. However, too many businesses overlook the obvious when they establish their payment controls. Instead, they focus on the receivables system or on petty cash—two sources of liquid cash.

The best control measures for the payables system involve separation of responsibilities. We want to be sure that if someone wants to abuse the A/P system for his or her own benefit, that person can't do it alone. Beyond that, there are deterrents and ways to discover fraud *after the fact*. However, if two people in the right jobs intend to defraud the company using A/P system, there's not much we can do to stop them.

The accounts payable system exposes you to such illegal acts as insertion of nonexistent vendors and submitting false invoices. Additionally, vendors' invoices can be doctored to reflect a larger balance than is actually due. An intermediary receives the payment checks from the company and cashes them. The vendor gets paid the correct amount, and the perpetrators pocket the difference.

Separating Duties

This is the best way to maintain proper internal controls in the payables department. We want separate people and independently monitored controls for:

- payment authorization
- disbursement
- accounting

That makes perpetration of a fraud require collusion between at least two people.

Accounts Payable Responsibilities

Assignment of your A/P responsibilities doesn't require an army of people. That's often not possible for small businesses. Instead, follow the rule that no single person has authority to

- Enter payables • Sign checks • Disburse money
- Reconcile the checking account

You can safely combine some of these responsibilities as long as there's an *independent* control to act as a deterrent to fraud. It's almost like saying, We trust you, but if you breach that trust, we'll find out immediately.

In the following list of A/P duties, notice that no single person has complete control over authorization, disbursement, or accounting.

Accounting

The accounting staff enters invoices into the A/P system. They review receiving documents and purchase orders to determine the accuracy of the invoices. Some firms require an authorized signatory to sign the receiver and invoice before it is entered prior to entry into the A/P system. This action prevents vendors from sending invoices for purchases that were never ordered, that never arrived, or on which there's a dispute.

Disbursement

The disbursement officer acts as the authorized signatory on all A/P checks. Often this person is the controller, treasurer, or CFO. He or she reviews and approves the invoice package and payment check prior to disbursement. Many companies designate the signature on the check as approval of a disbursement.

Custody of the signature plate but not the check stock serves as another disbursement control. That prevents someone from writing and signing a check without proper authorization.

Custody

Two documents in the A/P system require independent custody:

- Prenumbered check stock • The check register

Use prenumbered check stock issued and controlled by someone independent of the entire A/P function. Return all damaged or voided checks to the check stock custodian. Log the check numbers. Account for all gaps in the numbering sequence. Record voids or damaged checks in the register. Place the actual check stock in safekeeping or destroy it under the payment officer's supervision. This prevents people from just taking a check or two and writing it to themselves.

Canceling invoices

Smart managers cancel paid invoices with a PAID stamp. Others actually perforate invoices to eliminate the possibility of future use.

Prenumbered purchase orders

Prenumbered P.O.s identify specific orders. The A/P staff matches these with invoices before entering them into the payment queue. Someone independent of the purchasing and A/P function maintains control over the P.O. stock. Account for gaps in the numbering sequence.

A/P performance statistics

Routine reporting of A/P balances acts as a control mechanism. It ensures that company policies regarding payment times and discounts taken are being followed. It allows management to keep an eye on which vendors get the company's business. Many companies track such A/P performance statistics as

- Average aging on A/P balances
- Specific vendor balances
- Discounts taken and missed
- Cash required in the next month to stay current

Management review

Qualified and independent personnel perform regular reviews of the A/P system. Anyone inside the company who knows the various ways the A/P system might be abused and is independent from its function can do this check. Focus the review on compliance with the system of internal accounting controls and with management policy toward accounts payable.

Agreement among all ledgers

One important control over A/P is the agreement among all three points in the system:

- Vendor account cards   • A/P subledger
- Accounts payable account in the general ledger

Have someone independent of the A/P system document and review this balancing each month. If any of the three doesn't match the other two, there's a problem. Figure 14-2 demonstrates one way to reconcile these accounts.

INVENTORY

The control system for inventory focuses on monitoring its flow throughout the firm. Companies that have ragged documentation of inventory movement from raw materials to work in process to finished goods leave themselves open to pilferage. Poor inventory control gives people the impression that no one would know the difference if they took something.

Maintaining Records

The cost accounting system needs documentation of inventory movement anyway. The added benefit is that we know where our inventory items have gone. If they're not where the accounting system says they should be, a problem exists.

Figure 14-2
A/P Account Reconciliation

Vendor Acct. #	Vendor Name	Balance Due
100	Jones	$400
200	Andrew	300
300	Tobby	500
400	Maggie	400
	Total vendor balances	$1,600
	A/P subledger balances	1,600
	Difference	$0
	G/L balance in A/P	1,600
	Difference	0

Many manufacturing firms have a rule on the shop floor regarding inventory: It doesn't move without a work in process sheet. This policy forces all material movement throughout the manufacturing process to be accounted for.

Physical Inventory

We identified physical inventories in Chapter 10 as a time-consuming but necessary exercise to compute cost of goods sold. They also serve as a deterrent to pilferage. There's only one way to verify that goods are where the accounting system says they are—by physically going to the warehouse and looking at them. Often we find that goods were moved to another location, were sold, or just disappeared.

Make sure that those to whom you assign the task of conducting the physical inventory don't work in the warehouse. Doing otherwise is like allowing the fox to guard the hen house.

Using Prenumbered Receivers

Many companies insist on prenumbering all receiving documents used to confirm receipt of goods. They require these *receivers* before authorizing the entry of an invoice into the A/P system. Just as with the company check stock, someone independent of the receiving function issues and logs the prenumbered receivers. This person also accounts for all gaps in numbering sequence. The numbering sequence allows us to tie an invoice to a specific item received.

INTERNAL CONTROL OF CASH

Cash is the most liquid asset a company has. We've already identified the cash controls associated with receivables and payables. The only other major source of cash exposure for most companies is the investment account.

Many firms make short-term investments of excess cash. Be sure there is adequate separation of the investment function and the recording of each transaction. Otherwise, embezzlement of the often large sums involved might not be discovered until it's too late.

The person responsible for investing the firm's cash must have the appropriate qualifications as well as the firm's authorization. The board gives formal authorization to engage in *specific types of securities transactions.* Most companies do this through a resolution usually recorded in the board minutes. The investment officer must be clear about what securities transactions the board has authorized. Any others require further board approval.

Personal Accounts

It's not a good idea to allow your investment officer to have a personal trading account at the same brokerage firm the company uses. There is a risk that profitable trades might be channeled away from the firm's account. If you do allow it, make sure that someone in the company independent of the investment function reviews the person's personal account statements. If the investment officer views that as an invasion of privacy, tell him or her to take the account to another brokerage firm not used by the company.

Establishing Dual Control

We want two people involved in the company's investments. One executes the trades; the other receives the brokerage confirmations. The same dual control should exist with cash transfers. One person does the transfers, and an independent person confirms them. Still another independent person in the accounting department records them.

Reconciling Cash Accounts

Regardless of whether they're brokerage accounts or checking accounts, reconcile all cash accounts monthly. The account statements should go *unopened* to someone independent of the transaction's execution. That person performs the reconciliation and resolves any open items. Someone independent of the transaction function reviews the reconciliation.

Controlling Petty Cash

Many firms have elaborate systems of checks and balances, vouchers, reconciliations of receipts, dual control of the cash box—you name it—to protect petty cash funds usually valued at less than $1,000. We want the controls used for petty cash to match the risk of loss.

Here are the most effective petty cash controls used by small businesses.

Recording vouchers

Vouchers go into the petty cash box whenever money goes out. That's how we keep track of why funds left petty cash. The sum of the cash plus the vouchers at any point in time should be the standard petty cash box balance.

The vouchers enter the accounting system when the petty cash fund is replenished. The accounting entry is

Expense accounts as documented by the vouchers	X	
Petty Cash		X

When the box is replenished, the accounting entry goes like this:

Petty Cash	X	
Cash in Bank		X

Make sure you have a written policy regarding the balance of the petty cash box.

Reconciling petty cash

Reconcile the petty cash fund periodically by someone independent of the function. Do the reconciliation in writing and maintain it in a file.

Establishing the amount

Keep the petty cash amount as low as possible. The more money involved, the more controls you'll need. Use petty cash only for very small transactions. Employees should not ask for petty cash advances to fund business expenses. That's what expense reimbursement is for.

Practically, however, small businesses employ people who do not have the means to fund the company's business expenses. In these cases, it's usually better to draft an expense advance check than to dip into the petty cash box.

Identifying Problem Signals

The problem signals listed in Figure 14-3 probably don't mean much by themselves. However, an accumulation of several identifies potential control problems associated with cash.

Figure 14-3
Cash Alarms

- Cash indicators such as the quick ratio, inventory turnover, and profit margin suggest a better cash position than is actually present.

- The company keeps excessive balances in bank accounts.

- The firm is often surprised by cash inflows and outflows.

- The firm engages in emergency borrowing.

- Short-term investment yields are lower than market.

- The company maintains more bank accounts than are necessary.

- Bank accounts are not routinely reconciled by someone independent of the cash transactions.

- The company's banking relationships are poor.

BEATING THE SYSTEM

No system of internal controls is foolproof. If it were, it would be so expensive and cumbersome to operate that no work would get done. The trick is to match the cost of controls against both the risk and the expense of a potential loss. A determined individual can beat the system for a time. Under controlled circumstances, we'll take that risk.

Figure 14-4 shows some of the more common ways management shoots itself in the foot with control systems.

Figure 14-4
Ways to Beat the System and Their Solutions

1. Failure to separate uncomplementary duties such as check writing and reconciliation of the checking account. The check writer is then free to write himself a check and forge the signature.

2. Failure to require personnel in sensitive areas such as receivables and payables to take a vacation. Or, if management does require this, the person's work is left untouched until he or she returns. Such failures don't stop frauds like lapping the receivables system.

3. Failure to cancel paid invoices. This opens the door for the same invoice being put through the system again.

4. Failure to control and safeguard inventory. Without accurate inventory counts and security for valuable inventory, the possibility of misappropriation exists. Further, the amount of the loss may never be known. Periodic physical inventories help identify unexplained shrinkage. Strict control of the warehouse also provides a deterrent against pilferage.

5. Sending wire transfer confirmations back to the person who ordered them. Confirmations should go to someone independent of the wire order. This ensures independent verification that the confirm is matched to the properly recorded entry.

6. Failure to verify new employees' backgrounds. In this age of litigation, honest references from past employers are almost impossible to get. Yet a diligent search usually uncovers the most obvious lies.

INTERNAL CONTROL CHECKLIST

The following Internal Control Checklist was reprinted from *The Cash Management Handbook* by Christopher R. Malburg, copyright 1992, with permission of the publisher, Prentice-Hall, a division of Simon & Schuster, Englewood Cliffs, NJ. Use it to conduct a review of the most vulnerable areas of your own company.

Figure 14-5

Date:

Internal Control Points

Control Point	Acceptable Yes/No	Workpaper Reference	Comments

I. Overall control environment:

   A. Is management's awareness of the importance of the control system appropriate?

   B. Does management stress the importance of internal control and compliance with procedures?

   C. Are personnel assigned tasks using appropriate policies?

   D. Does the accounting system provide means to identify, classify, record, and report cash transactions?

   E. Does the control environment:

      1. Segregate responsibilities appropriately?

      2. Record transactions correctly?

      3. Build checks and balances into the system?

II. Treasury policy manual:

   A. Does a treasury operations policy manual exist?

   B. Is it kept current?

   C. Is it adequate for the purposes of policy control?

III. Employee controls:

   A. Are there procedures to verify employee competency?

   B. Are there procedures to verify employee experience?

   C. Are employees' adequately trained?

   D. Are employees' bonded?

   E. Are authorization responsibilities listed?

   F. Are employees required to take annual vacations? While on vacations, are their jobs done by other employees?

   G. Are uncomplementary duties not executed by any single individual?

Control Point	Acceptable Yes/No	Workpaper Reference	Comments

H. Are employees with family ties prevented from sharing uncomplimentary duties?

I. Are employees held accountable for their work?

IV. Bank accounts:

    A. Are authorized signatories designated with due diligence?

    B. Are account reconciliations done regularly by personnel independent of the bank account? Are bank statements received directly by the person doing the bank reconciliation? Are the reconciliations reviewed by a qualified appropriate independent person?

    C. Is the number of accounts appropriate for the firm?

    D. Are compensating balances managed?

V. Funds inflows and deposits:

    A. Are cash receipts listed by the person who opens the mail?

    B. Are over-the-counter cash receipts compared against register tapes and a count of sales tickets?

    C. Does the bank confirm deposits directly to someone independent of the cash deposit function?

    D. Does the bank alert the cash manager to incoming wires? Are they recorded properly?

    E. Are cash receipts managed according to policy?

VI. Fund outflow:

    A. Are checks prenumbered and accounted for by someone independent of the disbursement function?

    B. Are custodianship of checks, check writing, authorization, signature, and accounting all done by separate people?

    C. Is there an appropriate disbursement approval and authorization process in place? Is it followed?

    D. Does the bank confirm with independent of the wire transfer function prior to sending out a wire?

Control Point	Acceptable Yes/No	Workpaper Reference	Comments

E. Are invoices marked "PAID" so they cannot be used again?

F. Is the signature plate controlled by someone independent of the disbursement and check stock custodianship?

G. Are checks sent out promptly after signature by someone independent of the check function?

VII. Petty cash:

A. Is the petty cash fund adequately controlled?

B. Are vouchers used for disbursement?

C. Are periodic reconciliations of the petty cash fund conducted by someone independent of the task?

D. Is the petty cash fund appropriate in size?

E. Is the fund kept in an appropriately safe place?

VIII. Trade credit:

A. Is there an appropriate trade credit policy?

B. Is the credit manager qualified for the job?

C. Do formalized credit authorization limits exist for all customers?

D. Are there credit authorization guidelines?

E. Are credit decisions reviewed by management?

F. Does a timely and accurate communication link exist between order entry, A/R, and the credit manager?

IX. Investments:

A. Is there a formalized investment policy?

B. Are investment securities of the type specified by management policy?

C. Do the investment maturities fit the current cash flow plan?

D. Do the returns of the portfolio warrant the risks?

Control Point	Acceptable Yes/No	Workpaper Reference	Comments

    E.   Are brokers' statements reconciled to the G/L and the investments ledger by someone independent of the function?

    F.   Do employees have personal accounts at brokerage firms used by the company?

    G.   Are brokerage confirmations sent directly to someone independent of the investment function?

    H.   Is collateral sufficient to secure positions?

    I.   Is the physical possession of investment securities appropriately safeguarded?

    J.   Are periodic inventory counts made of the securities portfolio?

    K.   Are securities registered in the company's name?

X. Financing:

    A.   Do nonroutine financing activities carry the approval of a board resolution?

    B.   Is the person authorized to negotiate financing

       transactions qualified?

    C.   Are terms of the financing in accordance with board authorization? Do they violate any restrictive covenants already in place?

    D.   Are documents with intrinsic value properly controlled and

       accounted for?

    E.   Are financing documents signed by authorized officers of the firm?

    F.   Are securities records properly maintained?

XI. Accounts receivable:

    A.   Does the A/R subledger tie to the general ledger?

    B.   Is there proper control of invoices? Are gaps in the invoice numbering sequence accounted for?

    C.   Is there a reliable method to ensure that all invoices are posted to the A/R subledger and the general ledger?

Control Point	Acceptable Yes/No	Workpaper Reference	Comments

D. Are receivables statistics computed and monitored?

E. Is there an effective control procedure for credit memos?

F. Are collections managed and aggressively pursued?

G. Are monthly statements sent to all customers?

H. Is there proper approval for all accounts that are written off?

XII. Accounts payable:

A. Is the disbursement officer independent from the accounting function?

B. Are purchase orders matched with receiving reports prior to authorization of an invoice for payment?

C. Are A/P statistics computed and monitored?

D. Does the A/P subledger tie to the general ledger?

E. Are trade discounts taken?

XIII.

Cash projections:

A. Are cash projections regularly made?

B. Is the cash projection integrated into the overall business plan?

C. Are projected receipts and disbursements compared against the plan, with differences explained?

XIV. Interest rate risk:

A. Have interest rate risk limits been established by the Board?

B. Is there a mechanism in place to measure and control interest rate risk?

XV. Insurance:

A. Are insurance reviews done periodically?

B. Are insurance claims analyses done periodically?

C. Is insurance coverage adequate?

Chapter 15

Monthly Financial Results

OVERVIEW

Chapter 15 shows how to extract financial performance information from the accounting system. It provides the reporting tools we'll use to keep track of the company's profitability. Included here are the standard financial statements such as the balance sheet, income statement and statement of changes in working capital. However, Chapter 15 takes the use of these standard statements a step further and discusses how to use monthly performance reports in conjunction with the firm's business plan. Monthly comparison of actual with planned performance creates focused, results-oriented analysis.

OBJECTIVES OF FINANCIAL REPORTING

The financial reports generated by our accounting system represent the end result of all this effort. Our objective is to use these statements, reports, analyses, and historical records to manage the company's profit. Further, the financial reporting system provides access to historical trends as well as monthly trends. We'll use these to make midcourse corrections.

The three most important aspects of the monthly financial reporting system are

- Accuracy • Timeliness • Consistency

Accurate Financial Results

Credibility is the most important attribute of our monthly financial reporting system. When the accounting department publishes the monthly financial results, there should be no question as to their accuracy. We want the company to base its operating decisions on information provided by the monthly reporting system. If we do not have confidence in the numbers, the effort and resulting reports are of little use.

Using the three-step process to guarantee accuracy

Accurate financial reporting doesn't happen just because we put all the right numbers in the right places and added them correctly. Nobody is that lucky. After all, every month, the accounting system generates hundreds of numbers. You need to verify that each belongs in the general ledger account in which it appears.

Three steps when combined and religiously followed can guarantee consistent accuracy of your monthly financial reporting system. Here they are:

1. *Account reconciliation.* Where possible, reconcile important general ledger accounts against outside sources. For example, certainly the book balance in the checking account(s) must reconcile with that of the bank's. However, if we carry this reconciliation process further into such accounts as sales revenue, cost of goods sold, accounts receivable and payable, and notes payable, we reduce the possibility of material error. Such errors embarrass those who make them and diminish the credibility of the monthly financial reports.

2. *Foot, crossfoot, and reference.* Footing is an accountant's way of saying that he or she added a column of numbers down. Crossfooting means adding a row of numbers across. Make sure that you check all accounting information by footing and crossfooting it. This may sound silly to some, but most professional accountants write a small "*f*" or "*cf*" under a column or after a row whose total they have just checked.

   Columns should add down and add across. For example, suppose the income statement presents three months of a quarter and the quarter total. Each month must foot down. Each row in all three months must crossfoot to the quarter total. The quarter total must foot down. The net income for all three months must crossfoot to equal the net income for the quarter. If they don't, something is wrong.

   Cross-checking numbers in the monthly reporting package is tedious. However, people reading these reports expect numbers that have the same name to be equal throughout the package. For example, the sales revenue reported on the income statement must equal the total sales revenue presented on an analysis report showing sales by product. Make sure that everywhere a number should *refer* to the same number somewhere else in the monthly results package, it does. Many professional accountants write an *"R"* after key numbers that are referred to elsewhere in the report.

3. *Conducting the eight-point test.* Once the monthly reporting package is complete, perform the following eight-point test to be sure it's free of the most obvious errors. Go right down the list, asking yourself these questions:

   1. Does the balance sheet balance?
   2. Does cash shown on the balance sheet equal cash on the statement of cash flows?
   3. Does the balance in the accounts receivable subledger equal accounts receivable in the general ledger and on the balance sheet?
   4. Does the balance in the accounts payable subledger equal accounts payable in the general ledger and on the balance sheet?

5. Does inventory as reported on the balance sheet equal ending inventory in the inventory control system?

6. Does cost of goods sold as reported on the income statement equal CGS computed as beginning inventory plus purchases less ending inventory?

7. Have all accruals and provisions been correctly computed?

8. Does the difference in retained earnings on the balance sheet between last period and this period equal net income or loss appearing on this period's income statement?

Timing

The second objective of the monthly reporting system after accuracy is that the reports be timely. Accounting reports must be relevant to be of any use. There's nothing less relevant than an outdated report. Complete and distribute the financial package just as soon after month-end as possible.

Most companies can close their books and have the financial results ready to go within two weeks after month-end. After that, the results lose their relevancy. Additionally, if we're going to make changes based on these reports, we want to do it sooner rather than later to get the maximum benefit. Late reports that identify a problem just prolong a money-losing situation.

Additionally, some companies with large staffs have a *flash report*. This is a projection of the month's likely financial results based on two or three weeks of actuals. It gives managers time to correct problems before it's too late and the month closes. We don't recommend this for small businesses. It takes too much time and involves too many people.

Using financial reports

A good way to be sure the content of the financial reporting package remains relevant is to talk periodically with the managers who receive it. Find out what they do with each report. Determine how it makes managing their particular departments easier. The answers will surprise you.

Many times managers take an accounting report and massage the numbers further to convert it into something that's really useful. Other times, the recipient just slides it under a pile of work without even looking at it.

Either situation is too expensive for small businesses. Make the information contained in the financial reporting package useful or stop generating it. A good example is idle labor costs. Older machinery has more downtime, and idle labor costs rise along with this downtime. Therefore, what the manager really needs is information on machinery downtime—the *cause* of increasing idle labor costs. Knowing this information places the manager in a position to do something to correct high idle labor costs resulting from machinery downtime. However, it was the symptom—labor costs—that the financial reporting system first identified as the problem. Astute managers took it from there.

Focus your financial reporting system on the types of decisions made using its information. Provide that exact information in the most useful format. Anything more than that is a waste of time and will just confuse already busy decision makers.

Making Your Monthly Reports Consistent

Your monthly financial package should present the same reports each month. It may be dull, but this isn't a novel we're writing. We want readers to become familiar with the format. After a few months they will be able to quickly find whatever numbers they need because they're always in the same place.

Maintain the same sequence of information in each month's financial package. A sample sequence might be

- Summary of key numbers
- Narrative explanation of financial highlights
- Comparative financial statements: balance sheet, income statement, and statement of cash flows all showing
  - Actual versus plan
  - Year-to-date actual versus YTD last year
- Supporting schedules and financial ratios
- Graphical analysis

Using the same format each month avoids confusion and promotes familiarity.

EXTRACTING FINANCIAL INFORMATION

Accounting information that flows to the monthly financial reports should have four characteristics:

- The data is accurate and reliable.
- The accounting system captures its information close to the source so that the data gets into the financial reports quickly and doesn't become subject to error or misinterpretation.
- All raw data is converted into useful information.
- The process of converting data to information is quick and easy.

This is where using an automated accounting system comes in handy. Not only does the system produce the company's routine monthly financial statements, it can also use the computer's power to extract and analyze raw data and convert it into useful information.

For example, the income statement shows total revenue for the month as one number for all products sold. However, the sales department could use a schedule showing which products were sold in which geographic locations. If the order entry system can't produce just the report required, chances are that the system can transfer the raw data to a simple spreadsheet program. Using this simple tool, conversion of data to information is fast and easy.

Our financial reporting system emphasizes efficiency. Small businesses can't afford an army of MBAs just to crunch numbers. For example, say it's important that we track actual idle labor time resulting from machinery being down. An easy way to capture and report that information is through a special general ledger account called *idle labor costs*. The cost accounting system captures these costs and posts them to the special account. Of course, the monthly financial reports probably don't separate the specific components of manufacturing labor. However, the accounting system can easily extract this information. Further, it's easy to compare actual monthly details with the plan. That's what makes the financial reporting system useful.

Creating Alternative Reporting Systems

What happens if the accounting system just cannot capture and report the necessary information? How do we get it? An inelegant solution is to create a manual log. Let's continue with the example of idle labor costs resulting from machine downtime. The log could include

- Name of employee • Labor rate • Date of downtime
- Number of hours idle • Total labor cost for the idle time

A personal computer in the production department could keep the log on a simple automated spreadsheet. Then the capturing and reporting mechanism becomes *semiautomated*. We can probably transfer the log to the computer on which the accounting system resides. The time this process takes should be minimal for everyone.

CREATING FINANCIAL REPORTS

Our monthly financial results always include a complete set of financial statements. If your firm has bank loans outstanding, the lending covenant may require periodic review of financial results. Investors usually ask to see the firm's financial statements as well. Additionally, future financing or even sale of the company requires a look at its financial history. Finally, the firm's management needs to study its monthly financial results.

Our financial reporting system produces three elementary financial statements. These are

- Balance sheet • Income statement • Statement of cash flows

Rather than take the time for an accounting lesson, we'll concentrate on how to make the most of each statement. If you can't create these statements or don't know how they work, please see a good elementary accounting book. The process isn't difficult if you've constructed your accounting system along the lines described in this book. Further, if you're using an automated accounting system, it creates the reports for you.

Relating Financial Statements

Financial statements tell a story. To do so, however, they must relate to one another. That is, all three statements interact. They each report on specific parts of the firm's financial performance during the operating period.

The accepted order of presentation for the financial statements is

- Balance sheet • Income statement • Statement of cash flows
- Statement of changes in working capital

This is a logical progression. Each statement builds on the previous one. Further, they all relate to one another.

Balance Sheet

The balance sheet shows the ending balance of each lead account in the general ledger. Balances appearing in the balance sheets are additive from period to period. That is, the ending balance in, say, accounts receivable in month 9 consists of

- Ending balance from month 8 • Plus credit sales during month 9
- Less payments received during month 9

The balance sheet is related to the income statement because income and expense items during the operating period change the balance sheet account balances. Cash paid out and received is certainly one of these.

The income statement presents credit sales as revenue. They increase accounts receivable on the balance sheet. Likewise, cash sales are a part of sales revenue on the income statement and also increase cash (but not receivables) on the balance sheet.

Invoices for expenses generally go into the accounts payable system for payment later. They hit the income statement as expenses and increase accounts payable on the balance sheet. Expense items that don't enter the A/P system but are paid during the current period increase expenses on the income statement and reduce cash on the balance sheet.

Income Statement

Our accounting system summarizes all the income and expenses during the period. The profit or loss then flows to the balance sheet. Corporations add it to (or subtract it from) retained earnings. For partnerships, profit or loss is added to (or subtracted from) partners' capital.

Note that the income statement does not recognize the cost of durable goods that are capitalized (depreciated over time). Instead, it shows only the amount of depreciation expense allocated to that period for capital items. The balance sheet links these expenses by showing accumulated depreciation for all capital assets. This equals the sum of all depreciation for all periods reported on the income statement.

Here's an easy way to verify the correct relationship of depreciation between the income statement and balance sheet:

1. Subtract current period accumulated depreciation (appearing on the balance sheet) from that of the prior period.
2. The answer should equal depreciation expense as reported on the income statement.

Note that the same relationship exists for amortization expenses of things like goodwill, prepaid rent, and points paid on loans.

Statement of Cash Flows

The statement of cash flows (SCF) identifies the increase or decrease in cash. We can trace it to the change in cash on the balance sheet. Here's how:

- Prior period ending cash on the balance sheet
- Plus or minus the increase or decrease in cash from the statement of cash flows
- Equals current period ending cash on the balance sheet

The statement of cash flows links the income statement and balance sheet. Since November 1987, under Statement 95, the Financial Accounting Standards Board (FASB) requires an SCF as part of a full set of financial statements. Small businesses that don't report their financials publicly are not bound by this requirement. However, the SCF does provide valuable information regarding disposition of cash, including

- The ability to generate future positive cash flows to sustain operations
- The capacity to pay dividends and return partners' invested capital
- The ability to meet loan requirements and attract future lenders
- Explanations for differences between net income and associated cash receipts and payments
- Cash and noncash investing and financing activities that result in changes to financial position

Most small businesses don't include a statement of cash flows in their monthly financial reporting package.

Statement of Changes in Financial Position

Results from both the balance sheet and the income statement come together on the statement of changes. Unlike the other financial reports, this one doesn't take operating information from within the accounting system. Instead, it *uses* the changes shown on the balance sheet and income statement. It's purely a mathematical product of the interaction between these two financial statements.

The most valuable presentation of a statement of changes for a small business is one that emphasizes the sources and uses of working capital.

Sources of working capital

The first step in determining all sources of working capital is to convert net income (which is not a cash number) from the income statement. Include in this section of the statement of changes anything from the income statement or balance sheet that is considered a source of working capital or cash. Add these items to net income to account for all sources of working capital. Here's a short list of the most common sources added to net income:

- Depreciation and amortization • Paydowns of accounts receivable
- Cash inflows from sale of capital stock, partnership contributions, and financing

- Reduction of inventory

Uses of working capital

Companies use working capital for such things as

- Paydown of loans • Purchase of capital equipment
- Prepayment of future expenses • Payment of accounts payable
- Tax payments • Payment of deposits

This part of the statement of changes focuses attention on the use of working capital throughout the reporting period. Note that it doesn't include routine operating expenses. These are already included in the net income number.

An easy way to make sure that all the sources and uses of working capital hit the statement of changes is to look at each line of the balance sheet. Make sure that the changes from last period to this period appear on the statement of changes.

Many analysts prefer the statement of changes to compute the ending cash balance. Do this at the bottom as follows:

Beginning cash + cash sources - cash uses = ending cash

Figure 15-1 shows a sample statement of changes. The first part of the statement demonstrates how working capital changed. The second part illustrates how cash changed. The third part reconciles working capital and cash.

Figure 15-1
Statement of Changes in Financial Position

China Diggers Corporation
Statement of Changes in Financial Position—Working Capital Basis
For the Period Ending December 31, 199X
($ in thousands)

Financial resources were provided:	
Working capital from operations:	
Net income	$ 50,000
Nonworking capital expenses:	
Depreciation	5,000
Amortization	3,000
Total working capital from operations	$58,000
Issuance of common stock	50,000
Proceeds from bond issue	25,000
Total financial resources provided	$133,000
Financial resources were applied:	
Purchased capital assets	10,000
Preferred shareholders' dividend	5,000
Common shareholders' dividend	15,000
Total financial resources applied	$30,000
Increase in working capital	$103,000

China Diggers Corporation
Statement of Changes in Financial Position—Cash Basis
For the Period Ending December 31, 199X
($ in thousands)

Increase (decrease) in current assets	
Cash	$20,000
Accounts receivable	50,000
Inventory	60,000
Total increase in current assets	$130,000
Increase (decrease) in current liabilities:	
Accounts payable	(20,000)
Accrued liabilities	(7,000)
Total decrease in current liabilities	($27,000)
Increase in working capital	$103,000
Financial resources provided:	
Cash from operations:	
Net income	$50,000
Depreciation	5,000
Amortization	3,000
Total working capital from operations	$58,000
Effects of changes in components of working capital on cash:	
Increase in accounts receivable	(50,000)
Increase in inventory	(60,000)
Decrease in accounts payable	(20,000)
Decrease in accrued liabilities	(7,000)
Cash from operations	($79,000)
Issuance of common stock	$50,000
Proceeds from bond issue	25,000
Total financial resources provided	($ 4,000)
Financial resources applied:	
Purchase of capital assets	$10,000
Preferred dividend	5,000
Common dividend	15,000
Total financial resources applied	$30,000
(Decrease) in cash	($34,000)
Cash as of 12-31-19X1	50,000
Cash as of 12-31-19X2	$16,000

China Diggers Corporation
Reconciliation between Working Capital
and Cash Basis
($ in thousands)

Increase in working capital	$103,000
Less: Increase in A/R	(50,000)
Less: Increase in inventory	(60,000)
Less: Decrease in A/P	(20,000)
Less: Decrease in accrued liabilities	(7,000)
Equals decrease in cash	$(34,000)

Notice the ending cash balance on cash basis statement. That number must tie with cash appearing on the balance sheet. When it does, it's a pretty good assumption that all three financial statements tie with each other. A complete month end reporting package follows this chapter and shows how this all works.

Supplemental Information

The financial statements and narrative explanations provide an overview of the company's monthly financial performance. Often the numbers appearing in the financials are compared with targets in the business plan. These serve as an indicator of progress toward realizing the company's plan.

Supplemental information, however, provides the background for much of what appears on the financial statements. We include here any information that clarifies conclusions drawn from the financial statements. Often charts and graphs speed understanding of trends that are forming.

Manufacturing and Production Expenses

The cost of goods sold number that appears on the income statement doesn't provide the detailed information needed to identify specific problems in the manufacturing and production departments. Many companies that are heavily involved in manufacturing and production depend on supplementary financial information every month.

A comparison of the cost of production for each item produced with standards established at the beginning of the year gets everyone's attention. Often the manufacturing information includes comparisons of actual and standard costs for

- Raw materials used • Materials prices • Labor used
- Cost of labor • Manufacturing overhead allocation

Such a comparative report for each item produced highlights any problems that could cause cost of goods sold to rise.

Profit Margins

Profit margins are related to each item's production costs. It does little good to control the cost of production if the company cannot maintain the targeted sale prices for each item. We want to know about any deteriorating profit margins while there's still time to correct them.

Production costs and sale prices work together to drive profit margins. The most useful reports on profit margins show the computation. That way it's easier to isolate problems. Figure 15-2 shows the format of such a report.

Figure 15-2
Report of profit margins

T-D-O Enterprises
Plumbing Fixtures Division
Report of Profit Margins
Period Ending July 30, 199X

Product	Sale Price ($)	Production Cost ($)	Gross Margin ($)	Gross Margin ($)	Planned Gross Margin ($)
Faucets	25.00	15.00	10.00	40	39
Drains	5.00	2.50	2.50	50	50
Stoppers	2.00	0.75	1.25	63	75
Aerators	4.75	2.25	2.50	53	51
Shower heads	60.00	20.00	40.00	67	63

This simple table focuses on specific problems with each product. Additionally, if trends appear, this type of information lends itself well to graphical presentation. For example, if the gross margin for stoppers shows a declining trend over the last six months, illustrate the problem using a graph that plots sale price, production costs and gross margin over that period.

Operating Expenses

Operating expenses fluctuate in line with sales levels and production expenses. That's why many companies like to see the operating expenses detailed in a supplementary report. The items on these reports don't appear on the income statement separately. Instead, they are combined with other expense items and reported as an aggregate total.

As we did with profit margins, managers often show the actual detailed operating expenses next to those in the business plan. That way it's easy to see those expenses that are climbing above the intended level.

Compliance with Lending Covenants

Banks and other lenders usually pay close attention to the terms of their loan agreements. Many contain specific financial benchmarks that the borrowing company must meet. Failure to comply can place the loan in default. That's why many companies produce a loan compliance report as part of their monthly reporting package. That way everyone sees potential problems while there's still time to fix them. Figure 15-3 shows a sample compliance report.

Figure 15-3
Loan Term Compliance Report

LP Partners, Ltd.
Loan Compliance Report
Period Ending July 30, 199X

Lending Term	Actual	Wells Fargo Requirements	Citicorp LOC Requirements
Current ratio	2.5	2.1	2.0
Times interest earned	5.6	3.0	6.0
Minimum working capital	$80,000	$75,000	$80,000
Total cash on hand	$15,000	$10,000	$10,000
Compensating balance—Wells	$25,000	$25,000	N/A
Compensating balance—Citicorp	$15,000	N/A	$15,000

Using this type of report, it's easy to spot problems. Notice that Citicorp requires interest earned to be 6 times. However, LP's actual for the month falls below that, at only 5.6 times. Technically, the company is in default on its loan terms. The bank could call the loan. In practice, that probably wouldn't happen. However, LP must secure a *written* waiver of the default from the bank. Then it must correct the problem.

Key Performance Indices

Different companies rely on different specific pieces of information to run their business. Additionally, their financial stability has a great deal to do with what's viewed as important enough to include in the monthly financial reporting package.

For example, companies in a cash bind pay attention to specific cash flow indicators, such as

- Accounts receivable aging
- Roll rates for accounts receivable
- Aging of accounts payable
- Certain asset ratios

Accounts receivable aging

In Chapter 7 we discussed ways of tracking receivables. The most common report used to accomplish this is the aging report. This shows all the accounts and where they stand in terms of elapsed time since the purchase.

Additionally, many companies focus on their largest accounts. For these they run special aging reports detailing the purchases and payments over the last month. The theory is that saving one account that makes up, say, 5 percent of total receivables from default is worth the time taken from twenty other accounts that combined are only 1 percent of the total.

Rolling receivables

Companies that manage their receivables often look at the *rate* at which accounts roll from one aging bucket to another. Over time they get a feel for the percentage of each bucket that won't pay during a given month and instead rolls into the next aging bucket. Figure 15-4 shows a sample receivables roll rate report.

Figure 15-4
Receivables Roll Rate

Standard LP Corporation
Analysis of Accounts Receivable Roll Rates
Period Ending July 30, 199X

Aging Bucket	Current to 30 Days	30 to 60 Days	60 to 90 Days	90 to 120 Days	120 Days to Write-off	Total
Current	$34,532					$34,532
30 days		$18,762				18,762
60 days			$7,963			7,963
90 days				$3,672		3,672
120 days					$1,643	1,643
	$34,532	$18,762	$7,963	$3,672	$1,643	$66,572

This report illustrates the dollars that rolled from each aging bucket during the month of July. Using this report the company can track results of their collection efforts.

Accounts receivable turnover

Many companies watch the velocity of payment of receivables and their replacement with new purchases. We call this *accounts receivable turnover*. Receivables should turn as fast as possible. That means that the company finances less of its customers' business. Here's the equation:

$$\text{Receivable turnover} = \frac{\text{total revenue}}{\text{average accounts receivables}}$$

Performance indicators

Many companies have special indicators that mean something special about their financial performance. The first of these is *return on assets*. This tells the earnings of a company's assets. If that number isn't higher than the rate obtained from investing the same funds (assuming the same amount of risk), then there's no point in remaining in business. Here's the equation:

$$\text{Return on assets} = \frac{\text{income before interest and taxes}}{\text{total assets}}$$

The second measure is income per employee. Small businesses can't afford unproductive employees. The income from their work must exceed their cost. Otherwise, the company is overstaffed. Many firms measure this statistic regularly to track productivity. Here's the equation:

$$\text{Income per employee} = \frac{\text{net income}}{\text{total number of employees}}$$

One of the most watched numbers for companies with inventory is its turnover. This index tells something about product demand. Ideally, inventory stays in the warehouse for just a short time before it's shipped to a customer. Here's how to compute inventory turnover:

$$\text{Inventory turnover} = \frac{\text{cost of goods sold}}{\text{average inventory}}$$

INTEGRATING ACTUAL WITH PLANNED RESULTS

Prepare your monthly financial reporting package using these guidelines:

- Keep the number of reports as small as possible.
- Highlight exceptions or deviations.
- Highlight significant progress toward goals.
- Keep the effort to produce the package minimal.
- Make sure the right people get the information they need to make decisions.
- Emphasize control over the company's financial operations.

Creating Comparative Statements

The financial reporting package must provide reference points to show the progress being made. The best way is to compare actual results with the firm's business plan. That way readers can easily spot deviations. Additionally, it's often useful to compare actuals with the prior month and year-to-date figures with YTD results from the same period of the previous year. Here are the most common comparisons:

- Current month actual versus current month plan
- Current month YTD actual versus current month YTD plan
- Current month actual versus last month actual
- Current month YTD versus last year YTD

Running Rate

Often companies like to ask, At this rate, how does the year-end look? One way to compute this is by extrapolating a running rate. This simply projects the current results forward to year-end. It's done using a ratio between actual results for the current YTD period and the number of months left in the year.

For example, say that in the ninth month our YTD sales of corkscrews were $3,000,000. At that rate, how many should we sell for the year? Here's the equation:

$$\text{Annualized sales} = \frac{\$3,000,000}{9} = \frac{x}{12}$$

$$\text{Annualized sales} = \$4,000,000$$

If the business plan calls for sales of $5,000,000, there's a problem. However, at least we've discovered it in time to act.

Creating the Monthly Reporting Package

Your monthly financial results package should include only the information needed to run the company. Beyond that, extraneous information isn't needed and just wastes everyone's time. Figure 15-5 (pages 252 - 259) shows one company's sample monthly report.

Figure 15-5

MTH Enterprises
Summary of Key Financial Information
for the Period Ending July 30, 199X

| | JULY B(W) | | | YTD ACTL B(W) | | | |
	JULY	JUNE	JUNE	YTD ACTUAL	YTD PLAN	YTD PLAN
TOTAL SALES	$1,043,754	$1,043,195	$559	$9,573,010	$9,079,206	$493,804
COST OF GOODS SOLD	128,325	121,876	(6,449)	4,207,674	3,994,014	(213,660)
GROSS MARGIN	$915,429	$921,319	($5,890)	$5,365,336	$5,085,192	$280,144
TOTAL EXPENSES	500,443	533,162	32,718	1,635,872	1,547,452	(88,420)
INCOME BEFORE DEBT SERVICE	$414,986	$388,157	$26,828	$3,729,464	$3,537,740	$191,724
DEBT SERVICE & OTHER ITEMS	282,600	211,800	(70,800)	635,400	847,800	212,400
NET INCOME BEFORE TAXES	$132,386	$176,357	($43,972)	$3,094,064	$2,689,940	$404,124
CASH	$1,855,639	$1,207,016	$648,623	$1,855,639	$1,800,000	$55,639
ACCOUNTS RECEIVABLE	159,981	180,000	20,019	159,981	167,000	(7,019)
WEIGHTED AVERAGE AGING OF A/R	31	33	2	33	30	-3
INVENTORY	96,420	125,000	28,580	$125,000	155,000	30,000
DAYS OF INVENTORY ON HAND	23	27	4	27	25	-2
INVENTORY TURNOVER RATE	13	10	3	10	13	-3
ACCOUNTS PAYABLE	136,060	155,000	(18,940)	$155,000	135,000	20,000
A/P AGING	59	62	-3	62	65	-3
A/P TURNOVER RATE	5	6	-1	5.6	6	-0.4

MTH Enterprises
Comparative Balance Sheet
as of July 30, 199X
Current B(W)

	JULY	JUNE	PRIOR MONTH
CURRENT ASSETS:			
CASH	$1,855,639	$1,207,016	$648,623
ACCOUNTS RECEIVABLE	159,981	180,000	(20,019)
INTEREST RECEIVABLE	559	0	559
INVENTORY	96,420	125,000	(28,580)
TOTAL CURRENT ASSETS	$2,112,599	$1,512,016	$600,583
PROPERTY, PLANT, & EQUIPMENT:			
MACHINERY AND EQUIPMENT	1,380,600	1,380,600	0
FURNITURE AND FIXTURES	140,000	40,000	100,000
LEASEHOLD IMPROVEMENTS	129,854	129,854	0
SUBTOTAL PP&E	$1,650,454	$1,550,454	$100,000
ACCUMULATED DEPRECIATION	(38,956)	(25,971)	(12,985)
PROPERTY, PLANT, & EQUIPMENT (NET)	$1,611,498	$1,524,483	$87,015
OTHER ASSETS:			
DEPOSITS	18,826	18,826	0
GOODWILL	773,760	773,760	0
LESS ACCUM. AMORTIZATION GOODWILL	(133,032)	(88,688)	(44,344)
ORGANIZATION FEES	200,000	200,000	0
LESS ACCUM. AMORTIZATION ORG. FEES	(120,000)	(80,000)	(40,000)
TOTAL OTHER ASSETS	$739,554	$823,898	($84,344)
TOTAL ASSETS	$4,463,651	$3,860,397	$603,254
CURRENT LIABILITIES:			
ACCOUNTS PAYABLE	$136,060	$155,000	$18,940
ACCRUED COMMISSIONS	28,355	0	(28,355)
PAYROLL TAXES PAYABLE	217	0	(217)
SALES TAXES PAYABLE	188	0	(188)
TOTAL CURRENT LIABILITIES	$164,820	$155,000	($9,820)
BANK NOTE	960,000	720,000	(240,000)
BONDS PAYABLE	840,000	630,000	(210,000)
SHAREHOLDERS' EQUITY:			
COMMON STOCK	761,048	750,000	(11,048)
RETAINED EARNINGS	1,737,783	1,605,397	(132,386)
TOTAL SHAREHOLDERS' EQUITY	$2,498,831	$2,355,397	($143,434)
TOTAL LIAB. & S/H EQUITY	$4,463,651	$3,860,397	($603,254)

MTH Enterprises
Income Statement
for the Period Ending July 30, 199X

	JULY B(W) JULY	YTD ACTL B(W) JUNE	JUNE	YTD ACTUAL	YTD PLAN	YTD PLAN
SALES						
SALES—SWITCH PLATES	$865,321	$835,102	$30,219	$9,156,782	$8,678,420	$478,362
SALES—CONDUIT	42,761	35,762	6,999	84,810	79,193	5,617
SALES—CABLE WINCHES	135,672	172,331	(36,659)	331,418	321,593	9,825
TOTAL SALES	$1,043,754	$1,043,195	$559	$9,573,010	$9,079,206	$493,804
COST OF GOODS SOLD	128,325	121,876	(6,449)	4,207,674	3,994,014	(213,660)
GROSS MARGIN	$915,429	$921,319	($5,890)	$5,365,336	$5,085,192	$280,144
OPERATING EXPENSES						
ADVERTISING	3,057	2,578	(479)	9,170	8,733	(437)
AUTO AND TRUCK EXP.	42,893	43,538	645	126,783	119,535	(7,248)
DEPRECIATION	12,985	11,985	(1,000)	38,956	38,956	0
AMORT. OF GOODWILL	44,344	41,386	(2,958)	133,032	133,032	0
AMORT. OF ORG. FEES	40,000	36,000	(4,000)	121,687	120,000	(1,687)
LEGAL AND ACCOUNTING	27,813	25,684	(2,129)	83,440	73,456	(9,984)
LICENSES	2,382	3,589	1,207	7,302	6,954	(348)
OFFICE SUPPLIES	20,145	21,152	1,007	63,457	60,435	(3,022)
SALES SALARIES	39,809	41,799	1,990	127,932	119,427	(8,505)
SALES EXPENSE	4,230	4,441	212	13,325	14,681	1,356
SALARIES—EXEC & OFFICE	153,859	183,582	29,723	568,371	521,559	(46,812)
PAYROLL TAXES	21,503	22,578	1,075	67,734	64,509	(3,225)
RENT	40,553	42,581	2,028	123,868	121,659	(2,209)
ENTERTAINMENT	4,055	4,258	203	12,773	13,168	395
TRAVEL	15,234	15,996	762	47,987	45,702	(2,285)
TELEPHONE	19,876	23,924	4,048	65,785	63,467	(2,318)
UTILITIES	7,705	8,090	385	24,271	22,179	(2,092)
TOTAL INDIRECT EXPENSES	$500,443	$533,162	$32,718	$1,635,872	$1,547,452	($88,420)
INCOME BEFORE DEBT SERVICE	$414,986	$388,157	$26,828	$3,729,464	$3,537,740	$191,724
INT. EXP. FROM DEBT SERVICE	318,600	247,800	(70,800)	743,400	955,800	212,400
NET INCOME FROM LEASING CO.	36,000	36,000	0	108,000	108,000	0
PROFIT BEFORE TAXES	$132,386	$176,357	($43,972)	$3,094,064	$2,689,940	$404,124

MTH Enterprises
Statement of Changes in Financial Position
for Period Ending July 30, 199X

	JULY
SOURCES OF CASH:	
PROFIT BEFORE TAXES	$132,386
ADD DEPREC. (INDRCT.)	12,985
ADD AMORT. OF GOODWILL	44,344
ADD AMORT. OF ORG. FEES	40,000
CAPITAL STOCK	11,048
ACCOUNTS RECEIVABLE	20,019
INTEREST RECEIVABLE	(559)
INVENTORY	28,580
BANK NOTE	240,000
BOND ISSUANCE	210,000
SOURCES OF WKING CAPITAL	$738,803
USES OF CASH:	
PROP., PLANT & EQUIP.	100,000
ACCOUNTS PAYABLE	18,940
ACCR. COMM. PAYABLE	(28,355)
PAYROLL TAXES PAYABLE	(217)
SALES TAXES PAYABLE	(188)
PAYDOWN OF BANK NOTE	0
BOND RETIREMENT	0
USES OF WORKING CAPITAL	$90,180
INCR (DECR) IN CASH	$648,623
CASH AT BEGINNING OF YEAR	$1,207,016
PLUS CASH SOURCES	738,803
LESS CASH USES	90,180
CASH AT END OF PERIOD	$1,855,639

MTH Enterprises
Statement of Cash Flows
for the Month Ended July 30, 199X
Increase (Decrease) in Cash

	JULY
Cash flows from operating activities:	
Cash received from customers	$1,063,773
Cash paid to suppliers and employees	(493,598)
Interest paid	(318,600)
Income taxes paid	0
Other receipts (payments)	36,000
Net cash provided by operating activities	$287,575
Cash flows from investing activities:	
Proceeds from sale of assets	0
Payments for purchase of equipment	(100,000)
Payments for purchase of real estate	0
Net cash used in investment activities	($100,000)
Cash flows from financing activities:	
Net increase in short-term credit	240,000
Proceeds from common stock issuance	11,048
Proceeds from bond issuance	210,000
Payment of long-term debt	0
Payment of dividends	0
Net cash provided by financing activities	$461,048
Effect of exchange rate changes on cash	0
Net increase in cash	$648,623
Cash at beginning of month	1,207,016
Cash at end of month	$1,855,639

Reconiliation of Net Income to
Net Cash Provided by Operating
Activities

Net income	$132,386
Adjustments to reconcile net income to net cash provided by operating activities:	
Depreciation and amortization	97,329
Decrease in accounts receivable	20,019
Increase in interest receivable	(559)
Decrease in inventory	28,580
Decrease in accounts payable	(18,940)
Increase in accrued commissions	28,355
Increase in taxes payable	405
Net cash provided by operating activities	$287,575

Computation of Cash Received
from Customers and Cash Paid
to Suppliers and Employees

Cash received from customers:	
Revenues	$1,043,754
Decrease in accounts receivable	20,019
Cash received from customers	$1,063,773
Cash paid to suppliers and employees:	
Cost of sales	$128,325
General and administrative	403,114
Total operations requiring cash payments	531,439
Decrease in inventory	(28,580)
Decrease in accounts payable	18,940
Increase in accrued commissions	(28,355)
Increase in accrued interest receivable	559
Decrease in taxes payable	(405)
Cash paid to suppliers and employees	$493,598

MTH Enterprises
Management Ratio Report
July 30, 199X

CURRENT MONTH

ASSET RATIOS
1. CURRENT RATIO:
    EQUATION: CURRENT ASSETS ÷ CURRENT LIABILITIES

CURRENT ASSETS	$2,112,599
CURRENT LIABILITIES	164,820
CURRENT RATIO	12.82

2. QUICK RATIO:
    EQUATION: (CASH + MARKETABLE SECURITIES + ACCOUNTS RECEIVABLE) ÷ CURRENT
LIABILITIES

CASH	$1,855,639
MARKETABLE SECURITIES	0
ACCOUNTS RECEIVABLE	159,981
CURRENT LIABILITIES	164,820
QUICK RATIO	12.23

ACCOUNTS RECEIVABLE RATIOS
1. ACCOUNTS RECEIVABLE TURNOVER RATE
EQUATION: ANNUAL SALES ÷ AVERAGE ACCOUNTS RECEIVABLE BALANCES

ANNUAL SALES	12,525,048
AVERAGE A/R BALANCES	169,991
A/R TURNOVER RATE	73.7

2. AVERAGE COLLECTION PERIOD
EQUATION: ACCOUNTS RECEIVABLE ÷ (ANNUAL SALES ÷ 360)

ACCOUNTS RECEIVABLE	$159,981
ANNUAL SALES	12,525,048
AVG. COLLECTION PERIOD (DAYS)	5

3. AGING OF ACCOUNTS RECEIVABLE
EQUATION: SUM OF (WEIGHTED AVERAGE % OF EA. AGING BUCKET X # OF DAYS IN EACH BUCKET)

A/R BALANCES BY AGING BUCKET:	AMOUNT	WEIGHTING % IN BUCKET	AGING BUCKET WEIGHTING
CURRENT	$50,000	31%	0
30 DAYS	79,981	50%	15
60 DAYS	10,000	6%	4
90 DAYS	15,000	9%	8
120 DAYS	5,000	3%	4
TOTAL A/R	$159,981	100%	31

INVENTORY RATIOS

1. AVERAGE INVESTMENT PERIOD OF INVENTORY
EQUATION: PRESENT INVENTORY BALANCE ÷ (ANNUAL COST OF GOODS SOLD / 360)

PRESENT INVENTORY BALANCE	$96,420
ANNUAL COST OF GOODS SOLD	1,539,900
AVG INV. PERIOD OF INTY (DAYS)	23

2. INVENTORY TURNOVER RATE
EQUATION: ANNUAL COST OF GOODS SOLD ÷ AVERAGE INVENTORY BALANCE

ANNUAL COST OF GOODS SOLD	$1,462,512
AVERAGE INVENTORY BALANCE	110,710
INTY TURNOVER RATE (TIMES PER YEAR)	13

ACCOUNTS PAYABLE
1. AGING OF ACCOUNTS PAYABLE
EQUATION: SUM OF (WEIGHTED AVERAGE % OF EA. AGING BUCKET X # OF DAYS IN EACH BUCKET)

	AMOUNT	WEIGHTING % IN BUCKET	AGING BUCKET WEIGHTING
A/P BALANCES BY AGING BUCKET:			
CURRENT	$5,000	4%	0
30 DAYS	25,000	18%	6
60 DAYS	75,000	55%	33
90 DAYS	31,060	23%	21
120 DAYS	0	0%	0
TOTAL A/P	$136,060	100%	59

2. AVERAGE PAYMENT PERIOD
EQUATION: ACCOUNTS PAYABLE BALANCE ÷ (ANNUAL EXPENSES ÷ 360)

ACCOUNTS PAYABLE BALANCE	$155,000
ANNUAL EXPENSES	392,620
AVERAGE PAYMENT PERIOD (DAYS)	142

3. ACCOUNTS PAYABLE TURNOVER RATE
EQUATION: ANNUAL EXPENSES ÷ AVERAGE A/P BALANCE

ANNUAL EXPENSES	$392,620
AVERAGE A/P BALANCE	86,970
A/P TURNOVER RATE (TIMES/YEAR)	5

MTH Enterprises
Management Performance Report
July 30, 199X

	CURRENT MONTH	PRIOR MONTH	CURRENT B(W) PRIOR	YEAR TO DATE	CURRENT B(W) YTD	YEAR TO DATE TARGET	B(W) TARGET
CASH AND ASSETS							
CASH	$1,855,639	$1,207,016	$648,623	$1,855,639	$0	$500,000	$1,355,639
MARKETABLE SECURITIES	0	0	0	$0	0	$0	$0
ALL OTHER CASH ITEMS	0	0	0	$0	0	$0	$0
TOTAL CASH	$1,855,639	$1,207,016	$648,623	$1,855,639	$0	$500,000	$1,355,639
CURRENT RATIO	17.78	9.75	8.02	17.78	0.00	15.00	2.78
QUICK RATIO	17.19	8.95	8.24	17.19	0.00	12.00	5.19
ACCOUNTS RECEIVABLE							
ACCOUNTS RECEIVABLE TURNOVER RATE	73.68	12.00	61.68	73.68	0.00	15.00	58.68
A/R RECEIVABLE COLLECTION PERIOD	4.60	21.00	16.40	4.60	0.00	25.00	20.40
WEIGHTED AVERAGE A/R AGING	30.94	33.00	2.06	30.94	0.00	41.00	10.06
INVENTORY							
AVG INVESTMENT PERIOD OF INVENTORY	22.54	4.00	-18.54	22.54	0.00	30.00	7.46
INVENTORY TURNOVER RATE	13.21	135.00	-121.79	13.21	0.00	12.00	1.21
ACCOUNTS PAYABLE							
WEIGHTED AVERAGE A/P AGING	59.13	60.00	-0.87	59.13	0.00	11.00	48.13
AVERAGE PAYMENT PERIOD	142.12	3.00	139.12	142.12	0.00	11.00	131.12
A/P TURNOVER RATE	4.51	100.00	95.49	4.51	0.00	8.00	3.49
MANUFACTURING PERFORMANCE							
MATERIAL PRICE VARIANCE	(45,000)	20,000	(65,000)	(10,000)	(35,000)	0	(10,000)
LABOR PRICE VARIANCE	10,000	(500)	10,500	5,000	5,000	0	5,000
MFG. PRICE VARIANCE	(20,000)	10,000	(30,000)	0	(20,000)	0	0
SAFETY STOCK	10,000	10,000	0	10,000	0	15,000	5,000
STOCK OUT COSTS	0	500	500	1,000	1,000	5,000	4,000
FINANCIAL PERFORMANCE							
WORKING CAPITAL	2,793,717	1,357,016	1,947,779	2,793,717	N/A	2,500,000	293,717
SHORT TERM BORROWING	960,000	720,000	(240,000)	960,000	N/A	1,500,000	540,000
LONG TERM BORROWING	840,000	630,000	(210,000)	840,000	N/A	2,000,000	1,160,000
INTEREST EXPENSE	318,600	247,800	(70,800)	700,000	381,400	35,000	(665,000)
AGGREGATE INT. RATE ON INVESTMENTS	0.00%	0.00%	0.00%	0.00%	0.00%	0.00%	0.00%
AGGREGATE INTEREST RATE ON DEBT	12.00%	11.95%	-0.05%		-12.00%	12.00%	12.00%
LENDING COVENANTS (1)							
DEBT COVERAGE RATIO	0.42	0.71	-0.30	4.16	-3.75	2.00	2.16
RATIO OF DEBT TO NET WORTH	0.64	0.99	0.35	0.64	0.00	1.00	0.36
MINIMUM CASH BALANCE	$2,000,000	$2,000,000	$0	$2,000,000	N/A	$1,000,000	$1,000,000
COMPENSATING BALANCE	$100,000	$120,000	$20,000	$100,000	$0	$100,000	$0
OWNER'S EQUITY	$2,498,831	$2,355,397	$143,434	$2,498,831	$0	$2,500,000	($1,169)
OWNER'S DRAW	$0	$0	$0	$0	$0	$500,000	($500,000)

MTH Enterprises
Schedule of Receivables Aging
as of July 30, 199X

	CURRENT	30 DAYS	60 DAYS	90 DAYS	120 DAYS AND OVER	TOTAL
FORD MOTOR COMPANY	$25,398	$1,232	$848	$167	$33	$27,678
COHEN CORP.	34,267	0	1,235	56	78	35,636
DRAGON, LTD	10,596	0	2,135	200	66	12,997
IBM	5,432	506	468	0	0	6,406
Z,C & W, INC.	4,498	232	1,568	23	133	6,454
INACOMP	8,006	768	0	0	0	8,774
EDISON CO.	7,898	1,105	1,235	46	23	10,307
TRAULSON, INC.	1,578	2,258	1,567	46	97	5,546
HONDA OF AMERICA	1,322	31	2,156	32	32	3,573
ASHTON-TATE	3,393	268	3,158	101	21	6,941
S/T	$102,388	$6,400	$14,370	$671	$483	$124,312
OTHERS	25,597	1,600	6,428	1,730	315	35,669
TOTAL RECEIVABLES	$127,985	$8,000	$20,798	$2,401	$798	$159,981

MTH Enterprises
Schedule of Receivables Roll Rate
as of July 30, 199X

	CURRENT TO 30 DAYS	30 DAYS TO 60 DAYS	60 DAYS TO 90 DAYS	90 DAYS TO 120 DAYS	120 DAYS TO W/O	TOTAL
CURRENT	$28,978					$28,978
30 DAYS		$1,200				1,200
60 DAYS			$4,160			4,160
90 DAYS				$1,201		1,201
120 DAYS					$600	600
TOTAL RECEIVABLES ROLLED	$28,978	$1,200	$4,160	$1,201	$600	$36,139

Elapsed time from sale to invoice based on sample of 100 sales: 2.3 days
Invoice entry backlog averaged through the month: 26 invoices totaling $12,345
Internal deposit float from time of receipt to time of deposit: 1.75 days
Value of internal deposit float:

Receipts from customers:	$2,400,000	
divided by 31 days =	77,419	day
multiplied by internal deposit float	1.75	days
Value of internal deposit float	$135,483	
Annual cost of internal deposit float at weighted average cost of funds of 8% :	$10,839	

MTH Enterprises
Schedule of Payables Aging
as of July 30, 199X

	120 DAYS CURRENT	30 DAYS	60 DAYS	90 DAYS	AND OVER	TOTAL
CHINA EXCAVATORS, INC.	$4,521	$596	$945	$325	$0	$6,387
AUTUMN'S CUP CO.	5,657	500	1,538	23	0	7,718
SO. CAL EDISON	6,536	5,688	1,357	1008	0	14,589
CA SERVICE CORP.	15,656	2,135	466	0	0	18,257
CORPORATE SYSTEMS, INC.	205	565	323	237	235	1,565
SOFTWARE SYSTEMS, INC.	1,756	3,056	2,358	0	989	8,159
MORGAN/RATHER PARTNERS	2,356	1,578	232	0	0	4,166
GENERAL TELEPHONE	5,658	2,358	3,235	1235	0	12,486
SPACE PRODUCTS PARTNERS	11,568	4,566	1,638	0	1056	18,828
ART DIMENSIONS	15,687	2,358	658	1,972	168	20,843
TOP 10 PAYABLES	$69,600	$23,400	$12,750	$4,800	$2,448	$112,998
OTHER PAYABLES	17,400	1,600	2,250	1,200	612	23,062
	$87,000	$25,000	$15,000	$6,000	$3,060	$136,060

Discounts missed:	$5,677	
Discounts taken advantage of:	$23,538	

Chapter 16

Accounting for Profitability

OVERVIEW

Increased profitability is the most important byproduct of an efficient accounting system. Chapter 16 illustrates how to use key pieces of accounting information (such as cost of goods sold and production costs) to manage profitability.

SEPARATING THE COMPANY INTO SEGMENTS

Owners of small businesses sometimes find it particularly difficult to delegate responsibility to subordinates. They feel that since it's their money on the line, they should make all the decisions. Owners who maintain an iron grip on all decisions often unnecessarily limit the potential of their companies. Nobody has all the answers. That's part of what employees get paid for.

Regardless of a company's size, delegating responsibility requires identifying the specific area each manager oversees. Management action requires *segmenting* the firm into individual units. For example, manufacturing companies often segment the business into

- Production • Purchasing • Sales • Shipping • Accounting
- Finance • Personnel

A single individual is responsible for each area. Using this technique, top management doesn't have to oversee the details of each entity within the company. This saves time and usually provides for better decisions. Those involved in daily operations are closer to the issues and must live with their decisions. Therefore, they take complete responsibility.

If your company has several divisions, a likely point for segmenting the firm is first at the division level. The division manager has complete responsibility for that division. The manager then segments the division based on logical areas of responsibility.

Even if your company doesn't have formally separated operating divisions, segmentation often helps manage such logical breaks in the business as sales territories, departments, branch stores, and product lines.

Segmenting the business into specific areas of responsibility helps limit the number of things each manager controls. Suddenly managers have the time to thoroughly manage such things as planning and resource allocation. They can control and direct their particular segments. Further, they can coordinate their efforts with those of other managers.

Segmenting the business also allows the business plan to reach a level of detail needed by each operating unit. By comparing monthly performance with the plan for each segment, those responsible can make required corrections.

Profit Centers

Many companies break some parts of their firms into profit centers. A profit center is a business unit whose management is responsible for both revenues and costs. The firm evaluates the manager of a profit center on the profit made by that unit. For example, many firms designate product lines as profit centers. They have both revenues and costs such as manufacturing, sales expense, and overhead allocations.

Managing profit centers allows for specific planning of profit targets. If a profit center misses those targets, the company is in a position to judge the impact. That's how many companies decide to discontinue product lines or close down stores, branches, or sales territories.

Effects on the accounting system

Installation of profit centers requires an adjustment to the chart of accounts. The accounting system must capture all revenue and expense information *associated with each particular cost center.* The best way to accomplish this is through the chart of accounts.

Account numbering in the chart of accounts includes the profit center designation. For example, say our manufacturing operation has three profit centers:

- T-shirts: 001
- Dress shirts: 002
- Casual shirts: 003

All revenue and expense accounts have either a prefix or a suffix designating the profit center. Using this numbering sequence in the chart of accounts, the firm allocates all revenue and expense items to the correct profit center. That way it's easy to generate an income statement for each profit center. Of course, this increases the number of accounts in the chart of accounts. Now there must be a set of account numbers for each profit center, with just the prefix or suffix changed.

Most automated accounting systems allow for designation of profit centers in the chart of accounts. They also provide for individual reporting for each as well as for the firm as a consolidated whole. It's almost like keeping a set of books *within* a set of books.

The monthly reports used to control the performance of each profit center look like complete income statements. They detail all revenue and expense items. Often senior management likes to see the income statement for each profit center side by side with a consolidated total to which the statements crossfoot.

Investment Centers

Astute managers carefully track their return on major investments. They want to make sure profit meets the criteria originally planned. Many profit centers are investment centers as well. For example, say a real estate company invests in a new hotel. It's easy to identify the exact investment for computation of the company's return. Further, the firm may treat each of its hotels as a profit center.

Segments that are both profit centers *and* investment centers don't require any further designation beyond the original segment's prefix or suffix in the chart of account income and expense categories. However, segments designated as investment centers *within* profit centers require one more level of detail.

For example, say the T-shirt profit center just invested in a modern automated sewing line. The company wants to track the performance of its investment. However, at the same time, the line is a part of the T-shirt profit center. The solution is to add a suffix to each expense account item in the T-shirt profit center's expense accounts. The suffix designates the particular cost as belonging to the new automated sewing line. Cost account numbers for production line maintenance look like this: 001-450-020, where *001* is the prefix of the T-shirt profit center, *450* is the G/L account number for maintenance costs, and *020* is the suffix of the automated sewing line investment center.

The company computes return on investment for the automated sewing line by subtracting production costs accumulated for this particular investment center from the costs using the old system. Divide the annual savings by the amount invested in the line. The result is the return provided by this investment center.

Monthly investment center reports from the accounting system often include an abbreviated income statement.

Cost Centers

Just as the name implies, we measure the performance of cost centers by their ability to control costs and the quality of the services they provide. For example, some companies designate the manufacturing department as a cost center. They track all costs associated with that department using the accounting system.

Just as we developed a prefix in the account number used for profit centers in the chart of accounts, that's how we identify cost centers. However, most cost centers don't generate much revenue, so we don't usually include the income accounts.

Using the prefix number scheme to separate particular cost centers, the accounting system can produce a monthly cost summary for each. Managers compare these with the departmental business plan *that also separates the costs projected for each cost center.* That way the person responsible for maintaining performance of each cost center knows just how things are going.

IDENTIFYING UNPROFITABLE SEGMENTS

When we create profit centers within the company, we generate the ability to quantitatively evaluate each segment's performance. The accounting system provides the actual monthly performance numbers. The business plan also includes performance benchmarks for each segment.

With this information, we can determine those segments that are worth keeping and those that bark like the dogs they are.

Using Segment Profit Margin

The accounting system generates income statements for each profit center. Using this information, it's not difficult to compute profit margins for each segment. Figure 16-1 shows how one company does it.

Figure 16-1
Computation of Segment Profit Margin

Dooby Writing Instruments, Inc.
Segment Income and Expense
For the Period Ending June 30, 199X

	Entire Company	%	Pen & Ink Division	%	Pencil & Lead Division	%
Sales revenue	$1,000,000	100%	$600,000	100%	$400,000	100%
Cost of goods sold	600,000	60	450,000	75	150,000	38
Contribution margin	$400,000	40	$150,000	25	$250,000	62
Fixed costs traceable to product lines	150,000	15	90,000	15	60,000	15
Gross margin	$250,000	25	$60,000	10	$190,000	47
Fixed costs not assignable to segments	50,000	5	35,000	6	15,000	4
Income before tax	$200,000	20	$ 25,000	4	$175,000	43

Using the segmented income and expense comparison report, it's not difficult to tell that costs of the Pen & Ink Division make it much less of a performer than the Pencil & Lead Division. Additionally, management can focus on the problems. For Pen & Ink, cost of goods sold is too high, providing only a 25 percent contribution margin.

Discontinuing Segments

Business segments that don't show the required profits or that incur losses get discontinued. Smart managers with several business segments treat them as an investor treats a securities portfolio—they eliminate unprofitable trades. This periodic culling maintains only the most profitable segments in the company and discards those that do not meet management's criteria.

However, often there's a good reason for keeping an unprofitable segment. For example, one segment, though unprofitable, may round out the company's offering to its customers. Those customers might not buy the firm's profitable products if they could not get everything from one vendor.

Discontinuing Product Lines

Small business owners and managers often find it difficult to choose the product lines they offer. Formerly profitable lines sometimes change over time. Further, the discontinuation of one line may affect the sales of another. Therefore, we need to consider all aspects of the decision. Let's look at an example.

China Diggers Corporation offers three product lines to the earth moving industry:

- Super-deluxe bulldozer blades
- Medium industrial grade bulldozer blades
- Diamond edge additions to bulldozer blades

CDC's product line P&L's look like this:

China Diggers Corporation
Product Line P&L
Year ending 199X

	Total CDC	Super Deluxe Blades	Medium Industrial Blades	Diamond Edges
Sales	$1,000,000	$600,000	$100,000	$300,000
Cost of goods sold	520,000	350,000	70,000	100,000
Gross margin	$ 480,000	$250,000	$30,000	$200,000
Fixed costs traceable to each line	200,000	90,000	40,000	70,000
Common fixed costs	$100,000			
Operating income	$180,000	$160,000	($ 10,000)	$130,000

CDC's board thinks if it eliminated the medium industrial blade line, the $10,000 loss would go away. Therefore, the board reasoned, the company's annual income would rise by that same $10,000.

However, the controller asked two questions:

1. What else could the company do with the facilities and equipment now used to make the medium industrial blades?
2. How would elimination of that line affect sales for the remaining two product lines?

The board didn't have an answer for the first question, but formed a committee to look into it. However, the marketing director thought that two things would happen if the medium industrial line was discontinued:

- Sales of the super deluxe blades would rise 10 percent
- Sales of the diamond edges would *fall* by 25 percent because many customers for the medium blades upgraded with the diamond edge to make them last longer.

The controller took this information and did the following incremental analysis:

China Diggers Corporation
Forecast P&L Effects of Eliminating
Medium Industrial Blades
Year ending 199X

Elimination of the loss from the discontinued line	$10,000
Additional gross margin from increased sales of	
the super deluxe blades ($250,000 × 5%)	12,500
Forecast increase in operating income	$22,500
Decrease in operating income from sales decline	
of the diamond edges ($200,000 × 25%)	(50,000)
Forecast decrease in operating income	($27,500)

The controller found that the medium industrial blades constituted a *loss leader* for CDC. Eliminating this losing product line actually *decreased* profit by $27,500. However, the jury is still out until the board answers the question of an alternative use for the medium industrial facility. Perhaps CDC could rent out the space or use it in some other way that would net more than the $27,500 loss already computed.

RESPONSIBILITY ACCOUNTING FOR PROFIT

One spinoff of segmenting the company is the assignment of specific areas of responsibility to particular individuals. The method provides a standard of performance against which to measure responsible managers. That's what performance specialists mean by *responsibility accounting*.

Using the accounting system to monitor segment profitability requires three steps:

1. Each responsibility center must have benchmark numbers against which to compare actual performance. Usually these standards come from the departmental business plan. Choose them carefully. The benchmarks should be vital to helping the department and company as a whole achieve the goals set in the business plan.

2. The accounting system must capture specific performance information for each responsibility center. Further, the information captured must be

the same as that contained in the plan. If not, management spends too much time trying to convert it for comparison to planned numbers.

3. The accounting system must provide *timely* performance reports for each responsibility center. It makes no sense to go through the work of installing a profit control system only to negate its usefulness by producing late reports. These reports should compare the actual results with those in the plan. Additionally, the company should make no secret of the fact that it intends holding responsibility center managers accountable for the results of areas under their control.

Increasing Cooperation among Departments

Responsibility center managers should understand three things about the evaluation system:

- The method used to capture performance data
- Their authority to make the changes necessary to achieve their goals
- The standards used to judge performance

Managers in different responsibility centers won't allow another center to adversely affect their performance. Figure 16-2 illustrates the change a profit management system using responsibility centers brought.

Figure 16-2
Responsibility Centers at MTH Enterprises

Prior to installation of its profit management and evaluation system, MTH's managers suffered from uncoordinated efforts that helped one department while damaging another. Particularly irritating to the production manager were rush orders coming from the sales department at each month end. To meet these shipping requirements, Production incurred overtime and labor costs beyond those anticipated in the plan.

In March, management created responsibility centers in both the production and sales departments. That month the controller charged *Sales* for the added labor costs incurred by the normal month-end rush orders. This situation forced the sales manager to explain why *he* incurred such unplanned cost overruns. March was the last month Production received rush orders at month end. Instead, Sales parceled them throughout the month by planning customer calls better.

Organizing Responsibility Centers

Organize your responsibility centers just as you do your organization chart. The farther down on the responsibility center chart we go, the more detailed and specific the responsibilities. Figure 16-3 shows a chart of responsibility centers for a three-store clothing chain:

Figure 16-3
Responsibility Centers—Trixie's Fashion Enterprises

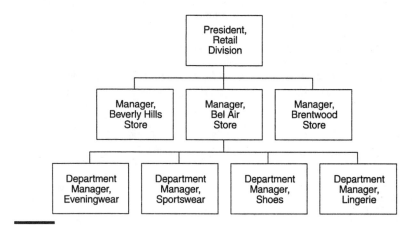

Note that each store is a separate responsibility center with its own income statement. Within each store, each of the four departments is a responsibility center as well. These also have their own monthly P&L reports. Using this technique, each manager knows his or her exact profit responsibilities. The business plan includes this level of detail for such income and expense items as

- Sales revenue • Cost of goods sold • Variable costs
- Fixed costs traceable to each responsibility center • Profit margin

Each line on every income statement adds to the next responsibility center like this:

- Evening + Sportswear + Shoes + Lingerie = Store P&L
- Beverly Hills + Bel Air + Brentwood = Retail Division
- Retail Division + Wholesale Division = Trixie Enterprises

USING RELEVANT INFORMATION

Most business decisions involve trade-offs between alternative courses of action. Scenarios of different revenues and expenses often cloud the issues. How many times do managers seeking to choose between two or more alternatives allow irrelevant information to creep into the process? Irrelevant revenues and costs are those that *do not* change regardless of the alternatives under consideration. They are irrelevant to the decision.

The only information relevant to a profit decision is information that provides an *incremental* difference between options. For example, say that Autumn Garden Tools runs a production facility in Darian. The Darian plant has fixed costs of

$11,000 a month consisting of depreciation, interest expense, and management salaries. Autumn must shut down the Darian plant for a month to retool. Costs of the engineering company to retool the Darian plant are $15,000. However, Autumn has the opportunity to rent a similar facility in a nearby town for that month. Net income from this production should be $7,000, and transport cost of miscellaneous tools to the new site is $1,000. Rent of the alternative facility is $2,000. What should Autumn do?

The answer is that Autumn comes out $4,000 ahead if it rents the facility and continues production. Here's how Autumn's controller conducted the incremental analysis:

	Don't Rent the Alternative Facitity	Rent the Alternative Facility	Incremental Benefit
Net income	$0	$7,000	$7,000
Costs and expenses:			
Fixed costs	(11,000)	(11,000)	0
Rent of facility	0	(2,000)	(2,000)
Transport of tools	0	(1,000)	(1,000)
Retooling costs	(15,000)	(15,000)	0
Income (loss)	($26,000)	($22,000)	$4,000

Notice that the two largest costs, the fixed costs and retooling, were irrelevant. That's because they don't change regardless of which alternative the firm chooses.

Make or Buy Decisions

Relevant costs enter into decisions regarding the use of company-owned manufacturing facilities to produce inventory. Often the cost of some parts or subassemblies is actually *lower* than what the company can make them for. However, you must factor out the irrelevant costs.

Let's continue with Autumn Garden Tools. The controller discovers that its Taiwan supplier can provide trowels for $3.50. However, it costs Autumn $4.90 to make them at the newly retooled Darian plant. Looks like a good deal, doesn't it? Autumn produces and sells 10,000 trowels a month. Here's how the controller figures production costs for these trowels:

Manufacturing costs:	
Direct materials	$10,000
Direct labor	12,500
Variable overhead cost	7,600
Fixed overhead cost	18,900
Total manufacturing cost for 10,00 units	$49,000
Cost per unit ($49,000 ÷ 10,000)	$4.90

Autumn's controller discovers that buying the trowels eliminates all direct materials and labor costs. Further, it removes $3,000 of variable overhead and $5,000 of the fixed overhead. Now the controller is getting excited. Then she decides to compute just the costs relevant to the analysis. They appear like this on the schedule:

	Make the Trowels	Buy the Trowels	Incremental Benefit
Direct materials	$10,000	$0	$10,000
Direct labor	12,500	0	12,500
Variable overhead	7,600	4,600	3,000
Fixed overhead	18,900	13,900	5,000
Purchase price of trowels @ $3.50		35,000	($35,000)
Total cost	$49,000	$53,500	($4,500)

Note that in this analysis—as so often happens in the real world—not all variable costs are incremental and some of the fixed costs are indeed incremental. Now it's more expensive to buy the trowels at the low price offered. The purchase decision's undoing is the portion of fixed overhead that remains regardless of who makes the trowels. Autumn continues making the trowels and saves the $54,000 per year ($4,500 × 12 = $54,000).

Accepting Special Terms

Small-business owners often wrestle with offers to buy at special terms. Buyers think they're doing the small company a favor by purchasing a significant part of its inventory. In exchange for this patronage, they demand a special price. These decisions also involve relevant and irrelevant costs.

Continuing with Autumn Garden Tools, let's assume that the same Taiwan vendor wants to buy Autumn's garden rakes for sale in that country. Autumn has the capacity to produce 10,000 garden rakes a month. However, it makes only 4,000, since that's all it can sell. Autumn makes the rakes for $3.00 each. Therefore, total monthly rake production cost is $12,000. Here's how Autumn's controller determines rake costs:

Manufacturing costs:	
Variable costs ($2.00 per rake × 4,000 rakes)	$8,000
Fixed costs	4,000
Total production costs	$12,000
Cost per rake ($12,000 ÷ 4,000)	$3.00

The Taiwan offer sounds interesting. The Taiwan company wants to buy 7,000 rakes a month and sell them under a private label. Since the sales territory is overseas, this won't affect Autumn's normal domestic sales. However, the offer includes a purchase price per rake of only $2.80. That's below Autumn's *produc-*

tion cost, reflects the controller. However, before Autumn rejects the offer, the controller analyzes the relevant costs:

	Domestic Sales	Domestic and Taiwan Sales	International Benefit
Regular sales at $5 per rake	$20,000	$20,000	$0
Taiwan order at $2.80 per rake		19,600	19,600
Manufacturing costs:			
Variable costs at $2 per rake	(8,000)	(14,000)	(6,000)
Fixed costs	(4,000)	(4,000)	0
Gross margin	$8,000	$21,600	$13,600

The Taiwan offer works even though it's below Autumn's normal production cost because fixed costs aren't relevant to the analysis. They remain regardless of how many units Autumn produces and sells. So it looks like a good deal. However, there are two points Autumn had better lock into the purchase contract:

1. The Taiwan company cannot under any circumstances market these rakes in the United States to Autumn's regular customers, thereby undercutting Autumn.

2. This is a confidential deal. The Taiwan company cannot disclose its price to Autumn's customers, who may demand a similar low price.

Opportunity Costs

Many analysts dismiss opportunity costs as irrelevant. After all, the company didn't choose that course of action, so how could it be relevant? That's a costly mistake. Most decisions involve benefits from other courses of action. They belong in the analysis.

Remember Autumn's make or buy analysis. From the facts it was apparent that Autumn should continue to make the trowels. However, let's change those facts just a little. Let's say that Autumn has an alternative use for the trowel production line. Without much change at all, Autumn could make small shovels and obtain a net profit of $10,000 a month. By continuing to make the trowels instead of buy them, Autumn incurs an opportunity cost. Now the analysis looks like this:

	Make the Trowels	Buy the Trowels	Incremental Benefit
Direct materials	$10,000	$0	$10,000
Direct labor	12,500	0	12,500
Variable overhead	7,600	4,600	3,000
Fixed overhead	18,900	13,900	5,000
Purchase price of trowels @ $3.50		35,000	($35,000)
Use trowel production line to make small shovels		(10,000)	10,000
Total cost	$49,000	$43,500	$5,500

Notice that the opportunity cost of using the trowel line for another product offsets the cost of purchasing trowels from the Taiwanese. Now the purchase option makes sense.

MAXIMIZING USE OF FACILITIES

For most small businesses, fixed costs don't change much regardless of the level of production or the number of hours the business stays open. That's why you see so many retailers extending their hours during economic downturns. The rent and other fixed costs like interest expense and property taxes don't change. That way they spread these fixed costs over a larger revenue volume. Profit margins increase for the company.

The only decision, then, when looking at more intensively utilizing facilities, is the *incremental* costs associated with staying open longer or adding more shifts. Such costs should stay proportionately the same as before. Labor expense may increase if you work the same people overtime rather than hiring more people. However, the lower *overhead cost per unit produced* falls to compensate for that.

The result is often that the company's profit expands by more intensively using its facilities.

DEALING WITH UNCERTAINTY

How many times has any business manager been 100 percent certain of the outcome of a decision? It doesn't happen very often. We take risk with the uncertain outcomes of our decisions every business day. The trick is to identify and quantify the risk and assess its probability. From there we can determine if the potential payoff warrants the risk.

Compartmentalizing Risk

Professionals compartmentalize a decision so that if they're wrong and it doesn't work out, the rest of the company doesn't experience a disaster. Assess the risk and outcome of a decision using these five points:

1. Identify the options under consideration—most decisions have several.

2. Define the possible outcomes of each option. Be sure to work these through to their logical conclusions. For example, in raising funds, one option is to get a bank loan. However, how does a future rise in interest rates affect that decision?

3. Identify the probability of the outcome for each option actually occurring. Rate these as highly probable, possible, or unlikely. If you multiply these probabilities by the outcome of an event (in dollars), you get the *expected value of the option's outcome*.

4. Assess the consequences of the option's not working out. If a given decision puts the company out of business, that's a consequence management isn't likely to accept regardless of the probability.

5. Assess the risk/reward tradeoff. For every risk, there's a reward. The larger the risk, the larger the potential reward must be to entice people. Make sure the potential payoff makes the risk acceptable.

Determining Risk

People unfamiliar with risk management techniques often don't know how to quantify it. The methods aren't difficult. Our purpose is to

- Quantify risk
- Adjust it to a point where the potential reward makes acceptance of the risk worthwhile
- Control the operation while it is in process so that the risk doesn't suddenly become unacceptable

Of course, small-business owners can't always control the risk they undertake. They're often too small to have that kind of clout. However, using this technique, at least we know what we're in for and we can make informed decisions. Figure 16-4 shows the concept of matching risk and reward.

Figure 16-4
Matching Risk with Reward

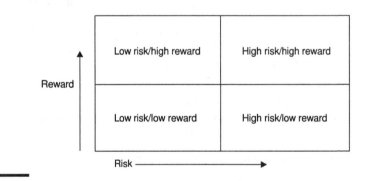

Many small businesses find themselves in the lower right quadrant of the risk/reward box. This is the lowest percentage decision. They're taking huge risk for little reward. Instead, increase the likelihood of winning by putting the decision in the upper left quadrant—low risk, high reward. Managers who leverage their money by borrowing the funds needed for capital projects do this.

Regardless of your business size, there are three analytical techniques you can use to quantify the risk of any decision. These are

- Multiple scenarios of an outcome
- Sensitivity analysis
- Simulation analysis

the example of the sales department that needed unit sales at midmonth to manage its progress toward each month-end target.

Timing plays another important role. The monitoring system should identify performance indicators that are critical to the rest of the business plan. For example, say the plan requires an increase in the line of credit to finance accounts receivable resulting from the sales plan. Without the increased credit line, the company cannot pay the vendors who supplied the raw materials needed to make the products.

Therefore, the monitoring system must provide a status report on such critical implementation items as the line of credit.

Identifying the effects of timing changes

Part of the plan monitoring system projects the impact of changes in timing. This task is easier if you put the plan schedules on an automated spreadsheet. Convert the timing change to specific quantitative shifts in the assumptions. Then run the planning model to determine how the changes affect key benchmarks needed to implement the plan.

There's often a cascade effect when one part of the plan changes. For example, watch what happens when sales goals lag their targets by a month or two:

1. *Accounts receivable*: We don't need the staff to handle the anticipated workload from increased sales for a month or two. However, the firm hired them in anticipation of the workload. Now they're on board and idle.

2. *Collateral*: Many companies secure loans with accounts receivable. The controller negotiated a loan in anticipation of the added receivables. Now the bank won't fund the needed draw until its collateral is up to the agreed level. However, the vendors demand payment. The company is headed for a cash crisis.

3. *Manufacturing*: The company has produced the goods specified in the sales plan. Now they just sit in the warehouse, gathering dust and eating up working capital.

4. *Raw material inventory*: Accounts payable rose as a result of the materials needed by Manufacturing. Some of this material is already in the finished goods that sit in the warehouse. However, the firm had not converted some of it to work in process before production slowed. If sales don't pick up and production resume, the company may sell the excess raw materials inventory at a loss just to get rid of it and generate some badly needed cash.

Monitoring systems with "what if" capabilities are invaluable for use in assessing possible options in response to deviations in the plan.

Units reported

The monitoring system must provide information in a form that managers can use in tracking and managing performance. Some measurements, such as finished goods inventory, require units. Other benchmarks in the plan, such as accounts receivable, make more sense in dollars. Still others, like sales volume, require measurement in both units and dollars. Make sure that the tracking system reports measurements the way managers need them. You don't want managers to have to go through extensive conversion computations just to use the monitoring reports.

Presenting the Results

Pay particular attention to the design of your plan monitoring reports. Tables are the best way to present most of the comparative information. That allows readers to see what actually occurred and compare it with what should have happened. Further, tables allow the system to make comparative computations for readers and point out deviations from the plan.

Graphs also provide a quick way to illustrate a trend or make a particular point. For example, let's say that Doobie International manufactures the tape cassettes used in professional recording studios. Doobie continues to hit its sales objectives. However, the margin by which sales exceed planned benchmarks each month is steadily decreasing. Shown as a downward-sloping graph, the trend is obvious. The implication is equally obvious—shortly Doobie's sales level is going to fall below the benchmarks by greater and greater degrees. Figure 17-1 makes this point. Notice how the line plotting actual performance trends down toward the level plan line. It looks as if sales will fall below the plan between the eighth and ninth months.

Figure 17-1

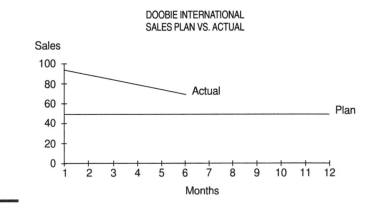

Pie charts are an effective method of showing the composition of a number. For example, say that Doobie wants to know what makes up the sales numbers in any particular month. Put the information in a pie chart. If you have the ability to cut out a slice, this provides a visual illustration of one particular component.

Most spreadsheet systems allow for pie charts. Many such systems also slice the pie at the touch of a button. Figure 17-2 shows Doobie's sales for the month of June.

Figure 17-2
Pie Chart

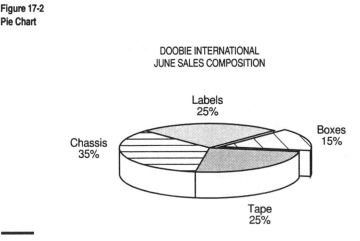

Chassis is the largest single sales component. However, perhaps boxes are the highest-margin product. Discussion in the financial results package may highlight this point.

CIRCULATING RESULTS

Your monitoring system should provide useful information, not just raw data. In many cases the readers draw conclusions as a result of the presentation's slant. That's what we want to a certain extent. However, the purpose of the monitoring system is *not* to persuade readers to accept the analyst's viewpoint. We want to give managers the exact information they need to track their areas of responsibility with the business plan. This usually means providing different pieces of information to different managers.

Tailoring Reports

Report formats vary depending on the needs of the readers. Not everyone on the monitoring system distribution list gets all the reports the system produces. Don't give this information to people without a need to see it. Additionally, let those receiving it know that this information is proprietary to the company and is *confidential.*

Therefore, tailor the monitoring reports to the specific needs of the recipients. If you don't, you run the risk of diminishing the importance of vital information because it's surrounded by less useful data. Further, the less sensitive information floating around the company, the better.

The planning team usually receives all of the monitoring system reports. Package this as

- Summary of monthly performance information
- Full set of comparative financial statements
- Information showing progress toward particular milestones on the implementation schedule
- All the special reports prepared for particular individuals that track their areas of responsibility

For example, the monthly reporting package that goes to the head of marketing might include the following:

- Summary of monthly performance—provides a quick overview of how the entire firm is doing
- Comparative income statement—supports the summary
- Milestone chart showing sales by product compared with the plan for this month, year-to-date, and this time last year, year-to-date—provides the specific goals for which the marketing department is responsible
- Detailed sales analysis by sales responsibility center such as territory and salesperson
- Inflow and outflow of balances into the accounts receivable system—shows how well the target market pays its bills
- Summary of A/R aging—shows the impact on cash flow from customers to whom the marketing department is selling
- Analysis of gross margin [(sales – cost of goods sold) / sales] by product for plan versus this month and year-to-date—demonstrates how product pricing ties with manufacturing costs to hit the all-important gross margin targets

CREATING THE REPORTS

Monthly progress reports of actual performance compared to plan are one of the most valuable tools in the business planning exercise. Some may complain that the program set forth here is too structured. That's the idea. We want a regular method of assessing the company's movement toward its planned goals. Management uses these monthly reports to make decisions regarding midcourse corrections.

With such usage and credibility, the business plan and the monitoring mechanism to ensure that it stays on course become tools. As management uses the plan, it often makes changes. The monitoring mechanism then reports these changes against actual performance.

Content of the Monitoring Reports

Include in the monthly financial results package only the information needed to run the company. Leave out all extraneous information—it just wastes everyone's time if it's not used. Figure 17-3 shows one company's sample monthly report.

Figure 17-3

PEACHES ENTERPRISES, LTD
Month of May 199X
Summary of company performance

	MAY ACTUAL	MAY PLAN	ACT'L B(W) PLAN	ACTUAL YTD	PLAN YTD	YTD ACT'L B(W) PLAN	YTD ACT'L LAST YEAR	MAY YTD B(W) LAST YR YTD
Revenue	$325,000	$315,000	$10,000	$1,357,000	$1,300,000	$57,000	$1,425,000	($68,000)
Cost of goods sold	173,000	155,000	(18,000)	732,000	700,000	(32,000)	775,000	43,000
Gross margin	$152,000	$160,000	($8,000)	$625,000	$600,000	$25,000	$650,000	($25,000)
Total expenses	111,435	105,900	(5,535)	605,675	567,500	(38,175)	636,967	31,292
Net income before tax	$40,565	$54,100	($13,535)	$19,325	$32,500	($13,175)	$13,033	$6,292
Dollars in inventory	$450,000	$455,000	$5,000	N/A	N/A	N/A	$500,000	$50,000
Units in inventory	15,000	14,000	(1,000)	N/A	N/A	N/A	30,000	15,000
Days of sales in inventory	15	20	5	N/A	N/A	N/A	22	7
Accounts receivable balance	$300,000	$275,000	($25,000)	N/A	N/A	N/A	$450,000	$150,000
Accounts receivable turnover	25	22	-3	N/A	N/A	N/A	36	11
Number of employees	26	28	2					
Direct labor costs	$25,000	$29,000	$4,000	$150,000	$174,000	$24,000	$180,000	$30,000
Total salary expenses	$32,000	$35,000	$3,000	$192,000	$210,000	$18,000	$250,000	$58,000
Cash balance	$50,000	$55,000	($5,000)	N/A	N/A	N/A	$40,000	$10,000
Available line of credit	$250,000	$250,000	$0	N/A	N/A	N/A	$200,000	$50,000

PEACHES ENTERPRISES, LTD
Month of May 199X
Comparative Income Statement

	MAY ACTUAL	MAY PLAN	ACT'L B(W) PLAN	ACTUAL YTD	PLAN YTD	YTD ACT'L B(W) PLAN	YTD ACT'L LAST YEAR	MAY YTD B(W) LAST YR YTD
SALES	$325,000	$315,000	$10,000	$1,357,000	$1,300,000	$57,000	$1,425,000	($68,000)
COST OF GOODS SOLD	173,000	155,000	(18,000)	732,000	700,000	(32,000)	775,000	43,000
GROSS MARGIN ($)	$152,000	$160,000	($8,000)	$625,000	$600,000	$25,000	$650,000	($25,000)
GROSS MARGIN (%)	47%	51%	-0.04	46%	46%	-0.00	46%	0.00
ADVERTISING	7,500	4,000	(3,500)	45,000	24,000	(21,000)	36,000	(9,000)
BAD DEBT EXPENSE	14,500	9,000	(5,500)	87,000	54,000	(33,000)	80,000	(7,000)
COMMISSION EXPENSE	26,500	25,000	(1,500)	159,000	150,000	(9,000)	142,000	(17,000)
DEPRECIATION:								
CORPORATE OFFICES	3,235	3,100	(135)	16,175	15,500	(675)	22,500	6,325
MACHINERY &								
EQUIPMENT	4,300	4,200	(100)	21,500	21,000	(500)	27,000	5,500
FURNITURE & FIXTURES	975	900	(75)	4,875	4,500	(375)	6,657	1,782
LEASEHOLD								
IMPROVEMENTS	1,750	1,800	50	8,750	9,000	250	11,100	2,350
INSURANCE	3,100	4,000	900	15,500	20,000	4,500	22,300	6,800
SALARIES & WAGES	33,575	36,000	2,425	167,875	180,000	12,125	184,060	16,185
PAYROLL TAXES	7,300	8,500	1,200	36,500	42,500	6,000	43,450	6,950
UTILITIES	6,100	6,500	400	30,500	32,500	2,000	40,900	10,400
TRAVEL & ENTERTAINMENT	2,600	2,900	300	13,000	14,500	1,500	21,000	8,000
TOTAL COSTS AND EXPENSES	$111,435	$105,900	($5,535)	$605,675	$567,500	($38,175)	$636,967	$31,292
NET INCOME BEFORE TAX	$40,565	$54,100	($13,535)	$19,325	$32,500	($13,175)	$13,033	$6,292
TAX ACCRUAL	17,000	13,000	(4,000)	7,730	13,000	5,270	5,213	(2,517)
NET INCOME	23,565	41,100	($17,535)	11,595	19,500	($7,905)	7,820	$3,775

PEACHES ENTERPRISES, LTD
Month of May 199X
Milestone Sales by Product
(Units sold)

	MAY ACTUAL	MAY PLAN	ACT'L B(W) PLAN	ACTUAL YTD	PLAN YTD	YTD ACT'L B(W) PLAN	YTD ACT'L LAST YEAR	MAY YTD B(W) LAST YR YTD
Blasting caps	267	260	7	1,335	1,300	35	1,200	135
Primacord (rolls)	153	150	3	765	750	15	2,150	(1,385)
Det. wire	75	100	-25	375	500	-125	1,650	(1,275)
Lead shields	226	200	26	1,130	1,000	130	500	630
Wireless ignition systems	67	60	7	335	300	35	300	35
High drive (40% dynamite)	51	75	-24	255	375	-120	600	(345)
Amonium nitrate	120	175	-55	600	875	-275	1,400	(800)
Magnesium pellets	199	200	-1	995	1,000	-5	750	245
Total units sold	1,158	1,220	-62	5,790	6,100	-310	8,550	(2,760)

PEACHES ENTERPRISES, LTD
May 199x
Accounts Receivable Flow

BEGINNING A/R BALANCE	$267,000
INCREASE TO A/R:	
CREDIT SALES 100	23,400
CREDIT SALES $100–500	76,875
CREDIT SALES $500–1,000	61,000
CREDIT SALES $1,000–5,000	55,000
CREDIT SALES >$5,000	10,000
TOTAL INCREASE TO A/R	$226,275
COLLECTIONS ON A/R BALANCES:	
CURRENT	83,250
30 DAYS	51,750
60 DAYS	39,756
90 DAYS	31,265
120 DAYS	8,345
OVER 120 DAYS	6,152
TOTAL COLLECTIONS	$220,518
ENDING A/R BALANCE	$272,757

PEACHES ENTERPRISES, LTD
May 199x
Summary of A/R Aging

	CURRENT MONTH	LAST MONTH	CURRENT B(W) LAST
CURRENT BALANCE	$114,356	$95,354	($19,002)
30 DAYS	40,687	64,595	23,908
60 DAYS	43,753	39,432	(4,321)
90 DAYS	36,535	19,786	(16,749)
120 DAYS	14,191	17,500	3,309
OVER 120 DAYS	23,235	30,333	7,098
	$272,757	$267,000	($5,757)

PEACHES ENTERPRISES, LTD
Month of May 199X
Analysis of Gross Margin by Product

	MAY ACTUAL	MAY PLAN	ACT'L B(W) PLAN	ACTUAL YTD	PLAN YTD	YTD ACT'L B(W) PLAN	YTD ACT'L LAST YEAR	MAY YTD B(W) LAST YR YTD
Margin analysis by product:								
Blasting caps:								
Gross revenue	$51,657	$50,689	$968	$142,000	$140,000	$2,000	$155,000	($13,000)
Cost of goods sold	30,410	27,656	(2,754)	119,833	28,500	(91,333)	70,900	(48,933)
Gross margin ($)	$21,247	$23,033	($1,786)	$22,167	$111,500	($89,333)	$84,100	($61,933)
Gross margin (%)	41%	45%	-4%	16%	80%	-64%	54%	-39%
Primacord (rolls)								
Gross revenue	$22,648	$17,689	$4,959	$80,000	$66,000	$14,000	$67,500	$12,500
Cost of goods sold	11,678	9,862	(1,816)	38,000	43,000	5,000	50,350	12,350
Gross margin ($)	$10,970	$7,827	$3,143	$42,000	$23,000	$19,000	$17,150	$24,850
Gross margin (%)	48%	44%	4%	53%	35%	18%	25%	27%
Detonation wire								
Gross revenue	$75,689	$70,658	$5,031	$420,000	$475,000	($55,000)	$483,000	($63,000)
Cost of goods sold	41,432	37,659	(3,773)	203,833	272,000	68,167	240,500	36,667
Gross margin ($)	$34,257	$32,999	$1,258	$216,167	$203,000	$13,167	$242,500	($26,333)
Gross margin (%)	45%	47%	-1%	51%	43%	9%	50%	1%
Lead shields								
Gross revenue	$27,965	$25,689	$2,276	$90,000	$67,000	$23,000	$75,500	$14,500
Cost of goods sold	14,356	13,598	(758)	40,000	43,000	3,000	51,250	11,250
Gross margin ($)	$13,609	$12,091	$1,518	$50,000	$24,000	$26,000	$24,250	$25,750
Gross margin (%)	49%	47%	2%	56%	36%	20%	32%	23%
Wireless ignition systems								
Gross revenue	$56,368	$53,689	$2,679	$200,000	$186,000	$14,000	$273,500	($73,500)
Cost of goods sold	27,659	20,689	(6,970)	148,833	163,000	14,167	145,250	(3,583)
Gross margin ($)	$28,709	$33,000	($4,291)	$51,167	$23,000	$28,167	$128,250	($77,083)
Gross margin (%)	51%	61%	-11%	26%	12%	13%	47%	-21%
High drive								
Gross revenue	$43,907	$41,398	$2,509	$195,000	$210,000	($15,000)	$175,000	$20,000
Cost of goods sold	26,879	27,986	1,107	85,000	78,000	(7,000)	110,000	25,000
Gross margin ($)	$17,028	$13,412	$3,616	$110,000	$132,000	($22,000)	$65,000	$45,000
Gross margin (%)	39%	32%	6%	56%	63%	-6%	37%	19%
Amonium nitrate								
Gross revenue	$36,898	$46,099	($9,201)	$165,000	$120,000	$45,000	$135,000	$30,000
Cost of goods sold	16,898	13,872	(3,026)	75,000	57,000	(18,000)	75,250	250
Gross margin ($)	$20,000	$32,227	($12,227)	$90,000	$63,000	$27,000	$59,750	$30,250
Gross margin (%)	54%	70%	-16%	55%	53%	2%	44%	10%
Magnesium pellets								
Gross revenue	$9,868	$9,089	$779	$65,000	$36,000	$29,000	$60,500	$4,500
Cost of goods sold	3,688	3,678	(10)	21,501	15,500	(6,001)	31,500	9,999
Gross margin ($)	$6,180	$5,411	$769	$43,499	$20,500	$22,999	$29,000	$14,499
Gross margin (%)	63%	60%	3%	67%	57%	10%	48%	19%
Total revenue	$325,000	$315,000	$10,000	$1,357,000	$1,300,000	$57,000	$1,425,000	($68,000)
less total cost of goods sold	173,000	155,000	(18,000)	732,000	700,000	(32,000)	775,000	43,000
Total gross margin ($)	$152,000	$160,000	($8,000)	$625,000	$600,000	$25,000	$650,000	($25,000)
Total gross margin (%)	47%	51%	-4%	46%	46%	-0%	46%	0%

Notice how the monitoring system reports only the parts of the company of interest to management. It purposely omitted the balance sheet and cash flow reports. However, in practice, the plan would normally contain these.

Timing of the Reports

Most small to medium-sized companies run their monitoring system at least monthly. Many firms conduct formal quarterly plan reviews. In that case the monitoring reports contain quarterly totals for both actual and plan.

Many companies conduct a midyear plan review. This is the most critical review. Think of it as halftime in a football game. Management assesses where the firm stands midway through its plan implementation. There's still time to correct deviations from the plan. Further, midyear is the time to incorporate into the plan new opportunities that surfaced in the last six months.

If your firm conducts an extensive midyear plan review, the monitoring system must produce two additional comparative reports:

- Midyear plan versus midyear actual year-to-date
- Midyear actual *annualized* versus total year plan

These two comparisons illustrate how the company is doing at midyear compared to plan and how the year will end up at this rate compared to the full-year plan.

Certainly the year-end reports from the monitoring system interest management. That's especially true when companies pay incentive bonuses for year-end performance. However, from a profit management standpoint, the year-end reports are less important—there's no time left to fix any problems.

CAPTURING INFORMATION

Design the monitoring system with the type of information and reports required in mind. You don't want to be in the position of needing information that's not readily available. Sometimes the implementation team needs information never before developed by the company. When that happens, you need procedures to capture the information, review it for accuracy, and put it into a format usable by the people who work with it.

Many people view data conversion for reporting purposes as busywork. However, companies that are serious about successfully implementing their business plan present the reason for this information frankly. Most people agree about its importance.

Techniques of Data Capture

Information captured by the performance monitoring system should have these attributes:

- It must be accurate and reliable.
- Raw data must easily convert into useful information.
- It must be available within the time frame required.

- It should be captured as close to the source as possible so that it doesn't pass through too many hands, wasting time and making it subject to error or misinterpretation.
- It should be verified by another party if possible.

The data most easily fulfilling these requirements comes directly from the firm's computer. From there, the system translates it into useful information. Some larger companies keep their performance information on a large computer. To work with it more easily, they may move the raw data to a personal computer where the software is more user-friendly. There, they convert the raw data into useful information.

Emphasize efficiency in your data capture. Watch the use of the reports and information coming out of the monitoring system. If no one uses them, then discontinue them. For example, let's say the production department wants to track idle labor hours due to machinery downtime against benchmarks it put in its plan.

An astute planner would have seen that benchmark in the beginning and designed a method of capturing it *prior* to starting implementation of the plan. A good way to do that would be to put such idle labor costs into a special general ledger expense account. This makes the data capture easy.

However, what happens if there is no computer, or if for whatever reason the cost accounting system cannot capture idle labor hours due to machine downtime? Now how do we get the information? One solution would be to create a manual log of employees who are idle because of machine downtime throughout the month. A simple log would include

- Name of employee • Labor rate • Date of downtime
- Number of hours idle • Labor cost for the idle time

You might even keep the log on a spreadsheet in the production department's personal computer. If possible, transfer this information to the computer on which the business plan monitoring system resides. The performance monitoring system can then electronically incorporate the data. The time such a procedure takes should be minimal for everyone. Further, the possibility of error falls because fewer hands actually massage the information.

Using Captured Data

If we take the trouble to capture information and report it to the company, it should be relevant. One way to be sure of this is to periodically talk with the managers who receive it. Find out what they do with it. Discover how they use it to track their particular benchmarks. The answers may surprise you. Often what you thought was useful information is marked up and further massaged to convert it into something that's *really* useful. Other times, the recipients just slide it under a pile of work without even looking at it because it tells them nothing they don't already know.

If either of these things happens, the monitoring system isn't doing its job. Make the reports useful or stop generating them.

Focusing on what people need

The monitoring system should provide what people actually need and use, not what they say they need. A good example is the idle labor costs described above. As machinery gets older, downtime increases, and idle labor costs rise right along with it. Therefore, what the manager *really* needs is information on machinery downtime, not raw data on idle labor hours.

Focus on the problem source, poorly maintained or aging equipment, not the symptom, idle labor cost. Provide the information necessary to make decisions. Look at the real use of the information and the decisions it supports. Then focus on just what's needed. Anything more than that is a waste of time and just confuses already busy decision makers.

USING ANALYTICAL TECHNIQUES

Most business performance monitoring systems employ ratios and statistics to provide an index of performance. By themselves, these measurements don't tell us a great deal. Their utility is in *comparison* with other companies or different time frames. Further, if your company has two or more different businesses, don't try to compare financial ratios. What may be an acceptable index for one business may not be for another.

The most commonly used performance measurements deal with parts of the balance sheet. Many already reside in the business plan as performance benchmarks.

Asset Ratios

Often companies focus on specific parts of their balance sheet. This is usually because their banks think these items are important. Many loan agreements require maintenance of certain asset ratios as part of the lending covenant. If that's the case, then the firm must certainly watch each of these performance indicators and keep them within the limits prescribed by the bank loan.

Quick ratio

$$\text{Quick ratio} = \frac{\text{cash} + \text{marketable securities}}{\text{current liabilities}}$$

This ratio tells the firm's ability to make payments without using cash generated from sales. It presents a worst-case scenario—no sales. Note that many analysts include either the current portion or the entire balance of accounts receivable in the dividend of this equation as well.

Current ratio

$$\text{Current ratio} = \frac{\text{current assets}}{\text{current liabilities}}$$

Use this ratio to show the ability to meet payment obligations due within the operating period with assets that we can convert to cash within that same operating period.

If you find these two ratios (or any others, for that matter) in a lending covenant, you should know well ahead of time if they're going to fall outside their specified ranges. Notify the bank if there's nothing you can do to prevent it. It looks a lot better to anticipate a problem and work to fix it than to appear surprised at bad news.

Finally, if your firm breaches a lending covenant, secure from the bank a *written* waiver of its rights and remedies against your company. Without a written waiver, you run the risk of the bank changing its mind and throwing the company into default.

Financing and Debt Ratios

- *Liabilities covered by working capital* (working capital provided from operations / total liabilities). This ratio illustrates the firm's ability to repay current liabilities using internally generated working capital.
- *Financial structure.* We measure two things concerning financial structure:
  - *Term financing* (fixed assets / short-term debt). If companies finance too many fixed (long-term) assets using short-term debt, two things can occur: The debt can mature before the assets have earned enough money to repay the obligation, and if interest rates spike upward, the cost of funds is likely to rise along with it, changing the assumptions used to justify acquiring the asset in the first place.
  - *Proportionate term of debt* (short-term debt / long-term debt). Ideally, long-term debt (sometimes referred to as the core borrowings) should exceed short-term debt. If it doesn't, the company is subject to a liquidity squeeze if it attempts to roll over maturing short-term debt when cash is scarce. This happened to some real estate developers during the early 1990s when banks all but stopped lending on real estate.

By tracking these benchmarks in the financial plan, you have positioned yourself to act in advance of a crisis. Further, many loan covenants require that the borrower not fall below specified levels on certain financial ratios. If that happens, the loan may be subject to immediate call and repayment. These are benchmarks to which you definitely pay attention. It's a good idea to have your financial plan compute them each month.

Aging Accounts Receivable

Weighted average age of accounts receivable = sum of (weighted average % of each aging bucket X number of days in each aging bucket)

This number (shown in days) demonstrates the weighted average time the company takes to collect its receivables. The fewer the number of days, the less cash the company has invested in receivables. Banks like this number because it provides an indication of the receivable portfolio's stability. Watch this statistic closely if a loan is collateralized by receivables. For example, a portfolio aged forty-five days has a higher probability of being collected than one with a seventy-five-day weighted average aging.

Accounts Receivable Turnover Rate

$$\text{A/R turnover} = \frac{\text{annual sales}}{\text{average A/R balance}}$$

This measurement shows how fast the firm collects its receivables. The faster receivables turn, the less cash this component of working capital consumes. The A/R turnover rate should interest the finance department.

Accounts Payable Turnover Rate

$$\text{A/P turnover} = \frac{\text{annual expenses}}{\text{average A/P balance}}$$

As with the receivables turnover, A/P turnover tracks the speed at which the firm pays its obligations. The higher the A/P turnover rate, the more cash escapes from the firm and the greater the requirement for working capital. Conversely, the lower this ratio, the more the company retains its cash.

Compare the accounts receivable turnover with the accounts payable turnover. If receivables turn faster than payables, your vendors are financing this portion of your working capital requirements—you are collecting money from customers before vendors require payment.

Aging Accounts Payable

Weighted average age of accounts payable = sum of (weighted average % of each aging bucket X number of days in each aging bucket)

The higher the number of days payables age, the greater the leverage derived from the company's vendors. This is another measurement of how closely the A/P department follows company policy regarding vendor payment. It's not usually good policy to pay obligations before they're due. During times of cash inadequacy, many firms stretch their payables. Further, using these and other A/P measurements, the controller can control the firm's payment policies even more precisely.

Average Payment Period

$$\text{Average payment period} = \frac{\text{accounts payable balance}}{(\text{annual expenses} \div 360)}$$

This measures the number of days of average expenses vendors have invested in the firm's accounts payable. The higher the average payment period, the greater the company's use of trade credit. Consider this as a free loan—the company uses its vendor's credit policies to finance part of its working capital requirements.

Average Collection Period

$$\text{Average collection period} = \frac{\text{accounts receivable balance}}{(\text{annual sales} \div 360)}$$

This ratio also provides insight into receivables collection efficiency. The average collection period tells the number of days of average sales contained in accounts receivable. The company wants as few days of sales as possible in receivables.

Average Investment Period in Inventory

$$\frac{\text{Average investment}}{\text{period in inventory}} = \frac{\text{present inventory balance}}{(\text{annual cost of goods sold} / 360)}$$

Many business plans focus on inventory control. The objective is to have as little money tied up in inventory as possible. The smaller the average investment period in inventory, the faster the inventory turns into disposable cash.

Inventory Turnover

$$\text{Inventory turnover rate} = \frac{\text{annual cost of goods sold}}{\text{average inventory balance}}$$

The faster a company's inventory turns, the faster its investment in inventory converts to sales and, further, the less valuable cash the company has tied up in low-demand stock.

MONITORING A FLEXIBLE PLAN

Sometimes negative variances aren't necessarily bad. At higher sales levels, the costs of commissions and other expenses are higher. Therefore, the firm may be over budget in some expense categories but still have a positive profit variance.

Be sure to watch the changes in expense levels when revenue is over budget. There should be some economies that cause expenses to climb at a *slower* rate. If that's not the case, then expenses may be out of control at the higher revenue levels.

Controlling a Flexible Plan

Flexible plans focus on the *relationships* between costs and expenses. Most planners define these relationships using percentages. For example, cost of goods sold is 55 percent of sales revenue. This defines the gross margin of 45 percent.

Flexible financial plans also allow us to maintain a valid plan despite changes in sales levels. That way the monitoring system always has a valid plan number against which to compare costs and expenses. The absolute value of the numbers may change—and that's all right—but the *relationships* remain the same. The monitoring system identifies deviations from the planned percentages and flags a problem. Make the decision to use a flexible monitoring format during the design stage of the business plan.

Chapter 18 demonstrates how to update your business plan.

Chapter 18

Updating the Plan

OVERVIEW

Business plans are living documents. Many departments continue through the planning year with little change. For them, extensive updating isn't necessary. However, in other departments, unforeseen circumstances necessitate a change to the plan. Often these changes cascade into still more adjustments to the targets and timing in other departments throughout the company.

Ignoring these changes and trying to make an outdated plan work is like navigating with an antiquated map. The milestones and landmarks have changed. The plan tells when to make midcourse corrections. However, outdated plans won't signal the need for change. The company will miss its overall targets.

Regular updates keep the plan relevant to current issues confronting the company. Obsolete business plans go stale if they don't accurately portray the business environment. Once enthusiasm has died, the business plan is almost impossible to revive.

Chapter 18 demonstrates how to update significant components of a business plan with new targets based on current results and recent developments. When managed correctly, the company achieves its main planning goals even though the *way* it gets there changes.

KNOWING WHEN TO UPDATE

How do you know when your business plan needs updating? A good indication is the differences between actual performance and the plan. If the differences accumulate to a point where the company cannot achieve the plan during the time remaining in the planning period, then the plan requires an update. Another sign is that the targets of some departments begin to shift frequently in response to missed or exceeded targets in other departments.

Scheduling Updates

Many companies schedule at least one update to their business plan sometime during the year. Often this update comes at midyear. Planned updates recognize the necessity of keeping the business plan consistent with the real world.

Companies involved in high technology or other industries where rapid change exists should schedule a plan update during the planning year.

Changing Assumptions

When basic underpinnings of the business plan change, the targets and milestones probably change as well. For example, let's say the plan bases its profit targets on sales projections. The sales plan identifies sales levels at particular points in time. However, if the plan miscalculated product demand (either up or down), the sales plan is no longer valid. There's no point in continuing to report deviations from sales targets for products for which demand has clearly shifted.

Instead, smart managers update the plan to determine what they can do *now* to reach the company's overall goals. This proactive approach helps cut losses short or allows the company to exploit new opportunities.

The fashion industry is a good example. At the start of each season, manufacturers and designers try to guess what will sell. If they guess correctly, their business plan may not require extensive updating. However, if they guess incorrectly and a line doesn't sell, the entire business plan may get revamped.

Changing Business Conditions

Business conditions change as the plan rolls out. Carefully constructed plans respond to these changes. The overall company goals remain unaffected. However, the individual targets required from each department may change. The most frequently seen environmental changes are

- Financial conditions • Technological advances
- Changes by competition • Union actions
- Regulatory and legislative actions

Financial conditions

Financial conditions change with the securities markets. For example, as the overall economy changes, the Federal Reserve adjusts its policies in response. The bond market moves as a direct result. As bonds move, the yield curve responds, and so do interest rates. Add to this the sentiment of lenders regarding general business conditions and the stability of specific industries.

All these forces combine to produce the market interest rate on which financing vital to achievement of the business plan depends.

Perhaps interest rates move, *but so do criteria lenders impose for the creditworthiness of borrowers.* Suddenly, the company doesn't qualify for the financing required at the rates specified in the plan. Perhaps the terms of the loan now require a larger compensating balance or more collateral to secure the lender's interest.

Another change in financial conditions that often requires an update of at least part of the plan has nothing to do with the company itself. *Customers'* ability to pay creditors varied with the economic environment. The cash flow plan assumed certain customer payment habits. If customers suddenly begin behaving differently than expected, the cash flow plan can stall. Updating for these events is a necessity.

Technological advances

Some industries enjoy rapid technological advances. The computer industry is one. Some types of manufacturing are others. The securities industry is still another. Often advances in the way a product is made or new materials produce unexpected downward shifts in manufacturing costs.

If your planners are up on the latest in their industry, most such advances won't catch them by surprise. Indeed, some of the most brilliant business plans anticipate the benefits of technological improvements. They capitalize on them, moving the savings to other parts of the company where they are needed to shore up some other part of the plan.

The impact of technological advances on business plans isn't limited to the production process. Often competitors build new innovations into their products. When this happens, it can drastically affect sales of companies whose products don't have the new wrinkle. For these companies, updating the business plan becomes a necessity. They may have to ram through a crash program to meet the competition's offering. Then the marketing department may have to figure out how to let customers know about it.

Changes by competition

Competitors don't always do what your business plan intends them to. Often they fire the first shot in what turns into a price war. Sometimes their advertising campaigns are so effective that they can significantly reduce your company's sales.

When this happens, the business plan must provide a measured response. Often this requires updating parts of the plan in order to maintain sales or counteract claims by competitors' advertising campaigns.

Union actions

Unions often disrupt even the most carefully thought out business plans. Job actions or unexpected demands in contract negotiations sometimes cause labor costs to skyrocket. Suddenly the gross margin drops to a point where it jeopardizes financial targets.

However, smart managers use the business plan to help determine just what concessions they can give to the union during negotiations. They put the financial schedules on an automated spreadsheet. Then they simulate the effects of various conditions. The simulations serve as a basis for updating the business plan after settlement of the negotiations.

Regulatory and legislative actions

These are often the most frustrating. Such changes can drastically affect small-business plans. Further, they often come as a complete surprise. Additionally, policies required for compliance with one government agency sometimes conflict with those required by another agency that also governs the company.

We see an example of this at the small community banks. The Community Reinvestment Act requires that banks lend to small businesses in the inner city. However, the Federal Reserve and the FDIC audit these same banks. The regulators criticize them for lending to small businesses in the inner city that don't meet their standards of creditworthiness. As a result, the business plans of these small banks must reflect inflated loan loss reserves (to satisfy the Fed and FDIC) for making loans to less creditworthy inner-city businesses (to comply with the Community Reinvestment Act).

Such dissonance created by competing government agencies often requires updating the business plan. This is also true of unexpected legislative changes. Sometimes companies depend on specific legislation to carry out their business plans. Real estate developers are a case in point. Zoning laws specify the types of structure allowed on certain property.

If a developer's business plan calls for an office building on land it owns and the zoning on that land suddenly changes to a less dense level, there's a major problem. Now the developer must apply for a variance or possibly change plans. Regardless, the timing of revenues and expenses slips as a result of the legislative change.

Changing Strategies

Sometimes companies must make major changes to their business strategy during the year. Such decisions cannot wait for the end of the planning year. Updating the business plan to include such decisions allows the company to track their implementation. It also allows it to better integrate the changes with the rest of the company's plans.

A change in business strategy might include the acquisition of another company or one of its products. It might include restructuring the firm's pricing strategy or the market it goes after. Any of these changes would require other adjustments in departments throughout the company. The best way to coordinate these changes is to update the business plan.

Department Changes

When separate departments change their plans and their targets, the rest of the company needs to know. For example, production departments that cannot meet targets sometimes subcontract out the difference to another manufacturer. The cost of production probably changes. To maintain profit margins, the sales department may have to adjust its pricing strategies.

Similarly, the accounts payable department may find that it cannot adhere to the planned policy of stretching all payables to forty-five days. Vendors supplying the firm with critical raw materials may establish a cash-on-delivery policy. If this happens, the cash flow plan must somehow pick up the difference in working capital required to run the firm.

A plan update—at least for the departments affected—identifies the change and helps determine the impacts. From there, the updating process makes adjustments that still allow implementation of the original business plan.

Notice that although a department's plan may change and be updated, the overall goals originally set forth in the business plan remain unaffected. We still want the company to hit its original targets. It would take major changes in critical departments to necessitate adjustment of these overall goals.

KEEPING THE PLAN RELEVANT

Updating the business plan keeps it relevant. Many plans fail because they don't reflect the current business climate. When this happens, management doesn't use the plan for its intended purpose—to help guide and control progress toward the company's goals. The monthly and quarterly reviews waste time.

Small companies that have operated for years without a business plan normally fly by the seat of their pants. They communicate changes in the operating environment as they happen. The business plan should record these changes almost as quickly. This doesn't mean redoing the plan every month. Rather, it means adjusting the targets and using the plan to coordinate efforts to ensure meeting the overall plan goals. *Then* the plan incorporates changes at its quarterly or midyear update.

Companies implementing a business plan for the first time regard relevancy as especially important. The design and implementation of a business plan was probably an uphill battle for these firms. They look at the plan with skepticism—as another way for the boss to exert control over the workers. Outdated plans supply their detractors with the excuse that they don't reflect the real world.

Updating the plan doesn't mean that management changes its original goals. After all, that's the point of making a business plan in the first place—to get the firm from point A to point B. The route taken changes, and so do the interim results, but the end point remains the same.

AVOIDING CONFUSION

People familiar with planning and the necessity of updating have doubtless heard the question, Now which version are we talking about? Confusion among the various updated plans and what each contains is a frequent problem. We don't want bewilderment over plan targets and their priorities. Everyone must sing from the same sheet of music.

The best way to avoid confusion is to keep the number of plan updates as few as possible—preferably just one update at midyear. Further, if possible, do not change the underlying goals of the business plan at that time. The various departments update their subplans to reflect changes in strategy and timing.

Everyone must identify each update as either the most current or one that was superseded. A good way to do this is to specify the revision date on the front of each updated plan. Keep a historical log of all updates. Anyone looking at the log quickly sees which is the most current. Include the update log in the front of the plan.

Another help is to summarize the changes in each updated version of the plan. Include this with the history log. Using the change summary, it's easy to see just what changed in each version and the results.

Consistency

The format of each updated version of the business plan should match that of its predecessor. This prevents having to modify the monitoring system with each plan update. Further, it ensures that the accounting system can capture all actual data against which management compares the updated plan. We don't want people to go through a laborious reconciliation of performance indicators prepared for one plan and for a new, updated version. This wastes everyone's time—especially when a performance incentive is on the line. People sometimes spend hours trying to reconcile two different plans.

Appendix I

Glossary

Accounting rate of return (APR): Relates asset investment to future annual income. Use this equation to compute ARR:

$$\text{ARR} = \frac{\text{annual cash flows} - \text{depreciation}}{\text{initial investment}}$$

Accounts payable (A/P): Used in an accrual accounting system to track the liabilities of the company. It is important in the business plan because paydown of A/P changes the balance of disposable cash contained in the cash flow plan.

Accounts receivable (A/R): Used in an accrual accounting system to track money owed the company. It is important in the business plan because receipt of A/R balances increases the balance of disposable cash contained in the cash flow plan.

Advance rate: A percentage of the loan value relative to the collateral asset securing the loan. Also called the *loan to value ratio.*

Audit: The examination of accounting records by an independent CPA organization for the purpose of expressing an opinion of the fairness of presentation of the company's financial statements in conformity with generally accepted accounting principals (GAAP).

Break-even point: The level of sales at which income exactly equals operating expenses. This is often used as the starting point for a small-business plan.

Capital acquisition plan: A schedule illustrating major purchases of machinery, equipment, real estate, etc. It usually contains items, purchase dates, delivery dates, and scheduled cash outflows.

Cash basis: An accounting method that recognizes revenue and expense at the time cash changes hands. This method differs from the accrual basis of accounting. However, when preparing a cash flow plan, a cash approach is used to determine *disposable* cash balances.

Cash capability: The company's ability to generate cash from all of its reserves and all available but as yet unemployed credit.

Cash conversion time: Used in business planning to determine the elapsed time required to convert a sale into disposable cash.

Cost of capital: The company's cost of borrowed funds. It is usually aggregated using the weighted average cost of all the firm's sources of debt financing.

This interest rate is often used in the business plan when projecting the cost of additional capital necessary to execute the plan.

Cost of goods sold: The cost associated with manufacturing or otherwise making the company's products available for sale. Sales revenue less cost of goods sold yields gross margin—a critical number in the planning process.

Depreciation: Allocation of the cost of a fixed asset to expense over the period benefited. It is used in accrual accounting systems to match revenues and expenses for each operating period. When preparing a cash flow plan, depreciation is added back to net income to arrive at total cash sources.

Economic order quantity: The order size that minimizes both carrying costs and ordering costs. The business plan should compute the EOQ and use it in the assumptions.

Float: The amount of funds contained in checks already written but not yet cleared by the bank.

Gain contingency: Used in business planning and presentation of financial statements. It quantifies a possible future favorable financial development for the firm, such as winning a lawsuit. GAAP does not allow the recording of gain contingencies as it does accruals for possible future losses. Instead, such possibilities require footnote disclosure; they are omitted from the financials.

Imputed interest: Computation of an effective interest rate on notes or obligations that carry no interest rate on their face or an unrealistically low rate. If the business plan is sent to third parties, its financial projections may require imputing interest on below-market loans.

Internal rate of return (IRR): The exact rate that makes future cash flows discounted back to the present equal to the investment in a capital asset. Using the correct IRR percentage, the net present value of the investment is zero.

Inventory: Goods held by the company for sale. Both beginning and ending inventory figures are used in the following computation of cost of goods sold:

Beginning inventory + raw material purchases + labor + overhead allocation – ending inventory = cost of goods sold

Learning curve: The assumption that the number of labor hours required decreases in a measurable pattern as the manufacturing process is repeated over time and people become familiar with it. Effects of the learning curve should be included in the overall manufacturing plan.

Leverage: Borrowing more than the equity owners have in the business or property. Many business plans assume a given level of debt leverage to finance growth.

Line of credit: A borrowing agreement that commits a bank to lending up to a specific amount when the borrower makes a demand for funds. Credit lines usually run for a specified period of time—one year is normal.

Mezzanine financing: An infusion of capital intended to prepare a company for a public securities offering.

Net present value: Excess of the present value of the cash inflows associated with a capital project over the initial investment.

Optimal reorder point (ORP): That point at which it's most advantageous to order more goods—raw materials, for example. Compute ORP using the equation

ORP = average requirement per unit of lead time X (lead time + safety stock)

Payback period: The length of time required to recover the purchase cost of a capital asset, used to determine the value of an asset investment. Compute payback period as

$$\frac{\text{cost of investment}}{\text{annual cash flow from investment}} \quad + \quad \text{payback}$$

Predetermined overhead rate (POR): The rate used to allocate factory overhead when planning manufacturing costs. Use the equation

$$POR = \frac{\text{annual planned factory overhead}}{\text{annual planned units produced}}$$

Regression analysis: A statistical method used to project sales, cash flow, and earnings.

Safety stock: Extra units of inventory a firm must carry to guard against stock-outs.

Tangible net worth: Book value of the company *minus* intangible assets. Use the equation

Tangible net worth = total assets − intangible assets − liabilities

Transfer pricing: The price at which goods and services are exchanged between divisions of a decentralized company.

Trend analysis: A method of forecasting sales or earnings using historical figures. It involves a regression whereby a trend line is fitted to a time series of data.

Appendix II

Organizations

International Association for Financial Planning
2 Concourse Parkway, Suite 800
Atlanta, GA 30328
(404) 395-1605

Institute of Certified Financial Planners
East Eastman Ave., Suite 301
Denver, CO 80231
(303) 751-7600

Planning Forum
P.O. Box 70
Oxford, OH 45056
(513) 523-4185

American Institute of Certified Planners
1776 Massachusetts Ave., NW
Washington, D.C. 20036
(202) 872-0611

American Institute of Management
P.O. Box 7039
Quincy, MA 02269
617) 472-0277

Association of Productivity Specialists
200 Park Avenue, Suite 303E
New York, NY 10017
(212) 286-0943

Appendix III
Bibliography

Abrams, Rhonda. *The Successful Business Plan.* New York: The Oasis Press, 1991.

Batchelor, Andrew. *Business Planning for the Entrepreneur.* New York: Tangent Publishing 1990.

Berle, Gustav. *Planning and Forming Your Company.* New York: Wiley, 1990.

——— . *Raising Start-up Capital for Your Firm.* New York: Wiley, 1990.

Bierman, Harold. *Cost Accounting: Concepts and Management Applications.* New York: Macmillan, 1990.

Blocker, E., and C. Stickney. "Duration and Risk Assessments In Capital Budgeting." *Accounting Review,* January 1979, 180–188.

Chamberlain, Neil W. *The Firm: Micro-economic Planning and Action.* New York: McGraw-Hill, 1962.

Collins, Frank, and Paul Munter. "The Budgeting Games People Play." *Accounting Review*, January 1987, 29–49.

Franz, Norman. *The Business Planning Workbook.* New York: Entole International Corp., 1991.

Greene, Charles N. *Management for Effective Performance., Englewood Cliffs, NJ: Prentice Hall, 1985.*

Kuehl, Charles, and Peggy Lambing. *Small Business Planning and Management.* New York: Dryden Press, 1990.

Larker, D. F. "The Perceived Importance of Selected Information Characteristics for Strategic Capital Budgeting Decisions." *Accounting Review*, July 1981, 519–538.

McKeever, Mike. *How to Write a Business Plan.* Boston: Nolo Press, 1992.

McLaughlin, Harold J. *Building Your Business Plan.* New York: Wiley, 1985.

Magee, Robert. *Advanced Managerial Accounting.* New York: Harper & Row, 1986.

Malburg, Christopher R. *Business Plans to Manage Day-to-Day Operations.* New York: Wiley, 1993.

— — — . *The Cash Management Handbook.* Englewood Cliffs, NJ: Prentice-Hall, 1992.

Mancuso, Joseph. *How to Write a Winning Business Plan.* Englewood Cliffs, NJ: Prentice-Hall, 1985.

Rappaport, Alfred. *Information for Decision Making.* Englewood Cliffs, NJ: Prentice-Hall, 1982.

Rice, Craig. *Strategic Planning for the Small Business.* Holbrook, Mass.: Bob Adams, Inc., 1990.

Stevens, Chris. *The Entrepreneur's Guide to Developing a Basic Business Plan.* New York: S.K. Brown Publishing, 1991.

Index

About the Author

During his management consulting career, Chris Malburg has explained countless complex business issues and their solutions to both executives and peer professionals. He has known and worked with senior executives both personally and professionally for over fifteen years. This background has provided Chris with a wealth of experience in financial operations.

A CPA with an MBA in finance, Chris is also a licensed NASD Financial Operations Principal. He runs an active management consulting firm, is president of Copralite Development Corporation, a southern California real estate developer, and is the general partner of the Lapin Development Group. Chris has worked with Fortune 100 companies as well as with many small to medium-sized firms. Chris has written seven other popular books and numerous professional articles.